GARAGE TO GLOBAL

INDIA • SINGAPORE • MALAYSIA

GARAGE TO GLOBAL

ASCENT TO ABSOLUTE ENGINEERING

SAMEER KELKAR

INDIA · SINGAPORE · MALAYSIA

ISBN
Paperback 979-8-89632-768-4
Hardcase 979-8-89673-424-6

Shailesh Sheth

Guide and Mentor

Shailesh Sheth was an eminent independent corporate advisor and a Board Member at Bharat Fritz Werner Ltd. In a career spanning over four decades, Sheth has earned the reputation of being the Guru of the machine tools industry.

Sheth's ringside perspective of the machine tools industry, and earlier association with Grind Master as an advisor placed him at a unique vantage position to guide and mentor the writing of this book.

Shailesh Sheth earlier wrote the book 'the Alluring Protege' about the journey of BFW.

Shailesh Sheth passed away on 12 September 2024. His thoughts continue to inspire many machine builders including Grind Master.

This book is dedicated

To every single person without whose support this journey would not have been possible.

To the Machine Builders and their spirit of perseverance and innovation against all odds.

To partners who trusted us when we did not have a track record.

To Appa and Ajji.

To Ram Bhogale and Mukund Bhogale.

To all colleagues and associates.

Contents

Foreword

Globally, it is observed that the Machine Tool Industry forms the bedrock of a strong and robust manufacturing ecosystem; Germany, Japan, France, United States, South Korea, Taiwan and China - all these countries house world-class machine tool companies that form the backbone of their domestic industrial ecosystem and also cater to manufacturing establishments world over. In the two decades starting the 1960s when an independent India was laying the foundations of domestic manufacturing sector, with the help of foreign technology providers, the public sector enterprises took lead in developing India's Machine Tool Industry. Despite large investments, little headway was achieved, and we could not keep pace with rapidly evolving technological advancements which gradually led to them to their decline. While this was a concern to many, select few technocrat entrepreneurs saw an opportunity and took it upon themselves to build grounds-up, India's own Machine Tool Industry. Hailing from Maharashtra, Mr. Milind Kelkar and Mrs. Mohini Kelkar form one such rare breed of engineer-entrepreneurs with commendable zeal and enthusiasm, the founders of GRIND MASTER.

It is with great pleasure that I introduce this remarkable book, which provides an insightful glimpse into the journey of Grind Master and the innovation culture that drives the company. For over 40 years, I have had the privilege of knowing the entrepreneurial family behind Grind Master - the Kelkars. From the early days of relatively simple automatic grinding machines to the development of highly sophisticated microfinishing machines and robotic grinding technologies, I have witnessed firsthand how Grind Master has evolved into a global leader in the industry. At Bharat Forge, we have been proud recipients of this indigenous technology, which stands as a true testament to 'Aatmanirbhar Bharat' - India's self-reliant technological prowess. Every new machine from Grind Master comes with multiple improvements, a continuous evolution that has helped the company rise to world-class standards.

One of the most intriguing aspects of their approach is their quality philosophy: **100-1 = ZERO.** This relentless pursuit of perfection reveals itself through the book. I also found the last chapter, which delves into Grind Master's **'Subhashita'**, particularly interesting. The saying, "sweat in Grind Master rather than bleed at the customer's end," reflects a principle that not only applies to them but is a guiding philosophy for any business striving for excellence.

As a technocrat with a deep interest in manufacturing technology, this subject has always been a source of joy and inspiration for me. I have always been keen to explore new developments, and during discussions for this book, Milind described the unique development of ballscrew superfinishing. Naturally, I was intrigued by how this was achieved, and I continue to be impressed by the breakthroughs Grind Master has brought to the table. Their global reach, with installations in advanced manufacturing centers in Japan, Germany, Canada, and the USA, is a testament to their relentless innovation and pursuit of excellence.

Today, as Indian Industry embarks on strengthening its manufacturing landscape, this remarkable journey of Milind and Mohini Kelkar serves as an inspiration to aspiring engineers, entrepreneurs and seasoned leaders alike. Their story is a testament to the power of vision, resilience, and unwavering dedication to quality – a legacy that continues to shape industries and lives. At Bharat Forge, we have always been committed to encouraging and supporting Indian technology, and Grind Master exemplifies what is possible when passion, ingenuity, and a commitment to continuous improvement come together.

I congratulate Sameer for capturing this inspiring story in such a profound and insightful manner. I am confident that this book will not only enlighten readers on the intricacies of forging success against all odds, significance of customer first philosophy and engineering excellence but will also inspire the future generations to embrace challenges with courage and forge their paths to greatness.

Baba Kalyani
Chairman & Managing Director, Bharat Forge Ltd.

Reviews

What does it take for two young engineers with a garage enterprise to build a world leader in core engineering sector, beating companies from developed world and selling in their own backyard? A lot. A lot more than excellence in engineering. A lot more than passion, hard work, grit, brash audacity, and constant learning. It takes self belief and faith in the chosen path for over four decades. In short commitment in the very extreme. "Garage to Global" is an inspirational, exhilarating and a very honest insider account of one such enterprise that broke every rule in the book, shattered every barrier in the way to beat the behemoths in machine tool industry and gain respect and orders from auto giants and industry leaders in every continent. A must read for every entrepreneur, engineer, manager, marketer, and sales person

Mukund Bhogale
Director - AITG
Bhogale Group

A very timely book. At a time when the Indian Manufacturing Industries are being challenged to increase their output to $1 Trillion and their share in the GDP to 20-25%, "'Garage to Global'" tells us, and more particularly the Technocrat led MSMEs, how they could break out of the mold and "Go Global".

The key to Grind Masters success has been their passion for "absolute engineering" — Perfect, pure, committed and assured engineering - to develop and provide comprehensive solutions to solve the customers problems in manufacturing industries. The author explains at length the struggles they had to undergo to get accepted against international competition and how they adopted an unrelenting commitment to the Customer's needs by installing and demonstrating their machines, not just in India but even in very challenging markets like China, Europe and Japan.

The book meticulously focusses on all the aspects which go to make a Globally competitive organisation - leveraging engineering design, adopting total Quality, sharp focus on the processes and continuous learning combined with a deep desire to train, develop and improve the quality of life, of all those who work for the organisation. A must read for all Technocrat entrepreneurs.

R Srinivasan
Machine Tool Industry Guru

'Garage to Global' is a multifaceted book that goes far beyond the technical achievements of Grind Master, offering readers a comprehensive view of the company's journey and evolution. It tells the inspiring story of a determined trio who transformed their dreams into a global reality. By focusing on the leadership journey, the book explores the synergy between personal values, strategic vision, and innovation that propelled Grind Master to become a global leader in precision manufacturing, particularly in deburring and superfinishing.

At its core, this is more than a business story - it is a testament to the power of purpose-driven growth, the pivotal role of leadership, and the transformative impact of people on an organization's success. The founders' philosophical foundation, especially the idea of "Absolute Engineering," shaped their approach to challenges and disrupted conventional thinking, not just in manufacturing but in how businesses can grow sustainably while remaining true to their values.

RameshBabu
Professor Emeritus
Indian Institute of Technology Madras

This book is a brilliantly written documentation of how Grind Master grew from a small domestic machine builder in India to one of the worldwide leaders in precision dimensioning and finishing technology. When I met the Kelkars at their modest plant in Aurangabad, India, back in 1997, I had worked on developing the Microfinishing Film Technology and was finding applications and partners.

It was so much easier to introduce to customers a new "turn-key system" that combined 3M Film Abrasives with new machine tools that were specifically designed to use those film abrasive products. I was introduced to Grindmaster at just the right time as the automotive powertrain component makers in India were convinced that statistically superior dimensional accuracy and surface finish consistency would be achieved with Microfinishing Film rather than wheels or stones.

In a few short years, nearly all of the automotive and diesel powertrain manufacturers became Grindmaster microfinishing customers. Since then, Grindmaster has continued to innovate and turn out machines with ever-increasing levels of dimensional and surface finish accuracy and consistency. story, and wish them continuing success!

Mark Sterner
3M Microfinishing Film Expert

• • •

The Entrepreneurial Family at the helm of Grind Master

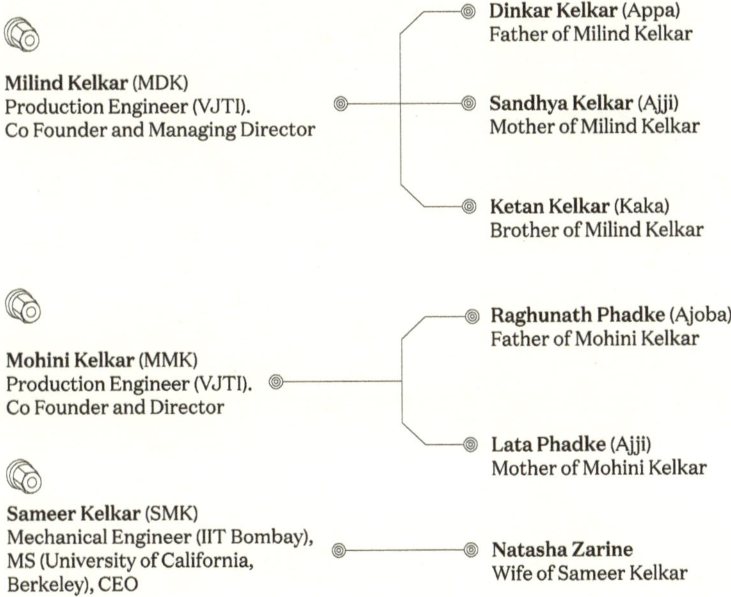

Introduction

'Garage to Global' – The Ascent to Absolute Engineering

This is the story of an Indian midsized firm – Grind Master, the world leader in metal finishing and deburring.

Grind Master operates in the historic city of Aurangabad#, which is home to the world-famous ancient caves of Ajanta and Ellora. The ancient city was once the capital of the Deccan region, and is now known as Chhatrapati Sambhaji Nagar. To break the shackles and leap into the future from this city with a loaded past must not have been easy. But Grind Master did it! This book tells us how.

This is a corporate biography, yes, but with a difference. It does not concern itself with recording the company's financial growth or its chronological evolution, which are equally fascinating aspects of Grind Master. Nor does the book claim a lofty 'I did it!' approach. Instead, in these pages, you, dear reader, will find an honest assessment of a company's journey narrated in all honesty, as it happened. Many aspects of this honest evaluation germinated from the pauses of life, in the absence of the pull of more urgent matters, as it typically happens. The sincere and deep introspection for Sameer Kelkar, the author of this book, took place at a time of important transitions. He was surrounded by the wilderness of the Himalayan mountains. While the mighty mountains always bring great perspective, Sameer was also ready to embrace fatherhood as he was welcoming his baby to join his family. Sameer's new and exciting role as a father forced him to re-examine his priorities. As you read along, these intriguing stories are bound to excite you, surely.

Reading this book feels like sitting across the table from the leaders at Grind Master for a free-wheeling, no-holds-barred conversation. The book takes you back to pivotal moments in the history of the company, narrated by the very people who lived the experience. These are not just a collection of stories. Hidden within them are

#The city of Aurangabad was renamed as Chhatrapati Sambhaji Nagar recently. For simplicity of narration it has been referred with the name 'Aurangabad' throughout this book.

also messages and learnings from business and life that are worthy of applying to any situation and for anyone willing to improve his life. The reader will enjoy these stories while also picking up new ideas and perspectives.

The founders of Grind Master were heavily inspired by the seminal work of Jacob Bronowski titled 'The Ascent of Man', a book that helps us understand human life by understanding the importance of science. This book, written over half a century ago, spurred a newly married couple to stake their future in pursuing their ideas and dreams. Along their journey, the couple uniquely branded their work as 'Absolute Engineering', a term that would do well to find a permanent spot in the new engineering vocabulary today.

This book is peppered with examples of how people drove projects, and not the other way around. Above all, at Grind Master, purpose prevailed over profits. The importance of people and purpose guide us back to the intellectual underpinnings of this company's story. The chapter titled 'Subhashita,' towards the end of the book, stitches together the myriad elements of the company's ethos and how it shaped the growth and direction of Grind Master over the years.

In India's industrial plateau, Grind Master is a relatively small company. Yet, its journey proves that size does not matter when it comes to achieving larger ambitions. India will become a force to reckon with worldwide based on entrepreneurship of this kind.

Growing from a garage to a workshop to a factory to a 10-acre campus, to making inroads in the most difficult market – China – and, above all, achieving global technology leadership in its field, are milestones of the journey that any company should be proud of – big or small. The title of this book "Garage to Global" uses both the words as adjectives rather than nouns - for it is the state of mind of the company that they reflect rather than the place of operation.

Grind Master has transformed from a company to an institution. In my various interactions with the Kelkar family, I found that every member of the family brought a unique set of talents that contributed to the company in a special way. I never heard family members address each other by their relationship – dad, mom or son – while at work. It was always Mr. Kelkar, Mrs. Kelkar or Sameer. In notations, their initials were used – MDK (Milind) or MMK (Mohini) or SMK (Sameer). It is a small detail but it went a long way to preserve a professional atmosphere within the company, ensuring that it didn't run like a family shop.

The book is largely written by Sameer with extensive inputs and fact checks by Milind and Mohini. It has been my pleasure to mentor them during this process. I hope you will find this book interesting, and take away the many rich insights it offers.

Absolute Engineering - Evolution of ethos of Grind Master

Absolute Engineering has been the North Star at Grind Master, guiding the company since its early days. It is truly intriguing.

- What does it really mean?
- How does it drive the organisation and its people?
- What does it mean for the customer?
- How does it impact QCD (quality, cost, delivery)?

A detailed examination of the concept is necessary. But first, let us define it.

The word 'engineering' is well known and understood, particularly in the manufacturing world. But what does 'Absolute Engineering' mean? The Webster's and Collins dictionaries define the word 'absolute' as that which is:

- free from imperfection – *Perfect*
- free from mixture' – *Pure*
- free from restraint or limitation – *Liberated*
- having no exceptions or excuses – *Commitment*
- free from any doubts – *Assured*

The Kelkars added to this the aspects of both engineering and the organisation. Absolute Engineering becomes, then

- Inclusive: it involves all concerned people in the organisation
- Comprehensive: it encompasses all aspects from product design to manufacturing

Ms. Ashwini Deshpande, Co-founder-Director of Elephant Design Agency, who originally coined the term, worked with the team at Grind Master. She was impressed by the pride that the entire team took in their work, both in the desire for precision and also in the technology that they created. This shared belief and confidence led to the use of the tagline 'Absolute Engineering', a term that was infused into the company's ethos.

The Kelkars built the company on the strong foundation of these attributes, including precision, inclusivity and top quality. These qualities form the basis on which every employee at Grind Master functions. These qualities are unquantifiable. What is apparent, however, is the ever-growing customer confidence in Grind Master. This is, without a doubt, credit to 'Absolute Engineering'.

The book tells the story of this journey, and how Grind Master achieved what it set out to do, while continuing to raise the bar and set new sights on the horizon for its dreams and hopes.

The Ascent of Man : Inspiring Grind Master

Mohini and Milind often visited the famous British Council Library in Mumbai. In 1978, they chanced upon the 'The Ascent of Man'. It is a 13-part, 1973 BBC documentary, subsequently published as a book with the same title. The work was created by Dr. Jacob Bronowski (1908 – 1974), a Polish-origin British mathematician and philosopher.

The work is an account of man's scientific and technological development through history. Greatly inspired by its messages, the Kelkars often returned to the book, using it as a constant guiding point. So impressed were they with the book that they bought several copies and gifted these to friends. Forty-five years later, 'The Ascent of Man' remains Milind's favourite, and is still a go-to for the Kelkars.

Drawing inspiration from Boltzmann

Amongst the many inspirational ideas embedded in 'The Ascent of Man' is one by Ludwig Boltzmann, the Austrian physicist most known for developing statistical mechanics, and for giving the statistical explanation to the Second Law of Thermodynamics (in 1877). His formula for the definition of entropy has been used ever since.

S = K Log W
S = Entropy
K = Boltzmann's Constant
W = number of microstates whose energy equals the systems' energy

Its usage led to the atomic theory, and continues to influence quantum mechanics today – around 150 years after it was first published. Science is building new knowledge on the shoulders of past giants. And Boltzmann is one such giant. The formula S = K log W became a part of his identity and was also inscribed on his tombstone in Vienna.

Boltzmann was known globally for his equation, which was taught worldwide in schools and universities. The universal appeal of such a formula inspired Milind and Mohini to create something truly novel, a global first in something. It became their main drive for innovating and attempting to go global early in their business. The passion and inspiration to create an identity worldwide led to their focused dedication towards improving machine tools in the decades that followed. This drive eventually became an integral part of Grind Master's DNA.

> *"Every animal leaves traces of what it was; man alone leaves traces of what he created".*

'The Ascent of Man' emphasises how man combined the arts and sciences, or even worked with imagination and logic to achieve a deeper understanding of, and a control over his expressions.

I share a few excerpts from the book here.

> *The men who made the weapons and the men who made the paintings were doing the same thing – anticipating a future as only man can do, inferring what is to come from what is here. There are many gifts that are unique in man; but at the centre of them all, the root from which all knowledge grows, lies the ability to*

> *draw conclusions from what we see to what we do not see, to move our minds through space and time, and to recognize ourselves in the past on the steps to the present. All over these caves, the print of the hand says: "This is my mark. This is man."*

Bronowski further elaborates on the colossal impact man has had through the use of his skills, quite contrary to the theories of contemporary times that rant about how man is misusing his skills to descend into oblivion! Consider what Bronowski says here below.

> *The hand is the cutting edge of the mind. Civilisation is not a collection of finished artefacts; it is the elaboration of processes. In the end, the march of man is the refinement of the hand in action. The most powerful drive in the ascent of man is his pleasure in his own skill. He loves to do what he does well and, having done it well, he loves to do it better. You see it in his science. You see it in the magnificence with which he carves and builds, the loving care, the gaiety, the effrontery. The monuments are supposed to commemorate kings and religions, heroes, dogmas, but in the end, the man they commemorate is the builder.*

Many argue that Bronowski's ideas are outdated and the world has moved on to more urgent issues today that are vastly different from what he wrote about. This may be too simplistic a view of the deeper meaning of his work. After all, man, his hands, skills, knowledge, and the desire to do better are all elements that continue to shape the world, and man, too.

Bronowski's ideas inspired the Kelkars, and they imbibed some core messages from the book.

- Whatever we do must leave such a mark that we are known for it even after we exit the scene.
- A venture can be an adventure, too.
- You should not be worried about doing something for the first time, because if it has not been done so far, it does not mean that it cannot be done at all.

- Whatever you make can always be made even better.
- All forms of work, even in metalworking, are an amalgamation of the arts and sciences.

These insights are an integral part of the work culture of the Kelkars and also the entire organisation of Grind Master.

Shailesh Sheth
Guide & Mentor

“

Cultural evolution; once it takes off, it goes as the ratio of those two numbers goes, at least a hundred times faster than biological evolution.

—

Jacob Bronowski,
The Ascent Of Man

01

Garage to Global

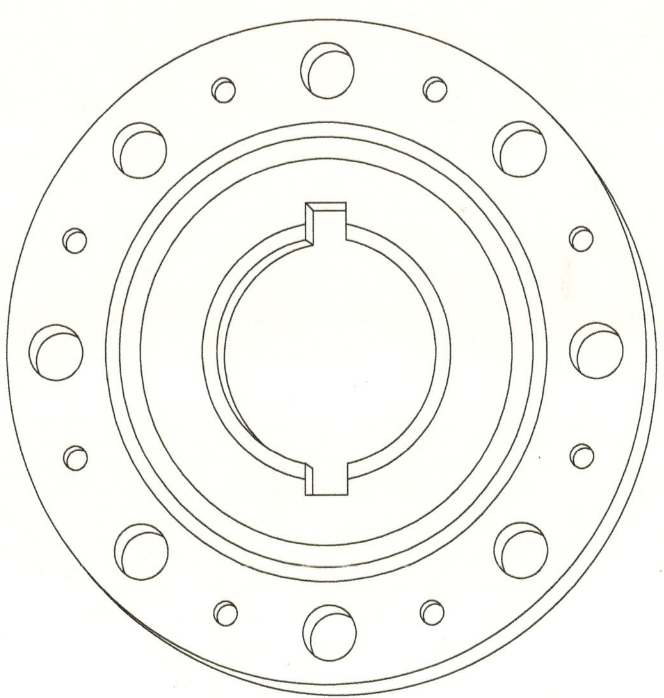

Shanghai, China. September 2009.

The room is in the bustling nerve-centre of an American automotive JV. A middle-aged Indian man and his elderly American counterpart burst in lugging a duffel bag that looks like it barely survived an encounter with airport security. Here, in a room accustomed to sleek presentations and polished pitches, this sight is... well, let's just say it's raising a few eyebrows, and some.

As the men unveil their treasure trove—a wood-and-steel contraption, that looks like it arrived straight out of a mad scientist's workshop—the room falls silent. The collective thought bubble is palpable: "What, on earth, have they brought us?" But Milind Kelkar, the Indian dynamo, and Mike Doyle, his American accomplice, are unperturbed. They launch into their pitch with the enthusiasm of kids showing off a new toy.

Their pièce de résistance? The 'Automatic Setup Change Prototype of the Crankshaft Microfinisher'. Here's the clincher: Instead of fancy simulations and glossy brochures, they have lugged along a tangible model. It was like watching a science show in a world obsessed with CG (computer graphics) – the real deal, no smoke and mirrors.

As Milind and Mike dive into the nitty-gritty of the model, the room comes alive. Skepticism melts into curiosity, giving rise to genuine interest. Step aside, fancy presentations and boring briefcases. Here are two men with enough passion to light up a room full of engineers with high energy. Cultural and national boundaries fade away at such moments when a common love brings people together. Science prevails.

Against all odds, the project is awarded to Grind Master, marking a pivotal moment in the company's history. This was not just another deal. With 30% of Grind Master's revenue at stake and a tight one-year timeline, the pressure was on. The days blurred into nights as Milind and his team burned the midnight oil to craft the perfect machine. Their dedication paid off when the crankshaft microfinisher, capable of producing one crankshaft per minute, became the first machine in the line to earn final acceptance from the client, Shanghai General Motors. The final acceptance is that coveted green flag to signal that everything is in order and every requirement is fulfilled.

Sowing the Seed

In 1983, or thereabouts, an automotive company called for qualified engineers to set up ancillary units for their business. Milind attended this meeting. But Milind was not content with being only a component supplier. He was keen on creating and selling a unique product. His interest in innovation was strong. The Kelkars decided to not ignore this drive, and went ahead to forge their way in a new domain. An entrepreneur is one who controls the what, where, how and when of business. Let us set up the context.

The Journey, Grit and Gumption

The automotive powertrain industry demands highly specialised machines with tremendous performance – especially reliability; these machines need more than 96% guaranteed uptime. The machines are used in highly automated production lines to produce critical components of cars – in this case a crankshaft, in high volumes.

Consider these numbers: 300,000 cars a year from one manufacturing line – that's 300,000 engines, 300,000 crankshafts, and a whopping 600,000 camshafts produced every year. It adds up to churning out over 1,000 crankshafts and 2,000 camshafts daily. That's 1 crankshaft and 2 camshafts every minute.

The automotive industry produces several million cars a year. It runs on a complex system, in which every machine is a crucial cog in the juggernaut of manufacturing cars. Any one cog breaking down puts thé entire production in jeopardy.

Typically, all the equipment in the production line requires a setup change to switch between two variants. This setup change time is an unproductive necessity. In dedicated production lines, the loss of time is not too significant, as the setup change is not required as frequently. However, as the automotive industry moves towards greater product flexibility, reducing the setup change time is gaining importance.

The crankshaft microfinisher, by nature of its process, is one of the most complex machines. The crank is a 'cranky' animal with a complicated process for the the setup change. Experts need to accurately replace over 100 bits and pieces of the machine during the switch. The project under discussion required, for the first time, that the setup change time be reduced to under 20 minutes. Herein was the challenge – and the opportunity.

September 2010. I stepped into the world of Grind Master. The machine, built with over 10,000 bits and pieces, stood proudly on the assembly floor as a testament to perseverance and innovation. It was not just a piece of equipment. It was a symbol of Grind Master's journey from obscurity to excellence.

Grind Master's evolution since 1984 – from humble beginnings to global recognition – is a story of grit and growth. The company and I were born in the same year. It makes my affinity to Grind Master even more special. I recognise a mirroring of our journeys. With each milestone, we have overcome our limitations to embrace innovation. The SGM (Shanghai General Motors) project was just the beginning, propelling Grind Master to the world stage.

Positioning an Indian company as a tech leader in the machine tool world is no easy feat. But with Mike Doyle's strategic moves, Milind Kelkar's innovative mind, and the Chinese openness to new ideas, Grind Master found its niche. The timing couldn't be better–amidst a post-recession resurgence, opportunities were aplenty for daring entrepreneurs. Each person here played a crucial role. Milind strived for excellence, and Mike partnered to find opportunities for the talent to shine. Mike Doyle continued to be associated with Grind Master from 2009 to 2012 and, during this time, introduced the company to the Chinese automotive industry.

Grind Master's journey isn't just about machines–it is about audacity. It is about seizing the moment, taking risks, and rewriting the rules of the game. As we continue to push boundaries and break barriers, our story resonates with anyone who dares to dream big in the manufacturing world. Grind Master started in a garage in 1984, and is recognised as a global technology player today. We went from Garage mindset to Global mindset.

"

It is important that students bring a certain ragamuffin, barefoot irreverence to their studies; they are not here to worship what is known, but to question it.

Jacob Bronowski,
The Ascent Of Man

02

THE GARAGE OF ENGINEERING MINDS

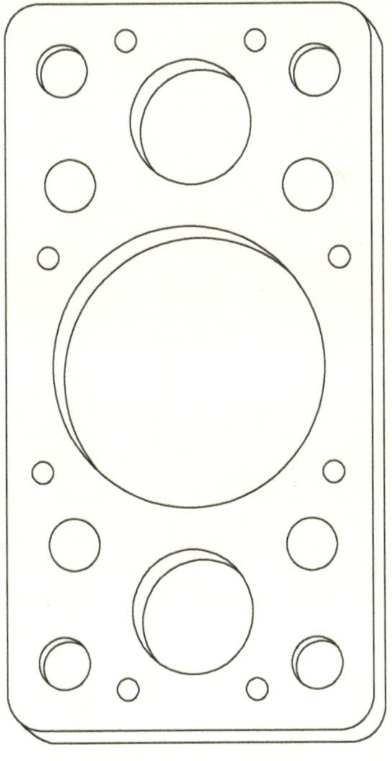

A Partnership for Life

Milind and Mohini met at VJTI (Veermata Jijabai Technological Institute) in Mumbai, both training in Production Engineering. Milind's journey to VJTI was not your typical stroll down the college corridor. He landed in Mumbai after being ousted from Garware College Hostel in Pune for some 'unsanctioned' activities like climbing down a bar from the third floor after lights out to go for a nightly snack. The gregarious Mukund Bhogale a partner in crime.

Mohini, the prodigy of her batch, was younger than her peers. She was promoted a couple of grades higher to match her calibre. She had initially set her sights on medical school but was thwarted by age restrictions. This was the plot twist that changed her life's trajectory. Fate had engineering in store for her. True to her nature, Mohini made the most of it! Mohini secured the seventh rank in the Bombay University exams in her first year, indicating a natural aptitude for engineering. This became a deciding factor for her to trade scalpels for spanners. She never looked back.

Milind, true to form, made quite the entrance into Mohini's life. Alongside several of his partners-in-pranks, including a close pal Ashwin, Milind and co would 'rag' their female juniors. Ragging consisted mainly of bombarding the juniors with questions like 'How many trailing zeros are in the number 5?' and 'What makes you think you'll make the most of the seat you have taken up in this engineering college?' It was a cunning ruse to charm the ladies while pretending to quiz them about math and engineering. The move worked.

The students turned into thick friends and formed a tight-knit group that explored the city on free days. The friends shared their passion for machines and took field trips, without fail, to IMTEX, India's largest machine tool exhibition. They ogled at the latest gizmos and gadgets, dreaming of the day they would build their own. Little did they know that day wasn't too far off.

After Mohini graduated in 1981, the couple tied the knot through a marriage-registration ceremony in Mumbai, surrounded by immediate family and a few friends (Milind's mischief-maker co-pranksters included). And so began Milind and Mohini's winding journey through the ups and downs of familial duties, engineering escapades, and adventures to last a lifetime.

The newly married couple moved to Pune to begin their work and life anew. Milind's role at Telco included setting up processes for various machines to ensure quality-control of parts. He also inspected the various geometrical parameters. This work gave Milind deep insights into managing machine alignments so they deliver the required accuracies. Mohini was a designer, working on several new machines at PMT Traub.

Milind was itching to start a business. He considered the rather crude scheme hatched in his hostel days by his mate Rattya Joshi – one of starting a timber business in Port Blair, Andamans. Mohini's mother heard this idea and said: "Andaman cha vikas nantar, aadhi magaslela Marathwada cha vikas kara" (Work on remote places like the Andamans later. You must first develop the backward Marathwada area.) This sound advice spelt the end of the Ukridge-like plan.

Dinkar Kelkar, fondly known as Appa, had been one of the first chartered accountants in Aurangabad. He wished for his son Milind to get into business and move back to Aurangabad. Meanwhile, Milind's best friend and childhood buddy Mukund Bhogale, another engineer who studied Chemical Engineering in Mumbai, had joined his elder brother Ram Bhogale to run Nirlep, a pioneering business in non-stick cookware started by their legendary father Nanasaheb Bhogale. Nirlep was facing several challenges in the polishing process for non-stick cookware, and this became an opportunity, a seed, for an engineering-led business.

Ram was already tinkering with the rather old polishing machines, and needed something more reliable. He urged the duo Milind and Mohini to design and build a polishing machine. He said, in his typical Hyderabadi Hindi style; "Kya kar rahe ho Pune mein? Aa jao Aurangabad. Aur kuch shuru karo. Buffing machine banaoge?" (What are you doing in Pune? Come to Aurangabad. Start a business.

Want to make buffing machines?) Ram had also advised Milind to minimise the capital investment, which was possible in the machine-building business.

Mohini designed a prototype machine by using a half-imperial size drawing board and a mini drafter, rigged up on a wooden stand, all of which was fabricated at home. Without any experience or similar products to look at, the prototype was created with innovative application, keeping in mind the custom requirement. For example, the polishing process was refined for Indian conditions, especially, to eliminate fire hazards.

Milind and Mohini took ten days off from their respective jobs in Pune to build this first machine. They put it together in a workshop called Shree Engineering. When the couple saw the first machine whirring to life and working exactly as they had planned, it infused them with fresh confidence and also the desire to create even bigger and better machines. It was this moment of creation – the working of the first machine – that nailed the decision for them. Milind and Mohini quit promising jobs in the manufacturing industry, in the bustling city of Pune, to pursue their passion for building machines.

Appa backed their decision, taking responsibility for the startup period by finding a nearby shed and offering the seed capital. The shed, which is the garage referred to in the title of this book, was incidentally associated with Honourable Kawade Guruji, who started MIT Aurangabad. Thus was born Grind Master. The company was initially called Precision Engineering when it was founded in 1984. In 1991, as the company grew and set its sights to eventual global expansion, it was renamed Grind Master. Throughout the book, I will continue to refer to the company by its name Grind Master.

The new place of work was located only a kilometre from the Kelkar residence. Mohini would ride her scooter back and forth while also keeping an eye on baby Sameer at home. Milind hired the first two employees, Vaijnath and Wagh, fitters with almost no prior experience. They both went on to stay with the company till retirement.

The first machines that were delivered to Nirlep raised the cookware maker's productivity by four times. Milind and Mohini continued to fine-tune the machines, and also innovated to design new machines – for example, the base grooving machines – to make them work even better. At the heart of this process was the Kelkars' determination to find solutions through innovation.

A journalist called Kumar from Business World once met Milind and Mohini to interview them as young entrepreneurs with big dreams of transforming the cookware industry. He saw the spark in their eyes and the vision to create lasting change and published an article on the enterprise

The young Kelkar couple recognise the unwavering support from their family when they decided to embark upon a difficult path where the goal was not yet visible. The Kelkars and the Phadkes unconditionally supported and encouraged the young couple with dreams in their eyes. This solid pillar of strength that was the family enabled Milind and Mohini to make the city of Aurangabad their 'Karmabhoomi'.

Karmabhoomi

Bhoomi is land. The Sanskrit words, Matrubhoomi and Janmabhoomi, refer to not only your birthplace or native but also the place that shaped your life in the formative years. This is where we form deep bonds with our culture and heritage, which go on to influence the rest of our life, no matter where we go. In a similar vein, the Karmabhoomi is the place referenced in Vedic culture to identify the place where our Karma or deeply entrenched soul connections are tied. This is where we work and build our career and professional life. This is where we fulfill our deepest aspirations and leave legacies behind from the work that we choose to do. Our Karmabhoomi is the place where life gets meaning and a deep sense of purpose.

'Begana Ladka Diwani Ladki'

'Begana' means explorer or rebel. He is someone who ventures on an impossible quest – enticed by its challenge. 'Diwani' is single-mindedly passionate in the pursuit of a mission. Dr. Anand Bhadkamkar, the then Secretary of Industries, Government of Maharashtra, used this phrase to describe Milind and Mohini. He recognised the couple's dreams and passions and used this phrase to acknowledge that they were on an unusual path.

The world of traditional manufacturing is set in its ways. To initiate any advanced technology to this setup, however helpful, was going to be challenging. Milind and Mohini saw the value of automatic polishing and grinding machines in greatly enhancing the quality and process of manufacturing. It would disrupt the status quo – rock the boat – of traditional manufacturing but also add great value and precision, among other things. As with most things new, Mohini and Milind had an even more challenging task of educating their clients, business owners and supervisors who would have to be convinced of this change. The automatic machines were advanced, and required a great deal of passion, perseverance, a touch of humour and, most importantly, the courage to take the leap of faith to use them.

Milind and Mohini initially worked on every small and big task themselves. This was primarily because there was no one to delegate to, and also because their early orders were only a few machines at first. This being a new company, it did not have a reliable ecosystem of suppliers. The trust-based relationships had yet to be built. Therefore, sourcing material for the machines became a major challenge. As was common in the '80s for small companies in the Tier II cities, hardware, motors and bearings were bought from the larger cities, Aurangabad and Mumbai in this case.

A part-timer managed the firm's accounting, and Appa's firm handled the audit. Milind read an expert book on accounting and taught himself how to read account statements. Then, with help from cousin Bipin Dada Chitale, Milind prepared the first project report to pitch to investors. The company received its first funds of under Rs 100,000 at exorbitant interest rates of 20% to 24%.

Mohini initiated the herculean task of making the machine drawings. Milind and Mohini then made the rounds of Chikalthan's workshops trying to bring to life the drawings. This is while surviving on 'chai gayab' biscuits at a café. Here's where much of the initial process-led learning came in. Many parts went to waste as the parts makers did not take into account the tolerance of the parts in the machine. The makers went by the general impression that it is sufficient for a part to look vaguely like the drawing, not be exactly as per the drawing – the infamous Indian 'chalta hai' attitude.

The numerous trial-and-error experiments forced Milind and Mohini to buy equipment and build a team to make the parts rather than outsource the process. When the company's order flow increased, they purchased the first machines – a lathe and a shaper – in 1987. Ravi Pasphulle and Meshram Rajput were the first two machinists at Grind Master. For now, the metal guarding was built manually end-to-end, with a hammer, and other tools. Later, a sheet metal working machine was added to the small but effective pool of machines, in 1989.

Two of the earliest employees at Grind Master, Jagannath and Dattu, were farm help and came from an agricultural background. They knew nothing of machines, leave alone how to work them. Milind built the first machines with their assistance, learning things on the go, including machine wiring. Milind was active on the shop floor and manually connected the first machines after a helpful tutorial from a family friend Rangnekar kaka (uncle). Milind would even manage the commissioning. These typically happened in some unfriendly environments in gala-type workshops that tended to be extremely hot and dusty. Milind would return from the tour with a bagful of soot-covered clothes and 'surma' (fine black powder) coated in the eyes from the buffing.

It wasn't only the hazardous physical working conditions that Milind had to contend with. Some of the businesses were run by proprietors with 'difficult' attitudes. Many were bigoted, ageist and generally unprofessional, treating a young vendor with disdain, and expecting total subservience in exchange for payments. Milind navigated these interactions with patience, focusing on the learnings from the experience and the deliverables on hand rather than letting words and varied personalities affect him.

Milind and Mohini remained focused on their goal of making top-class machines. They were even grateful for these difficult customer experiences as they helped renew Grind Master's 'can and will' attitude of making the machines they had promised clients. They were never distracted from their larger goal or the dreams that they set out to fulfill.

Catching the Winds to Sail Forth

1991. Mohini met Mr. Baba Kalyani (Padma Vibhushan Babasaheb Neelkanth Kalyani who went on to serve as chairman and managing director of Bharat Forge, the world's second-largest forging manufacturer) to present a proposal for an automatic grinding machine (king pin boss linishing machine). Baba Kalyani, renowned for his technical proficiency, instantly grasped the potential of integrating an adaptive floating belt grinding head into the machining process at his company. This innovation promised to revolutionise the intricate task of grinding complex components. Baba Kalyani identified the raw potential in the blueprint and endorsed the project with his pat on the back to Grind Master's efforts and dreams in pursuing it. Such an endorsement from a senior in the industry was the wind beneath Grind Master's wings.

The resulting machine was much appreciated, and led to spin-offs. Grind Master became the go-to for automatic linishing, ushering in dramatic improvement in productivity, safety and energy efficiency.

The journey towards this milestone had begun years earlier, in the cutlery sector, in 1986–87. Grind Master had initially focused on edge grinding for esteemed clients like Kishco and Jhalani Tools, and later catering to tool makers in Ludhiana and Jalandhar. The venture encountered a setback when local imitations flooded the market, eroding Grind Master's competitive edge.

Milind and Mohini's astute business acumen helped them identify the problem areas. Without wasting time, they pivoted away from the edge grinding machines for the cutlery sector. Meanwhile, belt grinding technology found new avenues in grinding forgings. Grind Master showcased a machine at IMTEX 1989 (the annual showpiece machine tools expo) to overwhelming positive feedback. This success gave them the confidence to develop the groundbreaking machine for Bharat Forge, signaling a new era of technological prowess for Grind Master.

Business volume increased at Grind Master, which was great. But it brought along some challenges in managing the business, including cashflows. The development of SPMs (special purpose machines) sometimes took longer than expected as it involved significant research. The company faced several periods of cash crunch as it awaited the realisation of funds. Milind remembers debating whether to fuel the car or go the extra mile using a scooter to save money.

Many customers were then somewhat immature. In a evolved business environment today, it would be wise to assume that such developments in a startup would receive stage-wise payments. However, in the 1990s, Milind and Mohini took bank loans at high interest rates. The business eventually came down to maintaining individual relationships. The couple would speak with each of their creditors, and explain their problems. This transparency helped build trust with business associates, and many suppliers extended support to Grind Master in these trying circumstances. Mr. Pramod Jalan of Hanuman Traders placed so much trust in Grind Master that after a few transactions, he told Milind, "Pay me when you can".

The one clear boundary that the Kelkars maintained was the separation of 'business money' and 'family money'. The two did not mix. Their personal expenses were quite basic, too. So, it was not difficult to maintain the boundary.

◎◎◎

Milind realised that Grind Master needed a product to get the cash flow going. He remembered a particular machine from Telco, built by a German company, that inspired a solution. It was a relatively simple gear deburring machine. The machine used floating, grinding and brushing heads, and was called 'nodding head' design that followed the gear profile while generating chamfer on the edges. The gear deburring machine was developed in 1988 for Bajaj Auto Gear division, and was a success.

For Grind Master, an enterprise that had not yet built two identical products until then, this machine was the first 'model' that could be replicated. Over the years, the company sold over 1,000 plus gear deburring machines across India, with several buyers ordering 20-25 machines.

Milind and Mohini's work received recognition from within the industry. Mohini, the lone woman entrepreneur in manufacturing – a man's world – received a number of awards. She received the **Parkhe Award** from the Maratha Chamber of Commerce Pune for the Automatic Double Ended Cookware Polisher, an award for creating an innovative product.

Mohini was about 25 years old then, and did not have the conventional looks of someone who could invent such a machine. Mr. Hastimal Firodia, the doyen who built the Rs 1000-crore Firodia Group of Companies, was a jury member at these awards. Mr. Firodia assumed that Mohini was a marketer or manager at the company, and asked to speak to an engineer so that he could ask technical questions. Mohini smiled and replied that she was the project engineer and could answer any technical query, much to Mr. Firodia's surprise and admiration. Mohini's ability to communicate well in English proved useful – writing and presenting to Indian and international companies without fear can be a limiting factor for entrepreneurs. Not for Mohini or Milind.

Grind Master also received the FIE Foundation National Award in 1992.

Some Hiccups on the Path of Hope

How is it to operate out of a garage? As a second-generation entrepreneur, I can perhaps never really empathise with the problems that come with the territory. The decision to move to a bigger setup – a workshop – came from an order that was impossible to execute in the existing premises. The contract was to build a rim polishing machine for a cycle manufacturer. It was a 25m long, 5m wide and 3m tall machine, developed after studying the global practices for such a machine.

Mr. Prakash Ratnaparkhi from Electronica Pune had been instrumental in introducing the client to Grind Master, and sealing the deal. The team dived headlong into the challenge despite being somewhat intimidated by the size of the machine. The machine also had new elements like complex castings and specialised belts that had to be developed with some iterations.

The first batch of castings produced for the machine did not get the desired results. An inspection left everyone at Grind Master jittery with a 'Potaat Gola Aala' – a knot in the stomach, in Marathi. It became urgent to find a good foundry. The larger foundries for automotive castings were not a good fit for this project. Special purpose machines needed castings in batches of one – they had to be flawless, neat-looking and also at a reasonable price. One of the foundrymen, fondly called 'Hasra Deshpande' (smiling Deshpande or one who is ever-smiling) in Pune, worked with Milind and Mohini to deliver the desired quality.

Similar struggles for machine parts became a part of Grind Master's journey. But Milind and Mohini did not lose hope, and kept their creative spirits high, always focusing on the solution rather than the problem. These experiences endowed Grind Master with a comprehensive knowledge of machine components. The Kelkars' expertise was building the way, brick by brick, or rather component by component.

The parts were finally ready, and the machine was coming together nicely. Now, Milind and Mohini were staring at a bigger problem. The machine, once built, was going to be bigger than their garage shed!

On a war footing, they found a new site to construct a workshop. Once the new floor was ready, they assembled the rim polishing machine under a tarpaulin cover for a roof!

The machine invoice value of around Rs 25 lakh was a huge start for Grind Master, and a big saving for the cycle manufacturer (Similar European machines would have cost 5-6 times with added custom duties of between 50% and 60%). As the young company cheered the dispatch of this project, little did they know that they were about to face a shocking hurdle. While in transit, the vehicle carrying the machine met with an accident right at the doorstep of the client's factory. When it was unboxed, the machine was found damaged.

Milind started for Chennai the moment he received the call, reaching to find the customer upset and blaming Grind Master for poor packing. Taking the rather nasty and inconsiderate comments in his stride, Milind assured the client that Grind Master would fix and re-deliver the machine on priority. While this took 2-3 months to complete, Grind Master faced a severe cash crunch.

The customer's payments were realised only after the repaired machine was delivered. One would expect a large company, standing to save a lot of money, would have been considerate towards a small-scale enterprise, but the world of business can be transactional with no margin for error. The client's team offered technical support as needed, and assisted in building a sound machine. With all the cost escalations, Grind Master ended up making a loss on this project but learned a great deal. The thrill of building a first machine of this size and complexity is priceless.

The rim polishing machine went on to become a successful product line at Grind Master in the coming years. Apart from bicycle rims, the technology could be applied to motorcycle rims. A Bangalore-based company that was contracted to manufacture rims for TVS, placed an order for a fully-automatic machine by offering a 10% advance. Grind Master built the machine by investing over 80% of the project's value. When ready to deliver, the client had vanished, and the owner was uncontactable.

When Milind approached TVS about this contractor, they indicated that this company was no longer a supplier! The owner had lost money in making movies and had shut shop. Through this experience, Milind and Mohini learned a harsh business lesson, albeit the hard way, amidst their machine-making enthusiasm. To taste the unpredictability of business first-hand was their silver lining in this misadventure. What came next is how they turned this experience into a strong determination to keep going.

The Kelkars eventually modified and sold the machine to Mandap International, a company in Faridabad. The only way Milind and Mohini could sell the specialised machines was by finding companies that made rims. They learned that big automatic machines required more investment, and the market demand for such machines was low. However, smaller semi-automatic machines were more suitable to sell in the Indian market. The unforeseen problem with the motorcycle contractor who disappeared had taught something useful to the Kelkars while also giving them a product idea.

In the years that followed, two station rim polishing machines each were sold to almost every company that made rims – Yoshika, Bagla Group, Atlas, and the suppliers to Hero and Honda. All these brands now used Grind Master's rim polishing machines. Some Taiwanese machines and a few Indian-made copies of Grind Master's design entered the market, and the Kelkars graciously exited the market having transformed it.

The journey from 1984 to 1991 was a voyage into uncharted territory marked by relentless exploration and innovation for the couple that completed their first decade, in life and business, together. This included bringing up a child with love, while crafting solutions that not just functioned but evolved into refined products. The couple knew that their work benefited from continuous research that was fueled by an unwavering 'bring it on' attitude. This way, a humble garage startup demonstrated its prowess in diverse fields, and pioneered the making of machines that were inspired by their European counterparts. Through it all, Milind and Mohini worked with minimal references for the machines. It was not unlike groping in the dark to find the power switch.

The birth of the name Grind Master in 1989 brought newfound focus to the mastery of polishing and finishing machines, further solidifying the company's identity. Transitioning from a garage to a workshop, it became clear that Grind Master had firmly established its presence and was here to stay.

Cooking up a Revolution

India's cookware industry grappled with the lack of scientific polishing solutions. This was a collective problem that every company within this industry faced. It included bottlenecks in polishing operations, inconsistent quality and poor labour safety in polishing shops, to name a few.

Determined to offer a solution, Milind and Mohini walked into the office of Dewal in Pune, with hope and the offer of a promise. By the end of that meeting, they had signed on Dewal as Grind Master's second customer. Many conventions were broken during this meeting. Two youngsters in their mid-20s walked into a factory without an appointment. They were not only welcomed but also given an order for business based on crude, hand-drawn sketches of a polishing machine. A huge amount of faith from both parties was riding on this transaction. The ultimate goal was to solve the company's polishing problem.

The utensils industry of the 1980s used primitive methods, plagued by inconsistent polishing, loose tolerances, and inadequate safety measures. There was great demand for automatic machines by manufacturers of pressure cookers and non-stick cookware. Most companies, often led by entrepreneurs, were eager for improvement.

The industry had been relying heavily on costly imported automatic machines due to the lack of specialised Indian-made options. Established brands like Nirlep, Hawkins, and TTK Prestige led the charge for innovation, demanding alternative solutions to polishing. Individual households apart, the cookware industry catered to the needs of India's burgeoning wedding market — each event requiring substantial cookware. With an eye on the market's vast potential, Milind and Mohini grabbed this golden opportunity to introduce advanced technology to India's cookware sector, thus laying the groundwork for a promising business venture.

The need for simple, robust solutions to automatic polishing made Hawkins, and other discerning brands, to collaborate with the young couple. Much brainstorming and work later, the Kelkars unveiled the concept for the DB400 model, which went on to become a bestseller. This was the first machine with an automatic cycle sequence controlled by relay logic. Milind and Mohini meticulously fine-tuned many key elements of the polishing machine, including work holding, polishing heads, and movement mechanisms. Grind Master initially produced 4-5 machines every year, each iteration an improvement over the previous version as it incorporated the refinements and implementations of the lessons learned. The DB400, which is multiple versions old now, is a staple in the pressure cooker manufacturing industry, boasting over 500 units overall in the cookware industry. This mean machine has cemented its status as the production machine of choice.

The stainless steel utensils industry faced its own challenges in polishing. Over 80% of the industry continues to rely on manual polishing in uncomfortable conditions. One of the largest in such steel utensils is one that is used to cook camel meat in the Middle East. Grind Master crafted a machine to manage the polishing of these large steel vessels.

Apart from nonstick cookware and steel, brass hardware parts require buffing. The company developed successful buffing solutions for hardware parts, including door knobs, door handles, plates, and more. Grind Master had delivered a lock polishing machine to multinational conglomerate Godrej in the 1980s, which is still in use. It was a first-of-its-kind mush head polisher, which had delivered polished locks (millions of them) for over 35 years. One thing was clear: if anything needed polishing, Grind Master was up for the task!

With business growing, Grind Master needed to ensure the backing of a reliable partner who could consistently deliver top-quality tools to complement the highly automated polishing processes. To this end, the company forged a partnership with Lippert, in Germany, in the late 1990s.

By the early 2000s, with several years of experience behind it, Grind Master introduced the indigenously developed Rotary index polishing machine for the cookware industry. This machine used rotary tables, higher power heads and an advanced controls system. Sivanesan, a South Indian company, partnered with Grind Master to develop these machines. Mr. Sivanesan and his deputy, Mr. Shankarnarayanan, a young man of 70, worked closely with the Grind Master team on the nuts and bolts of this machine.

Ahead of his time, Mr. Sivanesan was extremely energy conscious and believed in optimising motor power. Sivanesan and Grind Master found a mindset match as both parties had mutual respect and understanding that first-time developments may not always hit home in the very first time. The cookware industry had much to gain from indigenous technology, but some investment in R&D was essential. However, unlike Sivanesan, many companies expected magical results in the first attempt. Automation does not happen, well, automatically. It also needs the backing of huge management will. Sivanesan understood this well enough.

The Rotary index machine for polishing pressure cookers became popular in medium- and large-scale companies, not only in India, but also in Africa. Prashant Saraf and Bharat Pawade commissioned a machine for Tower Aluminum in Nigeria. Their workshop had a low ceiling, and the buffing process generated intense heat. The machine was designed to produce one part every 15 seconds (that's 240 parts an hour), and the engineers waited with bated breath to see if it, indeed, reached this target. After setting up, a production run resulted in the machine buffing 380 parts in one hour! At the end of the shift, the exhausted operator crashed on a bench, took off his sweat-drenched shirt, and declared, "I cannot work at this speed; please slow down the machine." This demonstrated the machine's strong production potential.

The renowned TTK group, maker of the Prestige brand of cookware, approached Grind Master, to provide an automation solution to their problem of loading and unloading. In 2013-14, Grind Master's Robotics group delivered several Robotic handling systems to the TTK group. This enabled the company to load one cooker lid every 12 seconds – a long way from the basic machines used for this purpose in the 1980s!

Rotary index machines have greatly evolved in the last few years. The most recent machines are more complex than their immediate predecessor – boasting over 10 stations with Servo axis for complete automation. Three of these advanced machines with contemporary design were delivered to Jindal Lifestyle (JSL). With this transaction, both Grind Master and JSL were promoting the concept of 'Make in India'. Mr. Jindal stated that his company would not invest in imported equipment, especially from China. He was looking for an India-made machine, which he found in Grind Master. Built with four decades of experience in cookware polishing, this top-of-the-line rotary index machine is considered a masterpiece.

Buffing machines have since diversified into numerous applications, sparking the emergence of several Indian polishing machine companies, most of them inspired by Grind Master's pioneering work. While Grind Master briefly explored other cookware industry requirements, it ultimately found the superfinishing and microfinishing product range more compelling.

Compared to China's advanced automation in cookware manufacturing, the Indian industry lags, owing to lower wage costs and less focus on health and safety. Chinese polishing machines have rapidly evolved, driven by local innovation and contemporary technology deployment.

The Indian cookware industry, particularly the unorganised sector, still operates sweatshops, where workers endure hazardous conditions and shorter lifespans due to prolonged exposure to fine dust. This grim reality underscores the challenges faced by buffing machine operators. Grind Master's automation solutions serve as a beacon of hope to usher in better times for the workers of this industry.

With its complete range of cookware polishing machines, Grind Master revolutionised the industry, automating the polishing of over a billion utensils, illuminating the path forward, and forging invaluable partnerships along the way.

The Sleeping Lala

While the DB400 was a standard machine, it wasn't an obvious choice of polishing machine for all pressure cooker manufacturers. It was not so much the technology that was under scrutiny but the prevailing social and cultural systems that business owners did not find the motivation to improve.

Mahesh Sahasrabuddhe, a sales and business development executive at Grind Master (now the pan-India sales head), vividly remembers a visit to a shed in the outskirts of Delhi, in the scorching summer of 2006. He went with another engineer, who worked in sales, Amol. Their car huffed and puffed its way to the dusty remote site. The 'factory' resembled the owner's home more than it did a place where cookware was manufactured. It was difficult for the two visitors to imagine this as a site of cooker production.

After keenly watching the machine videos and discussing the proposal, taxes, transport costs, and other specifics, the conversation finally shifted to the price. The parties settled on Rs 4.5 lakh. That's when things got interesting. The owner, around 60 years old, sat amidst a stuffing of blankets bundled up behind his chair. Suddenly, the pillows and blankets flew in the air behind him, revealing an old man, awakened from his slumber, who exclaimed, "Saade char lakh rupaiah kisi machine ka keemat hota hai kya, kyun mere bacche ko phusla rahe ho" ("Does any machine cost Rs 4.5 lakh? Why are you trying to con my kid?") The Sleeping Lala, or 'bade pappa' (elder uncle) had woken up. The fate of labour-intensive processes and 'bade pappa's knack for choosing the cheapest alternative were suddenly on the line. Transforming cookware polishing meant that Grind Master had to overcome such barriers, too.

“

Dare to be free, dare to go as far as your thought leads, and dare to carry that out in your life

Swami Vivekananda

03

BUILDING A SPECIALISED BUSINESS

Becoming a Custom-built Specialised Machine Maker

Through 1995, Milind carried a sheet of paper in his pocket everywhere he went. On this paper were listed the three projects that, if not completed successfully, would mean the end of Grind Master.

Crisis 1: Radiator trimming machine. In hindsight, Milind and Mohini realised that they should not have taken up this project at all. But this was in hindsight. It was only after robust experience that they understood that the radiator has a complex shape and trimming it without CNC technology was next to impossible. Grind Master used a hydraulic copying mechanism as an alternative, and though not the most optimal solution, the process had finally worked.

Crisis 2: Sole plate grinding on all sides in Russia. Grind Master had the idea of using floating heads to apply the technology of grinding to a range of parts, from connecting rods to sole plates. This led to problems at the customer site. The samples delivered for pre-acceptance had few burrs, and were possible to be belt grinded. But the jobs in real production had much heavier flashes, and were tearing into the belt.

Samad, a young engineer, having joined Grind Master straight out of college in 1993, was sent to commission this solution. There was a plague epidemic in India then, and Samad was quarantined for one week after he reached Moscow. The quarantine center was a kind of jail, where he was given food three times a day through a slit in the door. In the absence of mobile phones, it took some time for Grind Master and the client to ascertain his exact whereabouts, and to establish that he was safe. Samad then proceeded to work on site for a long time, converting the belt grinding machine into a carbide cutter machining system.

Crisis 3: Centerless finishing of annealed tubes. Tube size variants gave rise to a solution that solved several polishing problems. But it was too soon to cheer. Grind Master had not anticipated the impact of the material on the coated abrasive. Initial tests went fine. But during a mini-production run that was a part of the machine inspection, it was established that the coated abrasive belts did not last too long. In fact, the belts had to be replaced with almost every cycle, and the machine uptime was less than 50%. The solution to this criticality came from changing the coated abrasives on the belt. After experiments with various materials, the inputs from VSM, Vereinigte Schmirgel – und Maschinen-Fabriken AG, a reputed abrasives company in Germany, finally worked well. This success led to Grind Master's collaboration with VSM.

With two machines stuck on the floor for a long time, and a third in seemingly never-ending commissioning, Grind Master faced a severe and desperate cash crunch. We often say after surviving a tough trek, "What doesn't kill you makes you stronger." Grind Master had passed this existential crisis.

Grind Master took home four key learnings from this experience.

1. Don't try to do it all alone. Look for technology partnerships that can fastrack solutions
2. A specialised business works from nurturing a strong people-driven culture
3. Build a strong sales-led organisation to sell applications
4. Never, never, never give up

The next few years saw Grind Master transform to a 'custom-built specialised machine manufacturer', from being a 'special purpose machine manufacturer'. The creation of this identity helped clarify its DNA. The company would grow beyond an enthusiastic entrepreneurial garage venture into a focused organisation known for its trustworthiness and expertise.

Expanding Beyond Horizons

In two years, between 1995 and 1997, Grind Master looked almost unrecognisable. With speedy growth and expansion, the workshop was now brimming with people and machines.

Ms. Sandhya Pande was one of the first engineers that Grind Master recruited in 1992. Ms. Pande broke every gender stereotype in the book, and managed every aspect of machine assembly, from supervising technicians to building the machines and grooming interns and junior engineers.

Sudhakar Joshi joined the team in 1995 to manage the fabrication and machining activity. Senior in both age and experience, he ruled with an iron hand. After his retirement, many workers at the company breathed a sigh of relief while acknowledging, "Sir used to scold and shout at us, but he also knew how the parts were to be made."

Mahesh Sahasrabuddhe, who had interned at Grind Master during his engineering studies, joined the company along with three of his friends. This was the first 'graduate engineers batch' at Grind Master. Bharat Pawade recalls responding to an advertisement in Lokmat newspaper, and being interviewed by Milind in 1992. Pawade had initially planned his job at Grind Master as only a stop-gap as he considered the small size of the enterprise. But he went on to continue working as part of the Grind Master family for many years.

When asked to go to Malaysia to commission a machine in 1996, Pawade was scared and intimidated. He had never travelled overseas, and was apprehensive that he didn't know the local language. Mohini told him, "You understand this machine well, and are in the best position to do the job. One cannot progress in any work without focusing on the job at hand." Pawade started in the company as an ITI technician. With determination and the will to succeed, he learned English and computer knowledge, and now leads a team to build complete machines.

Grind Master developed its own style for nurturing a people-driven culture by putting together a motley bunch of people, not all of them having experience in the machine tool industry. This is the story of a company built on the back of ordinary individuals who performed extraordinary feats almost daily. It entailed pushing the self, and each other, beyond what is deemed to be one's capability. It is the attitude of 'can and will' that set Grind Master up for success.

With its growing reputation came better opportunities. Milind often said to the customer, "If the machine works, it is yours. If it does not work, the risk is ours." The company made a loss on several projects because it had decided to take on all the risks of the R&D activity. Milind and Mohini also absorbed, with a smile and plenty of grace, the cost escalations, machine modifications, and the occasional rejections. They benefited from tremendous learning throughout the process.

Through all these experiences and the high standard that Milind and Mohini set up for the company, Grind Master developed a strong identity as a technology company and solution provider. Over time, the company gained client confidence in its capability and understanding, which paved the way towards profitability and growth.

A strong sales and marketing faculty enabled the business to mature by leaps and bounds.

The 'Can Do and Will Do' Attitude

Grind Master has participated in every edition of IMTEX – the annual showcase exhibition of the Indian machine tool industry – since 1989. Owing to Grind Master's growing business, for the first time, the company had the desirable task of shortlisting client enquiries to identify the most promising ones.

Grind Master started its journey as an SPM (special purpose machine) maker but had to adapt quickly to becoming a maker of custom-built specialised machines. When a customer faced a unique challenge – as they did in most cases – Grind Master didn't simply throw its hands in the air and wait for someone to tell it what to do. The company got down in the mud and pottered about till it found, or devised, a workable solution. This attitude transformed the company's identity from an SPM maker to a specialised machine maker. Interestingly, the company's specialist identity was triggered by its necessity of finding a customer for a stuck-up project, known in the machine tool industry parlance as a project that is executed but is held up for various reasons.

An SPM maker applies his engineering ability and customer inputs to make a custom new machine. A specialised machine maker, on the other hand, develops the technology (often from scratch) to solve a specific problem. This know-how of solving problems is key to success. It was important that Grind Master be considered an expert in the industry. Several European and Japanese companies, relatively small in size, gained global reputation for being masters in a specific technology. Grind Master identified its core competence and had the vision of becoming a master in metal finishing.

Early in its journey, Milind and Mohini noticed the relief and joy they brought to clients when they suggested a solution. The promise of a solution, no matter how big or small, is enough to bring a sparkle to the eyes of someone who is gradually losing confidence and beginning to doubt the project itself. When Grind Master offered a solution, it was a revival of customer confidence when he starts to see that there is a way forward. The transition from 'they can do it' to 'they have done it and will certainly do it' is a big leap. This leap of faith led to many deals being successfully closed.

A sales team was emerging at Grind Master. Being a customised machine maker, the sales engineers at Grind Master needed a deep understanding of the process. Mahesh Toke, Abhijeet Pande, Mahesh Sahasrabuddhe and Nilesh Pathak (all from the machine assembly background) were recruited internally to the sales function. The modus operandi for this team was to attend to the enquiries that came through exhibitions like the IMTEX or by word of mouth. The new sales team divided up the regions across India to develop the relevant connections in their respective markets.

Mohini would guide the team, setting aside her role and love of engineering, to re-dedicate herself to the company's sales and business development. This was about having a conviction and commitment to doing what was needed for the company by venturing into unknown territory, and exploring the possibilities. The Grind Master team had developed the company culture of delivering what was committed to the customer. But, the company's direction would be determined by the orders that were pursued and received. The team learned along the way, with every client interaction. Mohini's patience in explaining concepts and ideas, over and over again, if needed, till the client absorbed it fully, created a benchmark of sorts for effective communication. In introducing new technologies, Grind Master realised, the truth needed to be, on some occasion, said a hundred times until it was convincing enough.

SPM builders usually do not typically develop a marketing and selling approach. They continue to be a 'jack of all trades'. Mohini's vision brought the entire team on to hyper-focus on what's important. This dogged determination, along with a clear path ahead, ultimately made Grind Master the master in specific fields.

The sales engineers at the company were home-schooled. They were learning by doing, as there was no prior format they could follow. The company, in this sense, was building the ship as it was also sailing. Mahesh Sahasrabuddhe, for example, had joined in the assembly department and had gained experience over eight years when he was transferred to the sales department. His region would be North India. Doing business in North India requires specific sensibilities. It demands knowledge of the way of talking with people, the cultural environment, and a unique decision-making process, especially in the un-organised sector.

Most of Grind Master's clients were family-run small enterprises, known in local parlance as 'Lala' company, typically helmed by a patriarch called 'Babuji' by one and all. Mahesh had strong machine and process knowledge. But this role demanded that he first understand the culture of the small companies before attempting to create business relationships. He also had language differences to contend with. It took Mahesh about two years to find his feet after which he was hugely successful. Initially reluctant to make this transition, Mahesh eventually started enjoying the process.

Mahesh shared with us some of his key learnings from these experiences.

1. Always keep calm. Meet a customer with an imaginary ice pack over your head. Postpone the discussion if you find that the ice pack has melted, but always remain cool

2. Always listen to the customer first, giving him ample space to talk to your ever-ready and patient ear
3. Do not be bogged down by something that is not in your control

This includes India's infamous traffic jams. Anyone in India has to face jams in the city and on highways. We have the choice to be frustrated by the situation or to calmly wait as we do something constructive during the wait, including relaxing. There are also many work situations that can benefit from a similar attitude.

His success in North India set up Mahesh for doing business anywhere in India. He had been the first engineer to transition to business development, and would go on to train many juniors, including me, in this field.

Mohini stayed the chief point of contact for the customers, developing a precursor to the CRM (customer relationship management) systems that were later adopted by the company. Mohini held the real market information, and also had knowledge of industry trends. Companies don't purchase capital equipment every year, or even often enough. Yet, being connected with customers even when they don't have an immediate requirement emerged as the key to building a strong relationship-led connection with customers.

The name Grind Master became synonymous with 'doing what it takes'. The company did everything in its power to fulfill its commitment of delivering complex engineering – whether it was absorbing cost escalations in R&D projects, or going out of its way to find optimal consumables, or the effort to train and retrain customer personnel to use the machine. Grind Master was known for its commitment to making every machine deliver as per expectation. This reinforced the company's reputation as a Solution Provider, over and above just a Machine Supplier.

The Focus: Centerless Finishing Machines

Centerless grinding machines, originally developed by US-based Cincinnati Machines, and others, had existed for long. However, the technology of centerless belt grinding was relatively new in the 1990s.

In 1991, a company called LMW Coimbatore wanted to develop a finishing solution based on this technology. Grind Master conducted a thorough study of imported wheel grinders, and developed the first centerless belt finishing machine in India. This machine was designed to provide finishing for the textile machinery shafts. The company went on to develop some small centerless machines for simple automotive parts.

Till now, Grind Master had traversed quite a journey. This included making Indian-origin machines for costly import substitutes, besides surviving several risky projects. Milind and Mohini felt the itch to gain advanced technical knowledge. They were aware that the European, American and Japanese companies had gathered a solid knowledge base from a variety of applications over decades. Collaborating with any of these companies that used cutting-edge technology would bring Grind Master up to speed with the contemporary thought process. Instead of reinventing the wheel, Grind Master could learn from those a little ahead on the path. From the mid-1990s, Milind and Mohini began conscious efforts to find suitable partners.

Vlademar Loeser (LOESER Germany) was keen to expand, and the recent opening-up of the Indian market was attractive. The company visited Grind Master's booth at the IMTEX in 1993, and expressed interest in taking things forward. Grind Master visited the Loeser factory in Speyer, Germany, and discussed a collaboration agreement. Loeser shared with Grind Master a design for their model – the RPS374. This was a centerless finishing machine with compliant heads. Loeser would charge no license fee but a royalty payment for every machine sold with this design.

The first machines that Grind Master built under this collaboration were all for the automotive industry – shock absorbers for two-wheelers, for example. Grind Master contributed significantly to refining the design with an acute observation of the process and regard for the machine's performance. While the European machine builders used coated abrasive belts for finishing, the Japanese automotive machines had experience with wheels. Being exposed to both technologies in India, Grind Master combined the best of both worlds, thereby using whichever process was most appropriate for the specific application.

The Loeser collaboration ended after running its seven-year course and did not continue for a variety of reasons. The royalty payments, while being made on the machines sold, were relatively small. The affordability of the Indian market was low, so the revenue was much lower than it was in the European market. The royalty payments, in this scenario, did not make sound business sense to continue.

Centerless Finishing: A Variety of Applications

Accord Corporation, a Singapore-based metal grinding company, worked with Grind Master since 1996 to sell a few semi-automatic machines. Accord was looking to promote its machines and polishing consumables in the Malaysian tube industry. Since Japanese machines were prohibitively expensive, an opportunity to develop machines for the Malaysian market came Grind Master's way.

A brief visit to the customer gave Grind Master's engineers the insights they needed to deliver as per the brief. The engineers observed the process and the machine used. They made sketches on site, and then returned to design, from scratch, a tube polisher with automation. The resulting design, delivered in 2000, was a start. Grind Master continued to deliver multiple machines to clients in Malaysia, cementing the strong relationship with Accord. Accord has continued to partner closely with Grind Master over the years. Mr. Y B Tan, who owns Accord, once visited Grind Master after a gap of several years. While planting a tree on Grind Master campus, he commented, "Let the growth of this tree be a symbol of our long-term partnership."

The success of the machines delivered to Malaysia was later replicated for the Indian market. India's tube mill industry had been using primitive methods. Basically, once the tube was out of the mill, two operators would hold the tube and index it, and a third operator used hand-held polishing tools to process the length of the tube. It was crude, to say the least, and left a poor finish quality with haphazard patterns and scratch marks on the tube. The operators also had a miserable time doing this day in and day out. A frugal simple design that was both affordable and manageable, was the need of the hour.

To meet this need, an early version of the Bestseller GCL series was introduced in India, in 2003. Amol Saraf, the sales engineer at Grind Master, commented, "The tube mill industry is small and well-networked. Once our machine was successful, we quickly started receiving calls from several other mills, demanding the same solution. Later, when our machine was copied by local manufacturers, customers would ask them 'Aapke pass ka Grind Master dijiye' (give us your version of Grind Master machine). Over the years, more than 1000 tube polishing machines were sold to tube mills. The machines were sold across India, Bangladesh, Malaysia and also Australia and New Zealand."

Round bars of specific kinds also need finishing operations. Steel bars, stainless steel bars and hard chrome-plated bars each need different types of processes. Venus Wires, a stainless steel manufacturer, was one of Grind Master's first customers from the bar industry. Grind Master developed a low-cost belt finishing series called LMCL that became popular within the industry.

Viraj Engineering, owned by Vipul Chitalia, needed a machine for the finishing process of hard chrome bars. His company was then a small workshop. Realising that finishing is required both before and after chroming, Grind Master suggested a change in their process and helped implement this incrementally. Vipul Chitalia once said, "I could enter the hard chrome business only because of Grind Master. My USP was the better finish of the material."

Mohini and Milind were attending a tax planning workshop when they received a call from one Mr. Kochhar. Known as Mamaji, he was instrumental in making Viraj Engineering one of the largest manufacturers of stainless steel bars. He wanted Milind and Mohini to immediately visit the plant near Tarapur. He half-jokingly said,

"Paisa kamaoge toh tax planning karoge, paisa kamane ke liye hamare liye machine banao" (It is only when you earn income that you can plan your taxes. Make machines for us to earn your income).

The meeting took place the following day, and led to several interesting projects for Grind Master. Mamaji's style was unique. He would invite Milind to Mumbai, and then fly him by helicopter to Tarapur. Mamaji used to maintain four elephants, feeding them puran polis (Maharashtrian sweet bread) after getting off the helicopter. Mamaji lived life on the fast track mode, wanting everything done immediately. He wanted to be two steps ahead of time, even getting off the car before it came to a halt fully.

Centerless finishing machines had several advanced applications, including precision finishing for hydraulics. Hydraulic tubes for telescopic cylinders are manufactured in large numbers and need fine finishing before and after surface treatment to increase their corrosion resistance. Such tubes are typically processed on centerless belt grinding and polishing machines. Grind Master applied the models developed, such as the FV series (model number), for such applications.

Hydraulic cylinders are manufactured in an environment that is similar to automotive manufacturing, and the machines are to be made highly reliable. Several machines of FH and FV models are in production in various companies like Wipro Fluid Power India, HYVA India, Taviller Turkey and Jagtar Singh India to name a few.

Centreless machines come with certain limitations. Large tubes and rollers, such as textile machinery rolls and water desalination pipes are difficult to process in these centerless machines through the feed concept due to limitations in feeding the big part. Grind Master developed an ingenious trolley machine concept for such applications, in which the part was rotated on rollers and the finishing heads moved longitudinally along the length on a trolley. Grind Master built from scratch a machine that had always been imported for, in particular, the strategic industries for advanced materials.

Grind Master further diversified its centerless finishing applications. Grind Master discovered many of these applications used by several advanced tube manufacturing companies when its engineers visited the Tube Fair in Germany in 2007, 2009 and 2011. These soutions were exhibited at this fair. The Indian engineers at the company were able to solve many new problems with a 'can and will' approach, resulting in the widest variety of products and applications.

Deburring and Beyond

Deburring is basically removal of unwanted material (called 'burr'). This unwanted material is not intended to be generated in the first place. The manufacturing process has certain natural defects that cause it to produce material called burr. This release of unwatned material is both uncontrolled and unintentional. 'Deburring,' therefore, is the process of getting rid of the burr. It is normally done after one or several of these processes: stamping or fine blanking, sintering or machining.

The deburring process has typically been left to the component maker's imagination. The flow sheets and drawings for manufacturing parts would indicate the various processes and machines that were to be used. These drawings would contain a generic statement with an asterisk that read 'All edges should be deburred'. But manufacturers rarely knew how exactly the deburring method was to be done. Years of neglect to this important operation has meant that deburring is one of the main causes for parts being rejected today. Awareness of this process is now increasing, and India's manufacturing industry is investing more in the deburring process.

Deburring machines for flat parts and for shafts started as an extension of the finishing business. The deburring process was carried out just before or after the finishing process, in most cases. Therefore, it was a perfect 'adjacent' product to develop.

For flat parts, Grind Master developed the CFG series – conveyorised belt grinding and finishing machines – discovering that this machine could also do deburring, especially of the heavy burr left during stamping operations. While this method worked for removing heavy primary burr, it left, by itself, a fine secondary burr. Grind Master's exposure to Lippert's advanced processes in Germany helped the engineers realise that brushes are used for fine deburring. There are a variety of brushes – Liprite wheel brush, abrasive bristle brush and wire brush. The abrasive bristle brush, in particular, was highly effective in generating a rounded edge – something that was not possible with abrasive belts.

Planetary deburring, which is based on the concept of planets revolving around the Sun while rotating on its own axis, inspires this sophisticated deburring technique. The rotary motion of the brush attacks the burr while the revolving motion ensures that all the burr in a complex part with pockets gets processed. The concept was so interesting to engineering that the first PDH (planetary deburring head) was more of a toy. Engineers imaged the Earth revolving around the Sun, rotating on its axis, experimenting with rotational speeds and testing deburring results.

Grind Master's sales team found new applications for this technology. They observed that tumbling methods were being used even for flat parts in several industries. So, they pitched the conveyorised deburring solution highlighting its consistency and throughput. The team conducted free tests for many customers to demonstrate the results. It was the sales team's persistent effort that slowly, but surely, these industries have changed its standard practice for the way parts are deburred today.

In 2013, Switzerland-based Hoerbiger ordered two of these deburring machines – one for the India plant and another for the company's Czech Republic plant. I led this project. One of the key processes is for the client to approve the design. To showcase the design, in particular the improvements made to the machines over the past few years, I needed to first understand the earlier models and improvements to the current design. I brought in a software expert to significantly improve the wear compensation methodology, and also the user-friendliness of the human-machine interface. We delivered precision deburring machines that performed well, achieving the requirement of generating a specific radius on the parts' edges. Deburring had gone beyond being just a process to remove unwanted 'burr'. It was now, also, generating a specific geometry on the part to improve its overall performance.

Deburring is a process that is sometimes of no value, low value or high value. The customer's understanding of this process and how he perceives it is also coupled with his ability to pay for it. Grind Master has, over the years in business, noticed a divergence in the market demand for deburring. There has been high price pressure from several Indian manufacturers for easy and cheap solutions, leading to Grind Master devising and delivering compromised solutions. Most of these have worked well. One of the few such solutions to have not worked was one delivered to a company in Pune. What works for low-production workshops does not always work reliably in high-volume production environments. The key, Grind Master learned, is to offer only the most appropriate solutions.

As a manufacturer, Grind Master felt deep regret having gone down this path to compete in the market, albeit successfully. As we attended to several complaints, owing mostly to the cheap-and-best, compromised and creative solutions, talented American innovator John Deere's words resonated for us, **"I will not put my name on a product that does not have the best in me."** These words kept coming back to us as we attended to customer complaints. After this, we made the difficult decision of selling the workshop machine series only for low-volume applications. For high-production applications, such as in the automotive industry, we sold only the advanced series.

Grind Master, understandably, lost many orders due to this approach. But all machines that were delivered since have performed well and received accolades. The deburring systems for the automotive industry's clutch-and-brake parts perform, essentially, the same application that we had earlier failed with. The method is known. But the rabbit hole goes deep. The machine needs a highly refined design to work flawlessly during the 24/7 production cycle. With support from Tom Campbell, a technical advisor for Grind Master in the US, the design was made even more robust. What helps in making the design more robust, is to identify every fault and failure mode. We took extensive feedback from the first such machine in the US. We improved the maintenance support for the machine and also the online support.

Katy Gasper, a manufacturing engineer from Burkland, Goodrich, Michigan, shared positive feedback, which offered the much-needed encouragement for Grind Master's engineers. The engineers' patience provided the essential time to continuously improve its functioning. Eventually, we were pleased with the result. We drove away from Goodrich, Michigan, elated that all the efforts had delivered the desired outcome.

Every machine part needs deburring but not all manufacturers are ready to pay for good machines and consistent processes. Grind Master believes there is a global niche market where its solution are appreciated. After learning the hard way, we have learned that there can be no compromise to good solutions, even in deburring.

A hundred minus one amounts to zero.

Our takeaway: Doing well is important rather than doing more.

From Workshop to Factory

An American advisor to Kirloskar Copeland visited Grind Master in the early 1990s. At the time, the workshop had been constructed by novices. We still live with some of the limitations of its crude design but at that time, it was worse. There were gutters on either side of the assembly area. The gutters were primarily used for laying cables, but they invariably attracted waste material, loose nuts, bolts, and dust, making it a rather ugly sight.

During the American's visit that morning, one of our technicians, Afsar bhai, a six-footer, was sitting at one end of the bay, hammering a bearing into a spindle housing. It appeared that he was at war with the bearing. The advisor calmly indicated to us, later, that it was not possible to do business with Grind Master in this environment. This was the first time the company received such honest feedback for its workshop. However, it was clear that to build quality machines for the automotive industry and for corporate customers, Grind Master's facilities had to step up.

We took the advisor's feedback seriously and immediately set in motion a slew of measures to fix the workshop premises. Major civil repairs were carried out across the premises to spruce it up. We also acquired the neighbouring plot of land to construct a new building with an office and a much larger assembly area. Importantly, the loading dock could now handle containers – an essential requirement for export business.

The company put in place a basic working discipline. We initiated a number of training activities, including one on assembly techniques. A lesson on '11 ways how not to tighten a bolt' was introduced to all technicians at the company. We started to conduct monthly meetings for all teams to share operational problems and brainstorm solutions. This initiated a culture of continuous improvement.

Another key initiative that helped was to introduce AutoCAD and then leapfrog into the 3D CAD tool. Amruta Ukirde, the first draftsman to train in this method, is still highly regarded for his accurate modelling of complex assemblies.

While the American from Copeland did not return to see the transformation at Grind Master, his Indian counterpart Milind Deshpande did, and must have shared a decent review. For, Kirloskar Copeland ordered its first superfinishing machine from Grind Master in the year Y2k.

Graduating to building machines for the automotive industry, and developing the superfinishing technology, Grind Master was well poised to gain from its growth years in Indian automotive that followed at the turn of the millennium.

1984 © *The garage of engineering minds - a bootstrapped operation*

1988 © Milind and Mohini with one of the first cookware polishing machines

1992 © Graduating to a workshop - building the first indigenous rim polishing machines

© Ajji and Appa - the rock solid foundation for Grind Master

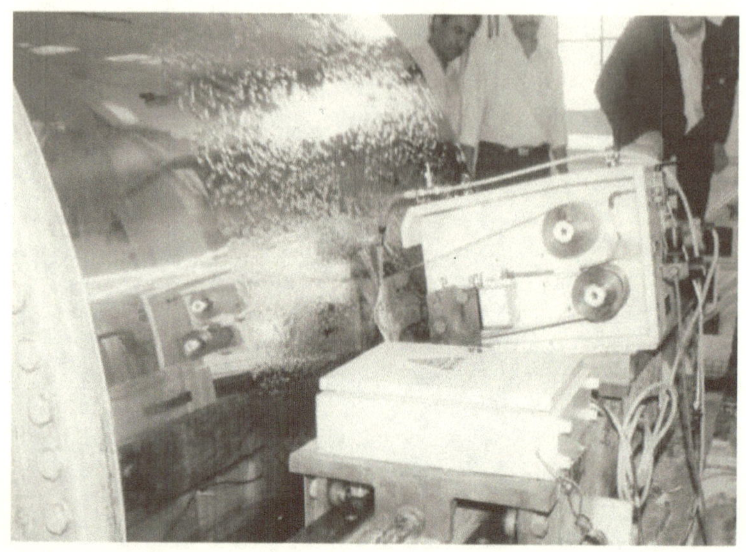

1992 © Deploying the First Superfinishing units to a diverse range of applications

1997 © 'I will bring you to the world' Milind and Mohini with Mark Sterner from 3M

2003 © A lifelong friendship based on Engineering - Milind and Tom Campbell

2003 © IMPCO collaboration agreement

“

We are all afraid for our confidence, for the future, for the world. That is the nature of the human imagination. Yet every man, every civilization has gone forward because of its engagement with what it has set itself to do. The personal commitment of man to his skill, the intellectual commitment and the emotional commitment working together as one, has made 'The Ascent of Man'

Jacob Bronowski

04

OPERATING AT THE FINISH LINE

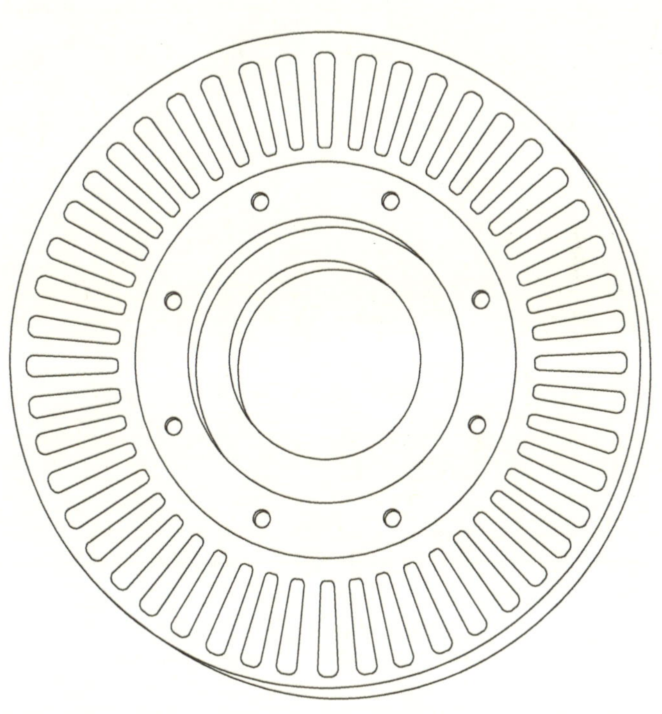

EMO 1989. EMO is the biggest machine tool exhibition in Europe. It is considered the go-to for the machine tool world globally. Milind was visiting the mecca of machine tools on a shoestring budget. The visit opened his mind to various global developments that were afoot in the industry. A couple of European machine builders had displayed the 'superfinishing' process using film-backed abrasives. Realising that this is a game-changer, especially for the finishing of precision components, Milind set out to develop the first indigenous superfinishing unit.

Milind has still safely kept the original design files with the various calculations, and gear ratios, forces and torques that led to this achievement at Grind Master. The rough draft of the paper workings that eventually transformed the company is a precious nostalgic treasure trove.

Only a few metal-finishing machine manufacturers worldwide had yet ventured into the superfinishing process. The market size for conventional metal finishing processes like buffing and belt grinding in developed countries was quite big. It was perhaps the highly fragmented nature of the Indian market that pushed Grind Master into developing superfinishing. Getting into the much higher precision class of superfinishing, placed Grind Master in a fairly small list of companies worldwide.

Microfinishing and superfinishing processes transformed the trajectory of Grind Master's journey. 'Buffing' or 'polishing' processes bordered between the categories of 'machine tools' and 'processing equipment'. Decorative polishing, on the other hand, was done on parts for purely aesthetic reasons. 'Micro-grinding' processes that include microfinishing, superfinishing, honing and lapping are considered the finest of machining processes, which is typically done after grinding. Milind and I later coined another term – NANOFINISH – a finish that can only be described in nanometers. NANOFINISH would become Grind Master's flagship product line. Developed from humble beginnings and inspired and supported by numerous partners along the way, NANOFINISH is a shining example of 'Make in India, Make for World.'

The industry had been using the honing process for internal diameters like crankshaft bores and cylinder bores of engines since the 1930s. When similar tools were applied to the diameters of shafts, the process was called external honing or lapping. A relatively soft stone with a fine abrasive oscillator was fixed parallel to the workpiece surface to finish the rotating workpiece. A combination of the Rotary motion and the oscillatory motion generated a 'cross-hatched' finish required to provide lubricating characteristics to the surface.

Later, during the 1980s, 3M, the highly innovative company famous for everything from Post-It sticky notes to ScotchBrite brand of products, invented the MICROFINISHING FILM. The company used the electrostatic deposition of fine abrasive grains on polyester-backed films. The abrasive film gradually became a tool of choice for fine finishing on shafts. 3M partnered with various machine builders to encourage the use of the MICROFINISHING FILM.

The first superfinishing units by Grind Master were sold as retrofits on lathes. They converted the turning machines into superfinishing machines. These machines would work best for customers who were low-volume producers and could make do with this kind of setup. One of the most interesting applications for superfinishing was in the machine glazed (MG) cylinder superfinishing for paper mills. The roller size was about 3 meters in diameter and 3 meters long. It was a part of a paper mill that produced high-quality laminated paper. The resulting finish was Ra of 10 nanometers.

The first opportunity to build a dedicated superfinishing machine came from TKAP – Toyota Kirloskar Auto Parts. In 1996, a team including a Japanese engineer approached Grind Master looking for 'paper lapping' attachment. They were scouting the market to find a solution in India. While known to the Japanese by a different name, the superfinishing attachment, already developed by Grind Master, had everything they needed. The machine built for this application would be a precursor to the bestselling SMP model range of machines.

A superfinishing machine is much more complicated than a metal finishing machine. It has many more parts, especially higher precision parts. Through history, technology upgrades have typically happened in response to the need. Necessity, as they say, is the mother of invention. Grind Master took up the challenge to deliver just what TKAP needed. For this, we used a recently launched software called Solid Edge to engineer the machine in 3D. It was a great way to design a sophisticated product. Through the use of this software, it became clear that components like headstock, tailstock and slides could be much more precise when built. The next step after the design was in making the parts and assembling them right. TKAP supported Grind Master through this journey, visiting the factory multiple times to witness the progress of the machine coming together.

IMTEX 2001. The Grind Master stall had displayed a superfinishing attachment with a hydraulic piston cylinder, finished to Ra 0.001 microns. Grind Master had applied for the Design Innovation award. Dr Suryaprakash, a mentor and guide for the IMTMA, insisted on taking the cylinder to the Zeiss booth to cross-verify the results claimed by Grind Master. The test was a huge success, which led to Grind Master being awarded the CMTI (Central Manufacturing Technology Institute) Design Award.

Grind Master had, over the years, established itself as a technology company, and a solution provider. It brought the great ability to do things differently. The company's confidence to interact with the external world and solve its problems resulted in organisational maturity. With the development of superfinishing technology, Grind Master started to operate at a high level!

I will bring your Superfinishing Machines to the World

1997 St. Paul. Minnesota. 3M headquarters.

Mark Sterner, a rather brilliant engineer at 3M, was part of the product development team that invented the microfinishing films. Mark encouraged and inspired Grind Master to grow its superfinishing business. His aim was to promote the abrasive film business in Asian markets. He had said, "I will bring your superfinishing machines to the world." And he truly did.

He organised a detailed five-day training for Milind and Mohini at the 3M lab in Minneapolis, in which he introduced them to the various applications and industries where these machines were required. These included automotive, hydraulics, rotogravure and rolls, among others. 3M labs had many superfinishing machines. Milind and Mohini were exposed to a whole world of possibilities the abrasive film opened up to Grind Master.

Amongst the various applications and machines that Milind and Mohini saw at the 3M technology center was a crankshaft microfinishing machine. A key new mechanism in this machine was the 'scissor arm', which was built to follow the eccentric diameters, like crankshaft pin journals, as the shaft rotates. A prototype of this kind of arm was designed and built by Grind Master in 2002. As fate would have it, a collaboration pushed Grind Master to the microfinishing world much faster than one could have imagined.

Mark spoke with Industrial Metal Products Corporation (IMPCO) about Grind Master. IMPCO was originally a family-run company, founded by the Judge family. Founded in 1937, IMPCO had been in the microfinishing technology since its inception. Even in 2003, the founder family member Norm Judge was a director in the company. The other directors were Dave Houghton, Dean Peters, Dave Howland and Jim Vasilenko. As luck would have it, IMPCO was looking to expand to the Asian markets, and Grind Master had all the potential to be a suitable partner for IMPCO's expansion plans.

Technical collaboration was not new to IMPCO. They had experienced success with their earlier collaborations in Europe (Evans and Price, which later became Neuteq) and in Japan (Nachi Fujikoshi). Their approach was to license the microfinishing technology, handhold the collaboration partner, and earn royalties from it. This strategy enables specialised machine tool companies to continue developing in their home markets while also taking their technology to geographically remote markets.

The IMPCO team clearly recognised Grind Master's unique 'can and will do' attitude that was embedded in its DNA. It also emerged during IMPCO's discussions with Grind Master that a recognised company in India would have a much better chance of introducing microfinishing technology to this market. There were only a few crankshaft and camshaft machines in India then. The cost of such imported machines was prohibitive for the Indian automotive and Tier 1 industry. Till then, it was common for companies to follow crude polishing methods – holding the shaft on a lathe and manually lapping the diameters.

The crankshaft is considered to be the heart of an engine. Therefore, automatic microfinishing, when introduced to the Indian market, would be a key process technology. Grind Master had a track record of introducing such innovations to the market. Grind Master, with its history of just under 20 years, was waiting for a moment like this one. The company could proudly introduce to the market a step-up in technology.

Milind and Mohini visited the US in the fall of 2003 to work out the nuts and bolts of the collaboration agreement with IMPCO. The couple returned home from their second ever trip to the US with a game-changing collaboration in hand. It was the vision of entering the high-precision automotive powertrain manufacturing business. In their mind and heart, they carried a great determination to overcome any seen and unseen challenges that such ambitions could bring.

Motivators par Excellence

The IMPCO-Grind Master collaboration happened at the right time.

India's landscape was changing. It was a common sight in the India of the 1980s and 1990s to find a car by the roadside, its bonnet open, and the driver pouring water in the radiator to cool the engine. Cars in the new millennium were comparatively far more reliable.

Family-owned and -run firms, especially those in which the directors are technology oriented, are pioneering in many ways. They have a greater appetite for risk (calculated risk). They have also encouraged the Indianisation of various technologies. Many such visionaries and leaders were the main motivators for companies like Grind Master to rise from the bottom up and make a difference.

Mr. Dayanand Netalkar was one such visionary. He led a crankshaft making operation, and had a critical requirement from an American customer. Grind Master stepped in to build a microfinishing machine for Mr. Netalkar's company. The process was not smooth and ran into rough weather. It came to a point when Milind decided to stay put on site until the machine's process results were achieved and the machine was stabilised.

Mr. Netalkar later said, "Grind Master made our life easy – first with microfinishers and later with balancers. Our relationship with Grind Master has been very friendly. I have given both positive and negative feedback, and they have been listened to. Being a nationalist, I do not like to send money abroad. Grind Master was one of the first quality Indian-made machines in the crankshaft line."

Over the years, the partnership between the Netalkar Group and Grind Master only grew. Satish Netalkar, Mr. Dayanand's uncle, when placing the order for Grind Master's first crankshaft balancer, said, "Your first microfinisher came to the Netalkar group. It was destiny that the first balancer would also come to us."

Grind Master also worked with several important companies to provide its technology. One such company was Precision Camshafts Limited (PCL) in 2001, which undertook polishing of camshafts for the Railways. Mr. Ajit Jain from PCL took the lead for this project with approval from the director Mr. Yatin Shah. PCL commissioned Grind Master to produce camshaft microfinishing machines. Grind Master offered the solution of a polishing tool, which was mounted to an attachment on a lathe. This innovative solution used a special felt wheel, and although crude, it solved the problem, and was appreciated by PCL.

After a few years, in 2004, PCL was looking for a finishing solution for an American automotive client. Grind Master, once again stepped in to install the first microfinisher for camshafts. Grind Master and PCL were able to overcome minor hiccups, and manage a smooth working relationship. Grind Master has provided scores of machines over the years to PCL. The relationship continues with the new generation leader at PCL, Karan Shah.

In 2005, I visited Bharat Forge's factory in Pune as part of my college visit from IIT Bombay. My batch of young students were taken on a tour to see the machines that matter. We stood before the latest crankshaft manufacturing line. In that line stood an IMPCO-built crankshaft microfinisher. The process engineer asked us to take turns to 'feel' the finish on the diameters of the shaft. He explaining that this new technology was key to getting the final result on the parts. I proudly said that this machine was actually made and installed by my father's company even though this machine was 'imported'. Those who stood around me stared at me in disbelief, many of them even dismissing my claims. The belief was that such specialised technology could only come from Germany, Japan or the US. I may not have been taken seriously then, but soon enough India was in the forefront of manufacturing and was building some of the world's finest machines.

Since 2006, Grind Master has built over 30 machines for microfinishing crankshafts for Bharat Forge Limited (BFL). Grind Master and BFL shared a great understanding of technology. The continued relationship was particularly possible because of the visionary, Padma Vibhushan Baba Kalyani.

BFL made a wide range of crankshafts, and Grind Master had the opportunity to develop many 'firsts' in this product range with BFL. A few years ago, while discussing a crankshaft microfinisher, a senior manager, while looking at Mohini's petite frame, commented, "This is a very heavy job for you. It is more than 200 kg." Within a few years, any apprehensions about Grind Master's ability had vanished, leading to a healthy, long-term partnership between the two companies.

Mr. Kalyani met Mohini at a CII conference where he delivered a talk on how innovations impact the machine tools industry. After his session, while interacting with some journalists, he introduced Mohini as the owner of the most innovative company Grind Master. It was heartening for everyone at Grind Master to receive such a glowing review from a technocrat like Baba Kalyani.

Mr. Kalyani is not only a seasoned technocrat but also understands the potential of Indian technology. He has a keen eye to identify Indian talent with the capacity to innovate. BFL has, over the years, encouraged the Indian machine tools industry overall by taking risks, especially by giving opportunities to builders of technology. They have also highlighted the lacunae in the system. In one meeting with IMTMA members, Mr. Kalyani spoke about poor workmanship plaguing the industry. He cited examples of leakages. Mohini stood up and affirmed that this perception of the Indian machine tool industry was outdated and that the industry had come a long way.

BFL grew by leaps and bounds since 2000. Grind Master worked with several senior managers at BFL. There were some disagreements along the way but the two companies have shared a trusting and understanding relationship for the greater good. There was great respect for each other's work and ethics. During the Covid-19 pandemic, when there was a shortage of oxygen cylinders, Mr. Baba Kalyani rose to the occasion when challenged by the PM of the country to quickly produce this critical item to fight COVID.

In its production line, BFL was missing the finishing machines. Grind Master stepped in and undertook the job on a war footing by first developing the process, and then putting together a makeshift system so that the prototype production could start. Grind Master then built a decent production machine. All of this was done within the span of a month. This was possible because of the cooperation of Milind from Grind Master and Kultar Singh from BFL. This collaboration was inspired by Baba Kalyani.

Such partnerships highlight the real potential of 'Make in India'.

Doing What it Takes

A highly specialised and niche technology, the microfinishing machine is not easy to build. To add perspective – a typical lathe machine contains about 150 parts while a superfinishing machine for geared shafts has 400 parts. A microfinishing machine for crankshafts has over 1,600 parts.

Right at the start of the collaboration, Milind had resolved to make the highly accurate parts for the microfinishing machine – there would be no deviations to the drawing. The company did not own any CNC machine nor was one available amongst vendors in Aurangabad at the time. The first machine that was considered for this purpose – a Mazak VMC – was expensive. Grind Master sought advice from those in the business, and the popular opinion was that investing in a CNC machine would not make economic sense considering the low volumes required by Grind Master.

Milind, being adventurous, decided to take the plunge. It was a bold decision but it turned out to be a practical one. It is always a good decision to build a company's internal capabilities. It was important for Grind Master to retain control over quality and delivery of precision parts. A machine is as good as the parts that go into it. Over the years, the manufacturing facility has been built with the help of various CNC machines. The essential know-how to develop the various machine parts has been an important part of this process, and was also developed internally. This is an example of choosing a path that was not taken by others before. Grind Master never hesitated to go down unknown paths albeit with caution to get surprisingly positive results.

Even before investing in the machine, the Grind Master team was always making quality parts using conventional means. Ravi Pasphulle, a highly skilled turner, would meticulously set true-cut with multiple iterations. He would take a long time but would get the part right. The assembly technicians would then scrape the flat parts to the required accuracy. It was always in Grind Master's DNA to do what is takes.

Grind Master had to step up its machine workmanship – assembly and testing. The customers for microfinishing were typically large automotive companies and were much more demanding than other clients. They were also well-versed machine-tool users. Mohini once asked Norm Judge at IMPCO how to improve the machine's aesthetics. Norm took a pencil and paper and drew a box. It was a simple principle: 'Make everything at right angles'. Building neat functional machines has since been the ethos of Grind Master's design. To make this possible, the company moved away from manual methods and started to use automatic CNC and laser methods for sheet metal working. We checked the machine assembly quality at multiple stages by introducing the key Machine Quality Record (MQR) concept for aggregates before assembling the sheet into the machine. We followed the process of continuous refinement with every machine built. It had to be better than the previous one.

Typically, in a technical collaboration, the licensor provides the engineering and design for well-developed products. The licensee is expected to build copies of this design following the given guidelines. There were a number of reasons why the IMPCO designs would not have worked in Asian markets. The microfinishing machine is, by nature, custom-built. IMPCO had designed the machines for the American automotive industry, which typically uses much larger engines than the Asian automotive market. The machines, therefore, also needed to be more compact for the Asian market. Over the years, Grind Master designed a range of machines by innovating based on IMPCO's references. It was a highly collaborative process of working on such projects with designs going back and forth with the different stakeholders.

Compared to the dedicated high-volume manufacturing elsewhere, Indian facilities produced a wide range of crankshafts in the same line. Machine flexibility and the ease of setup change were critical. The new range of machines, called the GBQ series (GBQ - Generating Bearing Quality was a term coined by IMPCO. It was used to designate a certain models as 'GBQ'), were more flexible than the machines built by IMPCO. IMPCO was receptive to the proposed changes, and the partners worked together wholeheartedly. Such an approach is often rare to find in technical collaborations where each party thinks it knows best.

Technology leaders in the developed world bring their designs to developing countries with a typically colonial approach of educating the natives. The collaborative partnership between IMPCO and Grind Master in the 2000s formed the basis to create a successful product range that had a cutting edge against its German and Japanese competitors. During this process, the Grind Master team became independent and competent to conceptualise and design new machines from scratch. From being a licensee, Grind Master had imbibed the microfinishing technology and gained the competence to not only customise machines but also conduct the process research.

Influx of Talent Boosts Grind Master

Mohini continued to spearhead the established metal finishing business, bringing in steady turnover for Grind Master. Milind dived deep into the new technology and built a new team. The team included some trusted hands like Lolewar and Ekshinge, and benefited from the influx of fresh talent that was experienced in building precision machine tools, particularly at Bajaj MTD (Machine Tool Division). It was in 2003 that Bajaj had started outsourcing many its activities, and the MTD was one of the sections that it scaled down.

Santosh Patil was one of the gems we acquired from Bajaj. An advisor insisted to Milind, "I do not know if you have a vacancy, but hire this man. He is good." Electrical Systems were, in those days, considered a part of peripheral systems. Consultants and contractors were accordingly engaged to deal with these systems. Santosh built the 'control systems' team from the ground up by grooming electricians, including Subhash Kalaskar, and engineers like Deven Rahangdale.

Electrical control systems eventually became an integral part of the machine. Prashant Yeole, a young controls engineer with experience in deploying CNC controls, working at Bajaj MTD, was inspired by Grind Master's growing reputation as a technology company.

He voluntarily left his assignment at Bajaj and sought to join Grind Master for the opportunity it offered him to innovate. His insights on building microfinishing machines using CNC technology played a pivotal role in helping the company to form partnerships with reputed companies like Fanuc and Siemens.

Milind recollects, "At a critical juncture in our discussions with Chen Jun Jie and Zhao Tao of SGM (Shanghai General Motors), there were hours of endless discussion about control systems. Prashant convinced them of the Fanuc CNC solution. This made a tremendous difference to the quality of the machines." Prashant expanded his role from control systems into design and engineering, and also materials, going on to take up the role of Milind's trusted partner – right hand – in the Microfinishing business.

The exodus from Bajaj MTD formed the bedrock of the new team at Grind Master. Suhas Kulkarni and Ramakant Dusane in design engineering, and Gangawane and Pawar in assembly brought new energy to Grind Master. Shedding the OEM culture, they imbibed the entrepreneurial culture of Grind Master. There used to be an unstated rule in the manufacturing industry that mechanical/ production engineers would be leaders. The machine tools industry that originally was mainly consisting of mechanical systems, was also steeped in this way of thinking. The 2000s saw a transition with the age of computer technology changing outmoded ways of thinking. Controls engineers went on to be an integral part of machine building. The key reasons for Grind Master being able to attract and absorb talent at this state of the company's growth was its flexible organisational structure and the space to explore new ideas and innovation.

Sowing the seeds for auto partnerships

Grind Master gained huge experience by building machines for a range of vehicles, including passenger cars, commercial vehicles, tractors, motorcycles, scooters and compressors. Indian corporates like Ashok Leyland, Tata Motors, Mahindra, Bajaj Auto, Hero Motors and Greaves trusted their Indian partner Grind Master to provide microfinishing machines for their projects. Grind Master's growing reputation also brought international companies like Musashi, Wabco, Delphi to consider the solutions offered by us. Component manufacturers like Happy Forging, MM Forging and AMTEK also took the plunge to invest in advanced machines made by Grind Master.

Just as things were ramping up for Grind Master's NANOFINISH business, the global recession hit in 2008. Distressed customers were wary of picking up the ready machines that stood on the shop floor. Many projects were cancelled or put on hold. Milind and Mohini led the company from the front, even at this challenging time. They inspired confidence in the staff that this was only a phase. They encouraged the company to use this time to diversify its product range by developing collaborations and refining systems. Grind Master emerged unscathed from the recession, not having to lay off employees or contractors, or cutting salaries. The strong trust within employees in the 'Grind Master family' stems from such resolve and commitment shown during tough times.

The automotive industry bounced back from the crisis with a bang. The Asian markets picked up growth quite fast and even became the manufacturing hub of the world. We had enough references and experiences by then that Indian and International automotives in India considered Grind Master's machines for their projects. Our company became a trusted partner, emerging from the recession even stronger than before.

A number of international automotive companies including Renault Nissan and PSA have trusted Grind Master's solutions over the years. In some projects, Grind Master faced stiff competition from German manufacturers. But we offered a technologically differentiated product, and prevailed. The confidence in our methodology, stemming from deep process research has been the key reason for our success. By 2012, we could look at a car model and tell if the crankshaft or camshafts was microfinished on our machine.

Grind Master's German competitors used to build machines with both stones and films. Grind Master firmly believed that the film-backed abrasive process was superior in multiple ways, including its process-reliability, low maintenance, and user-friendliness.

A major American company was setting up a new camshaft manufacturing facility for heavy diesel engines and approached Grind Master for finishing solutions. Large camshafts demand the most stringent finishing requirements in the industry. The process development for this project took time and several iterations, but the delivered solution was stable and was much appreciated.

The story of India's automotive growth can be traced to a flagship company that has pioneered and led the increase of car usage in India. This company brought to India the culture of quality manufacturing. It is none other than Maruti Suzuki. From the humble Maruti 800 to the rugged Maruti Gypsy, the brand offers a range of bestselling cars that are much loved for their reliability.

Despite Grind Master's successes in partnering with various other automotive brands in India and China, the opportunity to build machines for Maruti Suzuki eluded the company until the mid-2010s. When Grind Master finally got the chance to work with Maruti Suzuki, it derived several experiences and learnings. The first is that the Japanese way of working is slow but sure.

Grind Master delivered the first deburring machine that was to replace an old machine in an existing line. When 3-4 of Grind Master's deburring machines had performed well, Maruti Suzuki seriously considered Grind Master's microfinishing machines, too. The auto company replaced its first camshaft lapping machine that was supplied by a competitor. It found that Grind Master's machine delivered much better results with its good-quality build. The company also appreciated Grind Master's strong service support. This cemented Grind Master as a trusted supplier for Maruti Suzuki with the former building and supplying dozens of machines for crankshafts and camshafts in the past few years.

For Grind Master, its projects for Maruti Suzuki have been a learning experience in professionalism and good planning. Grind Master noticed how Maruti Suzuki runs its entire operation like clockwork, giving ample time to the engineers to build machines. It is a matter of pride and success for Grind Master that it had the opportunity to work for a true champion of the Indian automotive industry.

Grind Master worked at expanding its superfinishing product line launched in 1996. This included building machines for inline shafts and cylinders. These technologies were entirely homegrown. The superfinishing technology evolved and refined over the years. The sales team found newer applications for superfinishing. From small synchrocones to large piston rods, the team developed custom solutions for every application.

Additionally, Grind Master also provided solutions to the gear pump industry for its gear pump shafts that required deburring and finishing of diameters and faces in the automated machines. This solution is used by about ten manufacturers worldwide. Grind Master having pioneered film-backed abrasive-based face finishing technology turned out to be a highly reliable method for this industry.

Grind Master's multi-station automatic machines were also attractive to automotive geared shaft producers, including SFL (Chennai), Gewis (Germany), Getrag, FAW and Geely (China). These are all the various applications in a range of industries that Grind Master's technology could successfully transform.

The foray into China

IMPCO had been observing the rapid strides made by Grind Master by leveraging some of its unique abilities. IMPCO started to source many components, including machine bases, housings, and microfinishing units from India. Its growing confidence in India-made products over time led it to outsource entire assemblies to Indian engineers. This eventually led to Indian engineers customising machines and fully building them from scratch.

IMPCO then considered Grind Master to build machines for the Chinese market, which was fast emerging as the largest Asian market. Grind Master built two machines, which were run off at IMPCO and from there supplied to China. It soon became apparent that with this roundabout system, it was the transportation companies that were making the most profit in shipping the machine across the world.

Would Grind Master consider including China and other Asian countries in its collaboration agreements? The opportunity was overwhelming huge. A bite too big to let go?

One evening, at around 9 pm, at the end of a 12-hour workday, Milind looked up from his desk and asked Prashant, "Prashant China mein business karenge kya ?" (Prashant, should we do business in China?)

"*Jaroor karenge!*" (Of course we should!)

“

Perfection is not attainable. But if we chase perfection, we can catch excellence

—

Jacob Bronowski

05

ENTER THE DRAGON

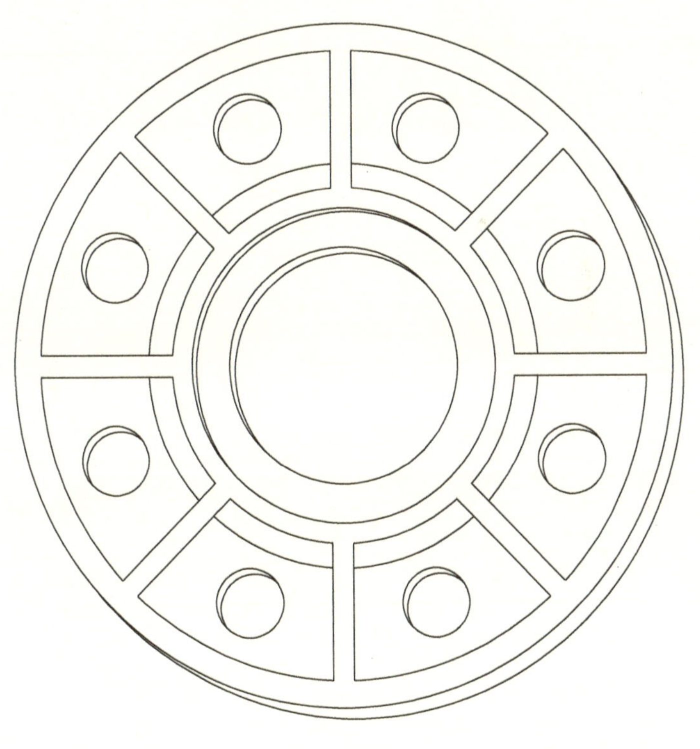

Milind was on a flight to Shanghai when he struck up a conversation with an African woman seated next to him. Mid-way through the conversation Milind talked about his work and the business visit to China. The woman clapped and exclaimed, "For the first time, I have met somebody exporting to China, and not the other way around."

The story of India exporting machines to China is so rare that it has, over the years, become a conversation starter for us. India's trade balance is in the negative. India imports everything from home appliances to consumer goods and automotive components like batteries and motors. The amount of exports is so limited that freight carrying charges from Mumbai Nhava Sheva to ports like Shanghai are negligible (while India's total trade amounts to about US $140 billion, India's trade deficit is about US $100 billion as of 2023-24). China produces goods with varying qualities and prices. Some low-quality 'Made in China' consumer goods have given the manufacturing giant a questionable reputation. The Chinese automotive industry, as seen and experienced by Grind Master (being an industry insider), is fairly advanced in technology and operations. Post 2020, Chinese companies are leading in the EV market. Names like Gotion for batteries and BYD for EV technology have made their mark in the automotive world.

Even in the early 2010s, when Grind Master first entered the Chinese automotive industry, China's manufacturing methodology was several years ahead of Indian manufacturing. China's abilities in project planning and management, manufacturing process engineering and efficiencies were a few notches higher. A part of the reason for this better quality was their comparatively higher volumes in production. At one point, China produced almost ten times the cars that India produced. It was clear that if Grind Master was serious about its aspiration to export machines globally, especially its specialised automotive finishing products, it had to first establish a reputation in China.

Between 2010 and 2015, automotive powertrain manufacturing was booming in China. Chinese automotive OEMs (original equipment manufacturers) like Great Wall and Changan, and joint-venture companies like SGM, SGMW, DPCA and DHAC were all setting up new facilities on a fast clip. They were making a high number of engines and gearboxes to meet the growing demand from both the domestic market and for export from China.

With Chinese manufacturing geared up for high volumes, they also needed to import specialised equipment to meet the reliability and process requirements. These imports were often processed with government subsidies and tax exemptions. Microfinishing machines came in this category of 'special machines' that were imported. German and Japanese companies were already supplying several machines to China every year. Most of these companies had set up a basic sales and service operation in China, and some were even manufacturing machines in China.

IMPCO, based in Lansing, Michigan in the US, found it difficult to compete in this area because of its geographical distance. There was stiff competition on prices, support and flexibility, too, which it could not meet from across the oceans. So, IMPCO handed over the Asia region operations to Grind Master. It was a once-in-a-lifetime kind of rare opportunity for Grind Master to partner on a project with a leading American company in a joint venture. The project in Shanghai was a foot in the door for Grind Master, and the years that followed were thrilling with work being done at breakneck speed to fulfill the commitments.

Every opportunity in the early years threw a new challenge towards Grind Master. Sometimes it was with the machine concept, and at other times, the layouts. Machines suitable for automation were in high demand at the time. It became a common requirement in the auto industry to have multi-station machines with integrated handling. For example, SAIC, a leading Chinese automotive, required camshaft microfinishing machines with up to four stations, generating a combination of Level 1 and Level 2 finish on journals and lobes, and also deburring of lobes. Such machines grew big and complex in terms of controls and software.

Automotive JVs of different origins had different requirements. DPCA, a joint venture of the French Peugeot Citroen, were quite European, whereas DHAC, a joint venture of Honda with the same Chinese company Dongfeng, had Japanese influence. Adapting to different requirements and customising machines for specific requirements became a USP for Grind Master. The European and Japanese companies were not willing or even able to execute the level of customisation that Grind Master could offer.

Grind Master faced the key challenge of meeting the process specifications of the automotives. Surface finish has an ever-growing complexity. The client would, sometimes, request a finish parameter that was not measured earlier. At times, the parameter would not even be known. It became important and challenging for Grind Master to first understand and then achieve the process reliability expected by the automotive clients. This had to be done using statistical measurement.

Milind took the lead in understanding what the parameters meant, and set up tests in the process research lab to demonstrate that it was achievable. He would document the various other process parameters. This speedy development was essential to prove to the customer Grind Master's technical ability and qualification to complete this project. This process demanded some amount of calculated risk-taking, which was backed by the attitude to take on the challenge and do what it takes to meet it. Grind Master can be proud of the fact that it always produced parts well within the tolerance specifications.

The execution of these first projects taught Grind Master many lessons. The Chinese automotives' expectations of machine quality, both build standard and workmanship, were higher than the expectations that Grind Master was used to till now. As a result, the company's quality systems had to be upgraded. We had to closely scrutinise the aesthetics, ergonomics and maintainability of the machine elements, including the enclosures, to build the right equipment. Each automotive company had its own standards for the use of electrical, pneumatic and other peripheral equipment. Each company also defines safety in its unique way.

Take, for example, the maintenance windows. Some companies expect the windows to be designed to fall when the screws holding them in place are removed. Some other companies need the windows to still stand in place even after removing the screws. Each company also follows specific standards for software programming to make it easy for debugging. For Grind Master to build the best machines for this industry, its engineers needed a deep understanding of specific skills in controls, safety engineering and software. As this work in automotives expanded, it became clear that what Grind Master did was not restricted to mechanical engineering alone. The company now needed engineers from mechanical, electrical/electronics and software to each play a strong role in successful project completion.

Milind led the efforts to build Grind Master's multi-talented strong core team dedicated to the auto industry's needs. The concept of a business vertical had evolved in the 2000s with the advent of microfinishing. But it was in the decade of the 2010s that the NANOFINISH team built its muscles and capabilities. It was a largely home-grown team. Every person on the team needed to step up to the challenge of building machines for the ever-evolving automotive industry. It demanded creative thinking on the part of the hired talent, and to figure things like using measurement instrumentation and refining the packaging process.

The first few machines supplied to China in 2009, 2010, and 2011, while being the best that Grind Master had ever built, had their share of problems. There were software bugs, fine points about safety, and issues with Chinese translations, to name a few. What the customer appreciated was the sincerity with which the issue was fixed and the fact that the process never failed and consistently produced quality parts.

Milind coined the slogan *'Sweat in India, do not bleed overseas.'* Fixing machine problems in remote locations in China was akin to bleeding. The time, effort, energy and money spent correcting the machines was disproportionate to the nature of the problem. Every bit of metal that was missing or needing replacement had to be first designed and manufactured in India, and then shipped and sent to China to set up on the machine. Between 2012 and 2015, on average, 4-5 service engineers from Grind Master were in China at any given point. Despite the problems, the team worked with a never-give-up attitude. It was perhaps this attitude that inspired and retained the customers' confidence. The client could see and feel the efforts that Grind Master took to resolve any complaint, big or small.

I joined Grind Master in 2010 and was introduced to this fast-growing business for the auto industry. When building a microfinishing machine with technician RR Kulkarni, I assembled many bits and pieces. For perspective, an average car has 600 parts. In comparison, a microfinishing machine has over 2,000 mechanical parts, and over 1,000 electrical and other peripheral parts. Each one has a function and must be done correctly.

There is much to learn from RR in his expertise as an assembler. He calmly goes about his task and does not get flustered by surprises. If some parts were not assembled as they should be, he would ask the designers about it in the morning Gemba meeting to find out the root cause of the mistake. If not, he would investigate if there was a misunderstanding in reading the drawing or if the part was not made correctly, to begin with. If RR still could not find an answer, he would present the problem to Milind, when he would be on his long shop floor rounds in the morning. Milind would have a solution to most problems, typically.

My next assignment was to inspect another machine for a Chinese automotive. It was no easy task to make an error-free machine of such complexity. I saw how a number of engineering streams came together to build this machine – fluid dynamics, heat transfer, kinematics, dynamics and manufacturing processes, all integrated with electrons. This was driven and integrated by software code.

Working on inspecting this machine was a great learning experience for me. I believed that my fresh perspective could catch errors that the engineers who worked on such assembling for years on end would overlook. I brought my novel way of inspecting the machine and working with experienced engineers like Shrirang Lolewar, I was confident that we had assembled a good machine that would wok flawlessly. It was not to be. We had taken but a minor step towards perfection. We were moving in the right direction but were far from perfection. The machine did bring up several issues and needed adjustment along the way. One of the complaints from the customer that the Chinese translation of 'microfinishing film' indicated 'cinema and the movies' was the least of the issues!

Machine assembly is the culmination of several months of efforts in design, materials procurement and manufacturing. If there is even a single issue in any one of these, it comes up as the machine is being assembled. When building specialised custom machines, several new parts are designed specifically for the project, depending on the level of customisation.

Typically, there are three levels of customisations, each with varying degrees of complexity in building the machine to specific requirements.

The process of conceiving a custom-built specialised machine begins at the proposal stage. Crafting a well-thought-out machine proposal is half the battle won. This is because a well-articulated concept that is aligned with customer needs ensures the project's success.

An automotive company issues an RFQ (request for quote) to technically qualified companies. The RFQ package is a set of documents (anywhere from 10 MB to 500 MB) that contains the standards and specifications. Apart from process requirements and component drawings, it contains the safety standards, list to be followed, floor plans, schedules, and numerous compliance forms. Understanding and completing a proposal package addressing the RFQ requirements was a major activity that demanded dedicated effort.

Milind and Prashant Yeole had been leading this process, carving time from building machines to creating proposals and then reviewing and finalising contracts. They took head-on the challenges in China. They travelled to China frequently – each making an average of one trip a month.

The project management process in the Chinese automotive industry was intense. Firstly, the customer would request 1-2 rounds of technical clarification meetings. This would be followed by meetings for bid opening and contract finalisation. Upon winning the project, there would be a kick-off meeting and detailed design approvals. Compared to the Indian automotive style of 1-2 hour design approvals, Chinese manufacturing engineers spent 2-3 days with each machine builder, going through all aspects of the project. To conclude the machine installation, detailed 3-5 day training programmes would be set up.

Usually in joint-venture companies, most project engineers would be conversant in English. However, in China, the original equipment manufacturers were sometimes not proficient in English. The meetings would last long, partly also because of the translation requirements.

Mike Doyle (who worked with IMPCO earlier and supported to launch Grind Master in China) had retired after giving us a strong introduction to the market. We were now represented by Micro-Poise Beijing (the Chinese arm of the American company that specialised in making tyre measurement systems). Mr. Dorian Liu was our face in the Chinese market. Balance Engineering (that made crankshaft balancing machines) was a subsidiary of Micro-Poise USA, and also had operations in China. Balance Engineering had established a strong team for sales and service for their products in China. Since our machines (crankshaft microfinishers) went to essentially the same customers, the synergy between Grind Master and Balance Engineering was obvious, and worked well.

China became a great learning ground for me to understand business development. I worked with Milind to make proposals and contracts, and took over some of the visits for project management in China. Prashant guided me during my first visit to Shanghai and the remote town of Xiangfan. The meetings in both these places were in-depth. I understood that there was much to learn, and quickly, about both technology and the style of doing business in this part of the world. When one puts oneself out there in the world in important situations, it forces one to be prepared. I got extremely busy between visits – reviewing documents and drawings, observing the machines, working out the details – I would not have been able to face the customer without doing this.

I remember an evening from that first visit to Shanghai. Prashant and I had taken the metro to see downtown Shanghai. We had successfully accomplished the mission at the customer's site, and having rented an apartment near the SGM factory for our team's stay, we took some time out for sightseeing. We saw the skyscrapers and the jazzy lights reflecting on the river. Cars, buses and trucks zoomed by on the intricate web of flyovers. Some of these vehicles were already fitted with the crankshafts polished on Grind Master's machines. With a full order book for the next two years, there would be more to come. At this moment, I felt a sense of deep satisfaction. *The underdogs had made it!*

Grind Master's business in China grew fast. Needless to say, it took a lot of effort from the company's engineers, and more. The small companies many departments creaked under pressure to deliver. Every department, from design to manufacturing and parts procurement, had their work cut out for them. The administration department, too, needed to address several challenges, main among them learning to export and import to and from various locations by navigating the government regulations and leveraging the export benefits. The machine tool industry's way of doing business is complex to understand, and invariably Grind Master felt that the regulations were made not keeping in mind the small and medium scale businesses.

Meanwhile, Grind Master's team expanded as new members joined the company. Radhakrishna Barde was one such, who came from Mazak Machine Tools company. Grind Master's machine assembly and testing team would handle the service of machines, including installation, commissioning and under-warranty service of machines. Barde was responsible for setting up a dedicated service team to coordinate the activities of the teams working on various active projects in China. Barde came from a controls background but also developed a good understanding of the process. With a customer-focused approach, Barde was a cheerleader for machine quality and understood the customer's needs. This became important in later years Barde formed and managed Grind Master's support business unit and later became the business unit head for NANOFINISH.

The Micro-Poise team consisting of Dorian, Mimi, Kenny, Leo and Natalie had been working on Grind Master products in China since 2009. They had developed a good understanding of the solutions, and a had developed a level of comfort with the Grind Master team. Dorian and Natalie who worked in the sales and business development departments, were, by 2018, able to clarify most customer queries without needing to involve the India team. The Grind Master India's management team did not need to travel as frequently to China, allowing more room for improvement of its India operations.

Micro-Poise Balance Engineering, however, hit turbulent weather. The company was taken over by Ametek, which decided to focus on the Micro-Poise tyre balancing business. As a result, the Balance Engineering crankshaft balancing business suffered. The operation in Troy, Michigan, was scaled down from 50 people to 5 personnel in a space of 2-3 years. Micro-Poise's loss became Grind Master's gain. Dorian and his team took a leap of faith by exiting the American multinational to form 'Grind Master China' in Beijing. This core team of Grind Master China continues to navigate the volatile Chinese manufacturing business in the post-pandemic world.

From being entrants to Chinese automotive manufacturing in 2010 to having a reference list of over 70 machines by 2016 was a highly significant achievement. Grind Master's customer list included SGM, SGMW, SAIC, DPCA, Great Wall Motor Company, Haima, BYD, Dongfeng, Cummins Wuxi, Changan and Linamar. Most of the customers had multiple machines from Grind Master, indicating a strong confidence in the technology, quality and the support that we were providing.

We had worked hard to catch up with the German and Japanese machine builders that had been making microfinishing machines since the 1950s. They had a tremendous head start and knowledge about the business. Initially, they regarded Grind Master as a low-cost Indian entrant. Over the years, there has been growing acknowledgement of Grind Master's capability. Our winning of contracts with minor price benefits indicated the strong technology basis of our selection. Some Europeans did not take to this change kindly. But the most significant company from Germany, developed good respect for Grind Master, and competes with us sportingly even today.

The partnership with Shanghai General Motors (SGM) had deepened to an extent that we won all the business after the first machine was commissioned in China in 2010. Over the years, attempts were made by several entities to dislodge Grind Master as a trustworthy supplier there, but to no avail. It is deeply satisfying as an Indian machine tool builder that it is the preferred partner over German companies even at times when the German competitor matched the price. We must be doing something right.

Mr. Bai Liguo, the chief crankshaft manufacturing engineer at SGM, who worked with the Grind Master team for many years, said in 2016, "We have over 12 machines now. The machines produce good quality parts. For every new project with Grind Master, they have ensured there is an improvement over the previous version of the machine. Grind Master has responded to every requirement of General Motors. The hands-on approach by Grind Master's owner also shows their commitment. We can cooperate for many more years to develop technology and good relations."

Senior engineer Mr. Zhao Tao, who was discerning about machine quality, especially when it came to safety, controls and maintenance, guided Grind Master's engineering of its first machine delivered to SGM. He said, "Over the years, the collaborative working between SGM and Grind Master resulted in good-value engineering and optimised concepts for the machines. Grind Master offered good service and support that gave us a lot of confidence to continue working on this business relationship."

The Chinese automotive industry perceived Grind Master's machines to be a good mix of quality and reasonable price (around 12%-15% lower than market rate), backed with strong after-sales service. Grind Master's build quality may not yet be considered at par with German machines, nor our marketing and branding meets European standards. A German or Italian machine is designed with aesthetics in mind. But Grind Master's machines are neat and functional. We make up for the lack with three key deliverables:

1. Process Research and Reliability: Grind Master believes in delivering excellent stable processes throughout the machine's lifetime. There are several instances when optimal process solutions were developed. For example, crankshafts for a major Chinese SUV manufacturing company did not require a Level 2 process. Yet, the European makers insisted on it as it was the standard for European automotives.

   Another example was when Grind Master used the Level 3 process for a major Japanese automotive that needed camshafts. It was the finest finish level used for automotive camshafts, and the company undertook rigorous testing in parallel to machine building to establish the parameters to be used. The automotive industry gained a lot of confidence in Grind Master when they saw the results of this project.

2. Customisation of machine design: Grind Master designs have been developed working with European, Japanese, Indian and Chinese automotives. They are thus truly international and can cater to all requirements. Grind Master is more flexible than the European and Japanese counterparts, bringing both ability and willingness to make customisations, whether in basic machine design, automation or tooling. This enables customers to gain exact solutions.

3. Service support: Experts from Grind Master are available for either machine debugging or process updates much more frequently than European machine tool makers. Grind Master's ability to offer retools and reconditioning of machines after a few years in operation gained it customer confidence. During the 2018-2021 period, Grind Master started remanufacturing —rebuilding machines making them as good as new — thus extending their operational life by 10-15 years. Customers valued this business practice.

ENTER THE DRAGON

From 2016 onwards, the automotive OEMs (original equipment manufacturers) in China started slowing down investments in IC (internal combustion) engines, instead outsourcing crankshafts and camshafts to Tier 1 suppliers – big Chinese companies like Tianrun, Fuda, Neijiang, or international suppliers like Linamar. The high flexibility of Grind Master's machines had great appeal for such companies. Some of these companies had been users of low-cost Chinese machines, but for high-quality crankshaft production they needed to use international machines.

While there were several Chinese component suppliers, only a select few were Grind Master's customers. I asked Dorian how he knew to identify our potential buyer. He said, "For me, it is very simple. I visit the factory and see if there are many imported machines from Europe or Japan, I observe their condition, and I see if the customer of this company is a good-quality buyer. If any of these conditions don't check out, we do not have a chance there." These are words of wisdom from the experienced Dorian.

Dorian is an interesting human being and professional. He has been the X factor behind Grind Master's success story in China. If we removed his role from the Grind Master story, it would have a different trajectory altogether. Dorian joined Balance Engineering in 2009, with a 5-6 years of experience selling other capital equipment for an international company. His exposure to the Chinese automotive industry came through two Americans, Dan Pappas (Balance Engineering) and Mike Doyle (IMPCO). Dorian remembers several interesting moments with them. Though these gentlemen would have taught him a lot about technology, Dorian's approach to customer management was quintessentially his own. China is a difficult market to do business in. I visited China numerous times and understood that no foreigner can teach a Chinese national how to work with other Chinese. Dorian's understanding of the Chinese culture and market helped Grind Master find its feet in a difficult foreign market. Pitching Grind Master's machines as a truly international product right from the start has also been key to this endeavour.

In the early years of his association with Grind Master, Dorian thought that his chances of cracking the big OEM projects like SGM were slim. Once these projects were successful, there was no looking back. We were in the thick of business in China.

There were only a few instances where Grind Master lost projects. We bid for a Korean automotive project in 2017 despite knowing that a Korean machine was preferred. We offered an aggressive price. The tender, strangely, was cancelled. In the re-tender, a Korean competitor company was suddenly 40% lower than us. This happened again for another project in the subsequent year. We knew that our machine was superior to the technology selected for the project, and we guessed that there might have been other considerations that were not strictly engineering.

Grind Master bid for a project of the largest private heavy diesel crankshaft maker, and lost. We had supplied three machines to this facility, and all were working well. Our NANOTOUCH Hybrid tooling, polishing fillet radiuses and side faces along with journals to a high specification had been a unique patented process technology that was relevant to 6-cylinder and 8-cylinder engine crankshafts. It was, therefore, no surprise that we were selected to make the fourth and fifth machine for this company. We signed the contract.

It was at this stage that a 'big guy' from this company visited Germany, and was hosted by our German competitor. The European impression played on his mind, we guessed, and a message was conveyed to the team to consider the German solution. The team did not want to cancel our contract, yet also could not ignore the big boss. Instead, they had the German make an offer at a price 5%-6% lower than Grind Master's bid. I chuckle at the desperation on display, sometimes, in the business world. This was German pride being challenged. While Grind Master eventually lost the contract, it will always be remembered as a memorable occasion when "the German bought the order from an Indian".

During 2018-2022, when the international machine market in China was not doing well, Grind Master considered the possibilities of competing in its Tier 1 and Tier 2 markets. As a business development professional, it takes a great deal of conviction and confidence to stick to the identity of being a top technology brand, especially when times are difficult to generate revenue.

As one of my several business visits to China was ending, and I sat at the Beijing airport reflecting on the four years of the pandemic, I had several insights. The Grind Master China team went through difficult times during the coronavirus pandemic as its related restrictions lasted much longer in China. A business based in Beijing during this restrictive period was tough. Business was also difficult. Apart from the economic slowdown that hit China after 2018, there has also been a dramatic shift in the automotive industry here with EV car sales affecting almost all customers of IC engines. Several makers even shut down operations while others reduced volumes ceding market share to Chinese companies like BYD (EV), Geely and Changan.

During the pandemic years, none of the Indian engineers were able to travel to China. Our service team in China, led by Kenny and Leo, installed and commissioned all the machines in this period, learning new technologies like superfinishing of hydraulics and steering systems completely remotely.

Geely and Getrag were two customers that were buyers of SPMS France Machines. After SPMS shut down in 2020, Geely started buying machines from Grind Master – first buying the gear shaft machines and later the crankshaft machine. Our first crankshaft microfinisher for Geely, delivered in December 2023, is a three-station microfinisher. Designed with various learnings of commissioning machines in Japan and America during the pandemic period, this type of machine used to take at least one month to install before 2020. The team was, thus, pleasantly surprised to be able to produce the first parts from this machine in a record five days. The machine was 'plug and play'. No amount of marketing activity can generate the kind of brand building that a result like this can.

During my recent visit to China for discussions, several curious people entered the conference room. I was a bit apprehensive about how I would be received. Instead, they congratulated me for delivering an excellent product. My heart swelled with pride. Geely had been always a European machine buyer. My earlier visit to this buyer was met with a great deal of skepticism. The accolades received now meant that Grind Master was very much in the game.

The China of 2024 is very different than the China of the 2010s. Chinese branded companies are technologically at par with any developed country. Companies like Geely, Changan, Great Wall, BYD have come a long way. They are asserting their brand worldwide by forming subsidiaries. I remember attending the Geneva Motor Show in 2008. A Chinese car similar to Rolls Royce Phantom was displayed then, and visitors commented on how the Chinese mimicked European and American technologies. While some companies copied, others took inspiration. Today, Chinese technology is considered to be several notches ahead of the rest of the world. Battery and EV software are examples of this.

I feel proud of our association with the Chinese companies here, partnering in their journey towards excellence. Grind Master made good progress in this time. My visit to China after a gap of four years was a revelation of sorts. Our reference base in China has grown to over 150 machines across the length and breadth of the country. As we took the train from Shanghai to Changsha, and later from Changsha to Beijing, there was not a town we passed, which did not have a Grind Master product.

I see a positive future for the Chinese automotive industry over the next few years. Hybrid cars are gaining customer preference, an ideal combination between EV and IC engines. New factories are being setup to meet his growing customer need, not only in China, but globally. Our team has stayed together, and built competences during these years in China. Grind Master China has emerged stronger from the pandemic, *ready to take on the next decade.*

“

All creations are done twice – once in imagination and then in physical form. Delving deeper in the imaginary creation leads to a precise physical form.

Benjamin Franklin

06

100 - 1 = ZERO

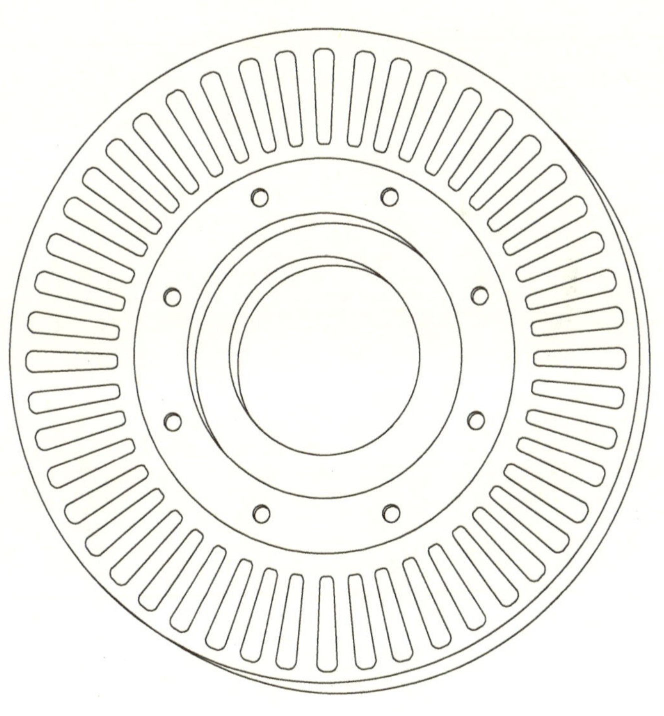

Quality policies are often elaborate, filled with many words relevant to producing good products. However, they don't always have the desired impact. A policy should spark curiosity and interest, ultimately leading to improvements. At Grind Master, our policy, **"100 - 1 = ZERO,"** instantly resonates with people. Many visitors take photos of the poster we have put up at our site. It is a talking point, and sparks discussions, both within and outside the office, about its meaning.

People frequently ask me about this phrase during campus interviews with fresh graduates. I explain that it means, "It takes 100 things done right for a machine to work well, but just one mistake for it to fail." This is a straightforward interpretation—all components in a machine must meet specifications and quality standards. However, when you think more deeply, this principle carries multiple meanings that apply to everyone's work within our company. And it all begins with a shared understanding of what "100" truly represents.

Defining 100

Defining "100" is important. Since most of Grind Master's machines are custom-built, deeply understanding customer requirements is key to conceptualising the right solution. If the appropriate process and machine are not selected correctly, the entire project is at a risk of failure. Metal finishing is a less understood field, and customers often approach Grind Master with a problem, rather than a specific machine requirement. For example, a buyer of a lathe machine typically specifies, "We require a lathe with 1000 mm ABC and 300 mm swing, with an auto turret and CNC control." In contrast, a buyer of a finishing machine might say, "We require a machine to polish a shaft to the exact specifications." What they are asking for is not just the machine but also the process and tools to achieve the desired outcome.

Grind Master's process research capabilities and extensive application reference bank enable us to select the appropriate process and method. The expectations for build standards, safety, and automation can also vary based on the country and culture of the manufacturing company.

The foundation for addressing these variables is our proposal-making process. For our range of NANOFINISH machines, Milind and I lead this process, with support from Chetan Shinde. Chetan is a young design engineer who has specialised as a product manager for several years, honing his skills. He approaches proposals with an open mind, asking pertinent questions and seeking answers. His methodology for proposal-making has evolved over the years, significantly upgraded with modern IT tools compared to the earlier years when proposals were hand-drafted, and cost estimations were done on paper.

When the sales engineer receives a request for quotation (RFQ) from a customer, it is often a detailed package. In many automotive OEMs, the RFQ may include over 100 files, including the standards to be followed. Sometimes, we must generate a detailed requirement to fully capture the customer's expectations.

The process of conceptualising a solution involves several steps:

1. Select the process after testing it in the lab
2. Choose the machine configuration options
3. Discuss the build specifications and optional items
4. Develop the final proposal

There are multiple approaches to solving a problem, and we usually have several machine solutions to consider. Presenting these options and discussing the way forward is a crucial part of Grind Master's interaction with the customer. Despite improving our systems and taking every possible precaution, the customer – and our understanding of their needs – remains an external factor that influences the definition of '100.'

A poorly conceived solution can cause significant problems at a later stage. We once had a project where a machine was delivered and installed, only for a senior manager at the company to see it on the floor and reprimand his team for ordering it. At that moment, all the effort we had put into conceptualising, designing, building, and proving the machine, had been rendered meaningless. What had initially seemed like a mutually beneficial project became a useless object within a matter of seconds. Our service engineers, who had been working hard to get the machine running, looked dejected and confused.

Poor project engineering in the manufacturing industry can sometimes lead to disastrous outcomes, and we must be prepared for such circumstances. In extreme cases, like the one mentioned here, it becomes impossible to achieve '100' because it was never properly defined. The result can only be zero.

Project Management

Grind Master learned effective project management from international automotive OEMs. Leading car manufacturers in China, for instance, would always conduct a mandatory two-day technical clarification meeting after submitting the preliminary proposal. This meeting involved five or six engineers – lead engineer, controls engineer, fluid engineer, tooling engineer, process engineer, and safety engineer – each highly knowledgeable about the company standards relevant to their discipline. They came well-prepared with specific questions about the proposal, drawing from experiences in previous projects. Despite the language barrier, we patiently communicated, ensuring mutual understanding as we explained the features of the proposed solution and took notes on action items. The entire process was constructive and collaborative, unlike typical buyer-seller interactions. And indeed led to defining the 100 to perfection.

This collaborative approach continued throughout the project's execution, including detailed pre-DAP (design approval process) meetings and DAP meetings. A typical DAP would span three days, during which we thoroughly explored every aspect of the project. Controls engineers and fluid engineers examined every circuit of the machine in detail, raising specific questions during the meeting. With five engineers from the customer's side and two from Grind Master, the DAP was a 150-man-hour exercise that led to a refined design.

In contrast, many projects only involve 10-12 hours for such activities. In one particularly poor example, a well-known automotive company in South India invited four machine suppliers for DAP meetings on the same day, with the project team shuttling between discussion rooms. It was no surprise that the production layout required multiple revisions, resulting in significant production delays.

We have also worked to instill a culture of detailed, collaborative communication with customers in our project management system. Grind Master insists that our teams proactively communicate, explain, and seek feedback from both buyer and end user. Continuous improvements are made in this area. For example, under the recent 'Make for World' programme, we established that machine software should be reviewed with the end-user during the engineering stage of the project. This required our controls engineering team to plan well in advance and demonstrate the software's functionality before the machine was built. The machine operators and maintenance engineers at our customer's facility in the US were pleased to receive user-friendly software tailored to their needs.

Explaining what the '100' means to the project team was a key step towards achieving these desirable results. A detailed kick-off meeting at Grind Master enabled the company to do exactly this.

Do Not Accept—"It Has Always Been Done This Way"

Nurturing a culture of questioning is crucial for growth. In the Indian culture, there is often deep respect for seniority, sometimes to the extent that engineers hesitate to question their seniors. However, Grind Master's principle of 'Absolute Engineering' is rooted in the belief that engineering facts should always supersede opinions. During their induction, graduate engineers are taught to question everything. Grind Master encourages young minds to not simply accept the status quo—"It has always been done this way" —and to ask "why" repeatedly until they reach the root cause and are satisfied with the answer. If their immediate senior cannot provide an answer, they are advised to escalate the issue until they get one. They are reassured that they should not fear 'rocking the boat'.

This mindset shift, particularly with the Millennial generation, brought about significant transformation within the company. Young and motivated campus recruits were not afraid to ask questions. Their willingness to challenge the norm was understood and accepted, not only by Grind Master's top management but also by a growing group of senior managers. This culture of questioning has become one of the foundations of the company's strong engineered solutions.

"If in Doubt, Build a Test"

Process research begins during the conceptualisation stage, which is referred to as Front End Engineering (FEE). This activity tests the key processes and develops the proof of concept for any dramatically new elements in a machine. We also encourage engineering teams to conduct an advanced FEE for any uncertainties that may come up during the engineering stage.

A recent example involved a machine for superfinishing EV shafts. Our engineers had conducted the process research on the dummy parts, and the machine was finalised based on this research. However, during the project kick-off meeting, we identified two key untested elements:

1. The process tests were conducted on dummy jobs, not on real parts. Could the actual parts be made available ahead of the production schedule?
2. A special chuck was to be used in the machine. Could it be developed on a fast-track to test before the machine was built?

Our engineering team took on the challenge and conducted an advanced FEE study. The results showed that both the process and the chuck design required fine-tuning. This work was completed ahead of schedule.

Grind Master's learning from this was golden. "If in doubt, build a test." This mantra of affirming and confirming the key elements as early as possible leads to faster and more accurate engineering solutions.

Productivity Equals Accuracy

Engineering teams know that to be productive, they must be accurate. Rapid product development and refinement are key to reaching world-class standards quickly. It took Grind Master over a decade – 10 to 12 years – to build internationally acceptable solutions in metal finishing and microfinishing. But we shortened that timeline to less than four years for our large superfinishing machines, and now the company is aiming to reduce the timeline to just two years for our upcoming bearing superfinishing range. When we launch a product, we ensure it meets international standards from the word go.

Engineering a complex machine with precision requires discipline. Design engineers are a unique breed. Often introverted, they may not say much, but they have an unyielding determination to get every detail right. Crafting detailed designs and preparing an accurate bill of materials (BOM) is a demanding task that requires focus and careful thought. Technology has evolved to assist designers – from hand-drawn sketches on tracing paper to sophisticated 3D CAD systems like Solid Edge, complete with FEA software for analysis. As control systems have grown more complex, tools like EPLAN have helped Grind Master navigate the challenges. But at the end of the day, it all comes down to the engineer in the hot seat.

Making modifications to a machine after it is built poses significant challenges:

1. Modifications create urgencies and disrupt the flow of other projects
2. Corrections rarely achieve the level of precision that is needed

When we began building microfinishing machines, the importance of getting the engineering right became clear. The international automotive market further highlighted our shortcomings. This led to a company-wide focus on doing things right the first time across all operational teams.

In our engineering teams, this focus resulted in a step-by-step, rigorous approach. Previously, controls engineering operated as a separate team, handling both electrical design and control software development. In 2014, we took a bold step by integrating controls design into the main engineering team.

Initially, there was hesitation – how could mechanical engineers guide electrical engineers and vice versa? But my background and experience in Switzerland gave me the confidence to say, "We are all machine engineers. Our expertise may come from different disciplines, but we are designing a product that depends on the seamless integration of brains and brawn."

We launched rigorous interdisciplinary training programmes to give engineers a solid understanding of fields outside their own expertise. My own background – a bachelors degree in Mechanical Engineering, masters degree in Controls, and experience in software development for machines – served as an example for younger engineers to aspire to. Almost immediately, coordination between the engineers improved, and Grind Master had a stronger, more cohesive team.

Quality Comes from a Strong Process

Quality isn't an accident; it comes from having a rock-solid process. A system is only as strong as its weakest link, so taking things step by step is critical. In engineering, that means following a workflow we've fine-tuned over the years. We start by sharing the Engineering Order between Mechanical and Controls Engineering, then move on to modeling and circuit design. We conduct thorough internal and external DAP reviews, hold manufacturing reviews for any tricky new parts, and finish up with a detailed bill of materials that gets peer-reviewed. This careful process leads to successful design releases. For us, success means one thing: accuracy. I always tell our designers not to rush in order to meet deadlines – precision is what matters most.

A Machine Is Only as Good as Its Parts

Getting everything just right in manufacturing isn't easy, but it is what sets us apart. A typical microfinishing machine has over 1,500 custom parts and over 2,500 commercially sourced components. Making sure all these parts are ready on the day we start building the machine is no small feat.

Before 2003, we could only manufacture lower-accuracy parts for metal finishing machines. But when we faced the challenge of producing highly accurate parts for microfinishing, Milind made a bold move. He invested in top-of-the-line Japanese CNC Machining Centers, which allowed us to craft precision parts for our microfinishing machines. We didn't stop there – we expanded our machine shop with CNC lathes and double-column CNC machines, continually improving our ability to make high-quality parts. Some of these components require specialised knowledge and tools, which we have developed and refined over time.

The real heroes here are our skilled machinists. Many started as fresh technicians or engineers and have grown into experts under the guidance of seasoned pros like Chandan Rajput and Arjun Kulkarni. These experts are the heart of our operation. Fixturing and programming in a toolroom setup is no easy task – each part is unique, and some dimensions demand extreme precision.

A few standouts deserve special mention. Uday Joshi became a master at producing tooling using VMC, designing and building multiple fixtures along the way. A.B. Kulkarni nailed the art of surface grinding, achieving incredible flatness specs. And Vilas Dabhade has recently perfected CAM programming for several components. These machinists are the backbone of our manufacturing process, ensuring every part meets the highest standards of quality and precision.

Ensuring Quality of Parts

Part Quality Assurance is the first critical step in inspecting a machine. No non-conforming part should ever pass through this stage. A dedicated team of inspectors examines every single part produced at Grind Master or by our suppliers before approving it for further use. Vyankuram Panchal leads this team with extensive experience, having mentored numerous technicians to become skilled inspectors over the years.

A crucial part of his role is to provide ongoing training on best practices and lessons learned from past mistakes. These monthly internal sessions, along with quarterly sessions at key vendor locations, often spark constructive debates that lead to better methods and continual improvements in our manufacturing processes.

Delivering the Complete Kit

The 'Manufacturing Business Unit' has a vital responsibility: producing the complete kit of manufactured parts needed to build a machine. They are not allowed to dispatch the kit until it is fully ready. Projects that involve many new parts are highlighted in blue, indicating the extra attention required.

One such project is the Superfinishing Hydraulic Cylinders, which includes a massive machine base over 8,000mm long and weighing nearly 10 tons—it's the heaviest part ever built by Grind Master. The team meticulously planned how to construct this enormous base using the available machinery, which required multiple setups. A special trailer is necessary to transport this colossal piece to Unit 1, where the machine is assembled. Before it leaves, the team gathers for a photo in front of the long base, proud of their work, knowing that every part has been tested and certified to meet Grind Master's exacting standards.

We Didn't Order Scratches

The definition of '100' for manufactured parts has evolved over time. When Grind Master sold our first machine in the UK in 2005, it performed its intended task. But soon after, we received a lengthy email filled with photos. The message was clear: "There are scratches and dents on the parts—these weren't on the drawing. Why are you producing them?" Our team gathered in the conference room, projecting the photos onto a big screen. The image that struck us the hardest was of a wear plate, a part notoriously difficult to produce to the required flatness. Written in blue permanent marker was a scribbled note: "Indian shit."

That feedback was both painful and powerful. Most of us probably didn't sleep that night. Milind certainly didn't, haunted by that image—both as a passionate engineer and a proud Indian. But instead of wallowing in hurt and talking about politics and racism, we turned it into resolve. The remark may have been a racist slur, but we knew the only way to overcome it was to accept the defects and fix them. The resulting changes in our manufacturing processes and part handling had a profound impact. Today, that same UK company continues to buy machines, sub-assemblies, and parts from Grind Master, confident that every part will be produced and delivered with care. Pat Cebelac, President of IMPCO in 2018, commented 'Parts coming from Grind Master are always perfect and none of our Chinese or American suppliers match the consistency of Grind Master'.

The Indian saint Kabir said:

"निंदक नियरे रखिये आँगन कुटी छवाये;
बिन साबुन पानी बिना निर्मल करात सुभाये"

(*"Nindak niyare rakhiye aangan kuti chhawaye; Bin sabun pani bina nirmal karat subhaye."* - Keep your critics close, let their hut be in your courtyard. That way you don't need soap and water to stay clean.)

This wisdom has become a motivation for our team.

The Machine Quality Record (MQR)

We learned about a key intermediate check system from our American collaborators at IMPCO—the Machine Quality Record (MQR). The MQR is a checklist used for each aggregate of the machine (an aggregate is a group of subassemblies that function as a unit, like a headstock or a pneumatic slide). This checklist must be completed to certify the full assembly and functioning of the unit. When assembling a machine with 3,000 parts, the MQR ensures that groups of 300-400 parts are certified before being added to the machine. This approach helps identify problems, part modifications, or omissions early on.

For instance, an MQR for a headstock includes measuring runouts and assembling all sensors on the headstock. These sensors are set and tested using a special electrical box designed for the purpose. Motorised headstocks are run for a few hours to check motor functioning and temperatures as part of endurance testing. Completing the MQR gives the technician a sense of ownership over his work. We've since expanded this system, applying it to all our products and every single aggregate of the machine. The rigour and discipline behind the MQR are what make it so effective.

Sweat on the Floor, Don't Bleed at the Site

After a machine is fully built and tested, it's time for customer inspection. The rigour of this process varies depending on the customer. For example, a typical machine for a Chinese automotive company undergoes a five-day inspection with 2-4 engineers on site. This inspection covers everything from a machine overview and operations to detailed process checks, including N1-N5-N30, and concludes with an endurance run. This thorough testing ensures the machine is fully ready for use.

However, there have been instances where machines were rushed through clearance and dispatched prematurely to meet urgent deadlines. In one notable case, a major Indian automotive supplier insisted on receiving a machine that wasn't fully completed, saying, "Finish it on-site; we need to show the OEM that we have the machine." Although we strongly opposed this approach, we eventually gave in and delivered the half-built machine. Completing it on-site took much longer, and I doubt it ever performed as well as a properly built machine. Looking back, we feel some shame for compromising our quality standards. This experience prompted us to make a significant change: we might take flak and penalties for delayed delivery, but we will never compromise on quality.

A Wake-Up Call

From 2005 to 2015, Grind Master's quality continued to improve as the team gained experience, but we still faced issues, even with machines we thought were built well. One project that stands out involved four camshaft microfinishing machines for a Japanese JV in China, built between 2018 and 2019. At the time, we had hired many new team members to meet the high production pressure. The headcount increase was disproportionate to our revenue growth, and building these specialised machines isn't easy—training newcomers takes time. Many of the new hires were contractors who didn't stay long. Until this point, the customer had been satisfied with our work, but these four machines were built in less-than-ideal conditions and dispatched hastily. Numerous field failures followed, harming our reputation. We had once been top-rated with this customer, but this project killed their confidence in us. It was a wake-up call that Grind Master couldn't ignore. We had to act fast to correct the situation.

Grind Master launched a major initiative to improve its execution methodology. The company decided to dedicate Shrirang Lolewar, also known as 'doctor', to focus exclusively on maintaining machine quality. With over 15 years of experience in machine building and testing, doctor played a crucial role in transforming our approach. Grind Master's ideas that had previously been implemented only in bits and pieces were now formalised into a comprehensive, updated system for machine execution.

A bold reorganisation of the machine execution team was central to this transformation. Santosh Patil, who had been managing the controls team, was chosen to lead the new direction. With over 20 years of experience in machine building and extensive international exposure, Santosh was trustworthy and reliable. The only hesitation was that he came from an electrical background, while machine assembly and testing is typically seen as a mechanical engineering function. Although initially tentative, I encouraged Santosh to take on this role, and the results soon spoke for themselves. Improvements in machine quality were quickly evident, and the phrase "Sweat on the floor, don't bleed at the site" became Grind Master's guiding principle.

We defined new methodologies and trained our technicians and engineers to implement them. We also established a clear process for control software development and deployment. This was possible because Grind Master started to treat software like engineering. We introduced software concept books to define software requirements and held software reviews by senior engineers to ensure standardisation across functions. Debanjan and Anklesh, both skilled programmers with several years of experience at the company, led this effort. By placing restrictions on how developers could programme the machine, we achieved faster, and more accurate, programming.

An independent machine inspection team carries out the final machine inspection and reports directly to the management. This team is highly empowered, and when operational heads have approached me citing customer concerns, I have solidly backed this team. Our commitment is clear: "Make the right machine. If there's any doubt, fix it. Test it. Only then will we send it out."

Do it right first time – every time

During the period from 2011 to 2019, Grind Master frequently sent its teams abroad to commission and support various projects. But when the Covid-19 pandemic hit in 2020, everything changed. Travel halted but the stability of Grind Master's team in India became a crucial advantage. Without the disruptions of frequent overseas assignments, our engineers could focus entirely on their projects by dedicating themselves to building quality machines.

I have always believed that Indian engineers need to be pushed to plan until it becomes second nature to us. We introduced a new system that forced managers to plan meticulously. The mantra was simple: "Do it right the first time, every time." This shift significantly improved productivity, reducing machine-building timelines by nearly 40%.

This transformation reminds me of a scene from the movie Million Dollar Baby. Clint Eastwood's character, a boxing coach, explains that to make a fighter, you have to break them down completely, stripping away everything they know, until they only listen to you and do exactly as you say. You teach them the fundamentals over and over until it becomes second nature, as if they were born that way.

We applied a similar approach in grooming our team – disciplining them, drilling systems and protocols into their work habits until it became almost second nature. Sometimes, the engineers' commitment to delivering a quality machine surprises even the management at Grind Master. Backed by a strong management team, the engineers learned to stand firm, even when facing customer pressure over delays. We have ingrained a company culture where quality is never compromised, no matter the challenge.

Customer-centric Commitment

Most of our machines are turnkey solutions, designed to deliver production readiness with specific cycle times and process reliability. Since these machines are specialised and custom-built, the commissioning is usually handled by the execution team members who were directly involved in the machine's construction.

Commissioning requires tight day-to-day planning, even in the face of uncertainties, at the customer site. Grind Master ensures that the site is fully prepared before deploying our team, and we closely manage and monitor the work and reporting daily. It's crucial to stay informed about real-time issues when work is progressing in a remote location. The service manager plays a pivotal role in this process, constantly balancing different approaches to problem-solving. They must guide the team remotely, support them internally, and maintain open communication with the customer.

Grind Master fosters the mentality of working for the customer as if on a war footing. In the world of custom-built machines, the final design validation often occurs on site, which means unforeseen challenges can arise that only surface during commissioning. When a component fails, production grinds to a halt, and our engineers must respond quickly. For example, when the deburring head in a machine we exported to the US failed after just two months, our team sprang into action. We built a new unit in just five days and shipped it via air, ensuring it was installed within ten days of the initial complaint. Although we acknowledged the failure, our swift response reassured the customer of our unwavering support.

Finishing machines are not as common as machining centers or lathes, so customer training is crucial and forms a key part of our deliverables. Over the years, our training program has evolved from basic, person-dependent instruction to an extensive, multi-day programme. This includes classroom sessions and checklist-guided activities on the machine, culminating in a certification that empowers specific personnel to operate our equipment.

After a machine begins production, teething problems often arise. For example, the variability in input components only becomes evident during mass production. We learned the value of offering production support periods from the international automotive industry. This approach facilitates the ramp-up of our production capacity while providing hands-on support to operators and fine-tuning processes. We've adopted these practices, offering production support periods and training personnel to optimise the output. We frequently visit customer sites, especially when a new design is deployed, to gather insights that guide our ongoing efforts. This feedback loop drives Grind Master's continuous improvement.

Transparency in communication with our customers is key to successful service activities. We strive to improve how we present problems and solutions, ensuring that our explanations are realistic while working tirelessly to resolve the customer's issues.

The Grind Master Way

The foundation of Grind Master's success lies in its unique system—the Grind Master Way—detailed in the Grind Master Management Handbook (GMMH). Every team member is not only trained in this methodology but also encouraged to contribute to its evolution. This collective effort over the years has created a dynamic, adaptable system that meets the changing needs of the times.

In the 2000s, Ketan Kelkar, the most systems-oriented leader at Grind Master, led the way in deploying systems, from basic computerisation to the early versions of ERP. After significant work on the quality system, we earned ISO 9001 certification. Building on this strong foundation, I introduced elements of Japanese methodology, like 5S and Kaizen, and refined our organisational structure. Simple yet impactful measures, such as creating Teamspace—a shared file folder system with strict access rules—transformed our information flow. The goal was clear: access any document within 30 seconds. A key step was digitising the Quality Manual into the Grind Master Management Handbook (GMMH), integrating the system into our daily work.

The GMMH outlines our machine-building process in six phases, each with 4-10 sub-phases. Specific project team members are responsible for each phase, ensuring that quality protocols are followed rigorously. A project only moves forward when the current phase is completed to the desired goal. Our Project Management System has evolved into a cloud-based version, complete with a customer portal and vendor portal that offer real-time access to relevant information without asking for it..

The GMMH is comprehensive, with SOPs that detail a wide range of activities. Each document has gone through at least 3-4 revisions, reflecting a living system of continuous improvement driven by those who work within it. Our 'systems people,' dedicated to nurturing this infrastructure, are passionate about implementing transformative changes, even if their methods sometimes seem idiosyncratic.

Over the years, digitisation has taken root, with industry-wide best practices implemented across various systems, from HRMS (Human Resource Management System) to VMS (Visitor Management System) to CRM (Customer Relationship Management) and ERP (Enterprise Resource Planning). Prashant Kawthekar and Tushar Joshi have been instrumental in driving these systemic improvements, constantly finding innovative solutions to automate processes.

Implementing ISO standards in other areas of our operation has also proven beneficial. In 2014, we adopted ISO 14001 and ISO 18001 for Environmental, Health, and Safety (EHS) management, followed by ISO 27001 for Information Security Management (ISMS) in 2019. The importance of safety in our operations and data security for both Grind Master and our customers cannot be overstated. Annual external audits and quarterly internal audits keep our team vigilant and proactive.

Systems and methodologies must evolve to stay relevant. A well-developed method serves its purpose for a time, but eventually, it must be replaced by a more advanced version. This continuous cycle of improvement ensures that our system remains contemporary, alive, and supportive of the organisation's forward momentum.

The Devil is in the Detail. And So Is God.

Grind Master's commitment to quality has always drawn inspiration from the Japanese approach. In the 1990s, we built a small Gear Deburring machine for Toyota, and their inspection process left a lasting impression on us. A team of six arrived to inspect this modest machine, and to our surprise, they spent an entire day just looking at it, carefully examining every detail. With pencils tucked behind their ears, they took notes and sketched observations. It was clear: the devil is in the detail, and so is God.

The Japanese companies we have worked with epitomise this philosophy. During our visits to Japan, we witnessed an extraordinary level of detail in everything they did, from logistics to planning each day down to the minute. Their strong desire to achieve 100% perfection was evident, and planning was their key to success.

Our understanding of '100 – 1 = Zero' likely began in childhood, instilled by parents who encouraged us to give our best to everything we did. This value shaped our lives, teaching us that the most important thing is to give it your everything. I can't recall a single task I have done half-heartedly, and the same is true for Milind and Mohini.

Grind Master's quality policy is a direct reflection of this core value. Passion and commitment to this philosophy are unwavering. It's not something we choose to do strategically – it's who we are. John Deere once said, "I will never put my name on a product that does not have in it the best that is in me." We live and breathe this principle every day.

“

Take up one idea. Make that one idea your life; dream of it; think of it; live on that idea. Let the brain, the body, muscles, nerves, every part of your body be full of that idea, and just leave every other idea alone. This is the way to success

—

Swami Vivekananda

07

CULTURE OF ENDURING EXCELLENCE

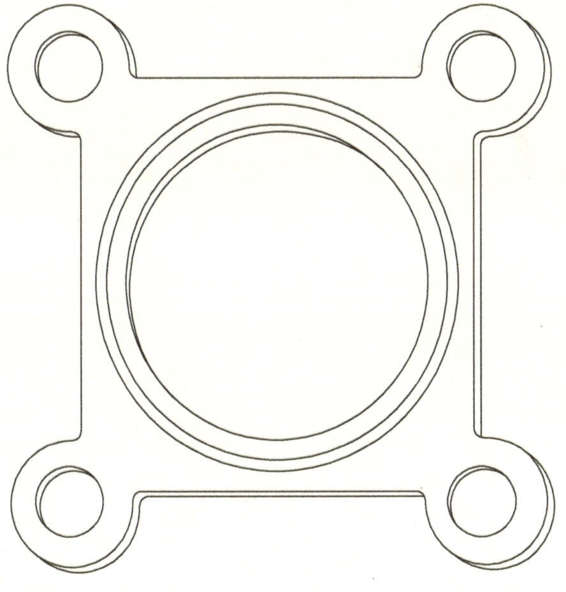

"We envision becoming a global technology leader by fostering a culture of enduring excellence, exceeding expectations through passionate and empowered people, ensuring sustainable and inclusive growth."

"100 - 1 = ZERO"
"Absolute Engineering"
"Passionate. Innovative. Trustworthy. Expert"

Aligning with the Vision

At Grind Master, our vision statement, quality policy, motto, and core values are not just words on a wall—they are the foundation of our success. The Kelkar family, alongside our dedicated machine builders, lives and breathes machines. This passion is woven into the very DNA of our company.

These guiding principles have been at the heart of our journey as the company was built brick by brick. While they were officially documented during Grind Master's brand building and vision mission exercises, these values have always been ingrained in our team's mindset. When it was time to define our mission, we found ourselves wrestling with ideas that didn't quite capture the full extent of our ambition. At one time, we focused on the only objective number available—revenue growth. We called it a BHAG, a 'Big Herculean Audacious Goal,' inspired by international management books.

But does revenue alone make Grind Master a global technology leader? Many Chinese companies mass-produce products inspired by European and American designs, scaling manufacturing efficiently. On the other hand, Swiss watchmakers like Longines, based in the small village of Saint-Imier in the Swiss Jura, have established a global reputation for technology and quality. The top-line number, so crucial to much of the corporate world, can often be misleading. We, too, wandered in pursuit of diversification for a time before refocusing on what truly matters—a culture of enduring excellence. This culture, driven by our people, is what defines us and will lead us to our goal.

What Does It Mean to Become a Global Technology Leader?

In Grind Master's early days, we sold machines labeled as 'Import Substitutes,' replacing European and Japanese imports with India. Later, we expanded into developing markets like China and Mexico. Even when we sold machines to Germany or the US, it was often attributed to India's 'low-cost advantage.'

For me, true global technology leadership means becoming a trusted partner in **developed countries** based on our **innovation and technology**. It means selling our machines in Japan against Japanese competition due to our process innovation. It means establishing machines in South Germany based on our product flexibility or conducting R&D in robotic grinding for an Australian foundry, achieving something unique at a global scale. We have reached a level of technology leadership in the Chinese automotive industry, where quality and technology are paramount. One customer, SGMW, expressed their perception of us by saying, "The 1% price difference wasn't significant, but the high-quality part finish and almost instant service convinced us."

Kailash: An Inspiration for a Culture

The Kailash temple at Ellora, a masterpiece of engineering, art, architecture and perseverence, embodies the values that drive us. The culture that created this monolithic structure represents the excellence we strive for at Grind Master. The sculptors of Kailash exemplify our ideal: Right the first time – every time. Every strike of the hammer and chisel had to be precise. The audacity to attempt such a feat inspires us to shed mediocrity and dream the impossible.

Our team at Grind Master is largely homegrown, with most members hailing from the surrounding villages in the Marathwada region. This region, known for its splendours like Ellora, Ajanta, and Devgiri Fort, has a rich history of pioneering and innovating technologies and art forms that were often centuries ahead of the rest of the world. It's a constant source of inspiration for us to create our own island of excellence.

Machine Builders: The Craft of Excellence

The machine tool environment demands resilience and a specific mindset. Only those who possess the toughness to endure can thrive in the challenging conditions we face daily. Those who can't keep up either leave or are pushed out within a few years. The success of our projects hinges directly on each individual doing their part with precision and dedication. Here, there is no "routine" work. Every day requires full awareness and active engagement. Technicians, engineers, and administrative executives who pass this litmus test earn the title of Machine Builder. Most other workplaces would seem uncomfortably easy for them.

Building special-purpose machines is inherently motivation-driven. The attendance machine at the factory's entrance only tracks if "bodies" have entered and left, but in our line of work, motivation isn't optional—it's essential. While mass production units might sustain operations with a less motivated workforce, our output in machine building would plummet to near zero without an energised, dedicated team that shares our core values.

Working in specialised machine building offers tangible results—products and solutions that you can see, touch, and feel. There's an inherent joy in creating something that works. After months of effort, when hundreds of parts come together and function as a whole, it feels magical. I recall a particular project during my time at Gudel Switzerland, where we were working on a European research project to build a new robot called the 'Gantry Tau.' This machine had unique kinematics and dynamics. I spent over four months developing the software to run it, focusing on the complex forward and inverse kinematics of the parallel arms manipulator.

Step by step, I deployed the software, and when the Gantry Tau moved with rapid precision, I felt an overwhelming sense of pride. At that moment, my career in machine building was sealed. I was on a machine high for days—a state of pure joy and bliss. Most machine builders experience this elation at some point, a feeling engineers in large corporations seldom get to know. In the machine building space, a small to medium-sized company can produce high-technology products, with a handful of team members truly taking ownership of the development. Each new creation brings a new high, as the creator falls in love with his creation.

The Principles of Engineering Are Supreme

Building specialised machine tools is an intense engineering endeavour. To compete with German and Japanese companies, we need engineering capabilities that not only match but surpass theirs in innovation. Cultivating a strong 'Absolute Engineering' attitude is essential. Milind often compares it to going to school every day—applying what you've learned and learning something new.

In our senior management team, we don't have any management graduates. Leadership here is earned through demonstrated excellence in engineering. Some of our best engineers are groomed to be managers, while others, more inclined toward individual performance, are encouraged to become lead engineers, gaining respect and growth through their technological prowess alone.

In our work, the principles of engineering reign supreme. Opinions must be supported by analysis and scientific reasoning. Systems are to be followed and challenged simultaneously. Challenging the system reinforces its validity if it's correct and updates it if it's outdated – this is the essence of continuous improvement. To foster this environment, we focus on the subject matter rather than personalities. Milind often reminds us, "Use of adjectives is not allowed except in genuine praise." Applying this principle in debates, which are naturally a part of meetings, brings the correct approach from all stakeholders.

Rocking the Boat: A Cultural Shift Led by Young Engineers

A wave of cultural change swept through Grind Master, driven by a young brigade of engineers who dared to rock the boat. Each year, our campus recruitment drive screens over 2,000 students, putting them through rigorous rounds, including objective tests, subjective exams, technical interviews, and final selections. We sought practical engineering mindsets and found the best recruits in regional engineering colleges in Aurangabad and Kolkata, focusing on students from mechanical, electrical, and electronics disciplines.

Final selections often take place at the Grind Master factory, where candidates are taken on a shop floor tour. What they think is a casual introductory visit quickly turns into a test of their observational skills. We ask them questions about what they noticed on the floor: Did they look inside the control cabinet? What elements did they see? Did they observe the tools used in the process? What was the most interesting mechanism they noticed? These questions reveal their passion for building machines. Are they true 'Machine Builders?'

Out of the 2,000 applicants, only six make the cut. Many of these top selections often come from students who have built robots or vehicles for inter-college competitions. One such recruit, Prajanya Kendrekar, first met me as the captain of his college's BAJA team (BAJA SAE is a competition organized by SAE international. Engineering college teams compete in building vehicles such as ATVs), which we were sponsoring. His enthusiasm and ability were evident, leading his team to success. His selection in our campus drive was unanimous. Despite being honest about his plans for further studies, he worked closely with me on Dynamic Balancing Machines for Crankshafts—a new technology we were mastering at the time. This advanced process required a deep understanding of physics, body dynamics, and vector mathematics.

In just two years, Prajanya had mastered the process and could independently lead projects. We implemented machines at select customers like Netalkar Power Train (NPT) and Bharat Forge. It was remarkable to see a fresh graduate, with only one year of experience, explaining the process to Mr. Satish Netalkar, the founder-owner of NPT, who had decades of experience in manufacturing crankshafts.

Prajanya later pursued Masters in Engineering at the University of California, Berkeley, and secured challenging roles at companies like Tesla and Rivian. He recalls, "During the rigorous interviews with Tesla, I was asked to present on any project. I presented Dynamic Balancing of Crankshafts. The team was surprised by the depth of my knowledge and the opportunities I had at Grind Master in such a short time. This played a key role in my selection." Prajanya, the son of a senior government officer, always impressed me with his ability to forge his own path and speak confidently in every interaction. His professionalism and confidence reflect the power, conviction, and fresh perspective of many young engineers. It's our responsibility to provide them with a platform.

The manufacturing industry often struggles to recruit and retain young talent. Common complaints include, "They don't want to work on the shop floor," "They prefer cushy jobs in software and finance," and "They change jobs every few years." As an employer, I've been tempted to make these statements myself. But deeper reflection has led to introspection, realisation, and action.

Motivated engineers learn quickly. Within 3-5 years, they develop strong machine-building skills and start craving more space and opportunities to explore their abilities. However, the manufacturing industry is often dominated by seniority, with most managers in their 40s or 50s. This generation gap can hinder the understanding and leveraging of young engineers' talents. In various industries, including Grind Master, I've observed 'semi-retired' individuals holding key positions, limiting the potential of younger talent.

When we initially launched the Fastrack programme, it shook things up significantly. Engineers with just a few years of experience were rapidly promoted in both designation and salary. In the first batch, four sharp engineers—Monoj Maiti, Debanjan Dhar, Sudeep Khadse, and Onkar Kulkarni—were promoted to senior engineer after just three years of experience, a designation that typically took older engineers 8-10 years to achieve. Within six years, they became lead engineers and managers. Monoj mastered fluid engineering, Debanjan took on the responsibility of control software for complex machines and spearheaded the development of the NANOSMART controller and Framework standardisation while Sudeep and Onkar were deeply involved in robotics, developing new technologies like offline programming software, scanning methods, and robotic 3D printing. They were at the cutting edge of developments at Grind Master.

As a young leader, I was sometimes criticised for giving opportunities disproportionately to the younger generation. But those objections faded as the performance and delivery of the Fastrack members spoke for themselves.

11 Ways a Fastener Won't Tighten—and How We're Closing the Gap

Grind Master is a tough environment, where we constantly push to develop and refine our abilities. When we benchmark our performance against international companies, we see a significant gap in our team's average capability, which directly impacts productivity. For example, productivity in our machine-building division is three times lower compared to German or Japanese companies. This gap stems from differences in training.

To address this, we start with the basics. We ensure that our apprentices and graduate trainee engineers (GTEs) are well-prepared for the challenges ahead. We brought in Mr. Kulkarni, a professional trainer, to design a GTE programme specifically tailored to Grind Master's needs. This programme, which spans six weeks of intensive classroom and shop floor training, immerses freshers in the art of machine building – the Grind Master way.

Akash Pramanik, from a village in Bengal, recently completed this programme. Educated in local colleges and passionate about machines, Akash was thrilled to join Grind Master. *"Now I feel like an engineer,"* he says, beaming with pride as he steps into new challenges armed with the fundamentals.

Our team had previously lacked management training, creating a gap when employees moved into supervisory or senior management roles. To bridge this, we launched the 'Fire' programmes in 2015-2017 – a rapid MBA-style series that groomed 15-20 potential leaders in each batch. Conducted by Dr. Chandratre, these programmes transformed many engineers into effective managers.

In recent years, we've shifted our strategy to focus more on internal training. We set a high benchmark inspired by the software industry – 50 hours of training per person per year – and we often meet or exceed this goal. Our monthly training calendar is packed with sessions on assembly, controls, engineering, materials, and manufacturing. Supervisors and managers also participate in discussions on challenges and solutions, reinforcing the Grind Master way of working. These trainings guide our team from good habits to a strong, positive culture. Some topics, like '11 Ways a Fastener Won't Tighten,' might seem basic, but are crucial. When every builder understands and uses the correct technique, the workmanship of our machines improves.

We constantly push our people to surpass their abilities. Our annual English and computer training, conducted over a two-month period, has been a game-changer for many. We noticed that some senior technicians understood technology better than the engineers supervising them, but they struggled to express themselves. With enhanced skills in assembly, testing, and processes, their experience was invaluable. After completing the English and computer training, their careers took off. Early adopters of this programme, like Bharat Pawade, Sunil Ekshinge, and Shrirang Lolewar, have become inspirations for younger technicians, embodying the spirit of 'learn and grow.'

Multitasking is another crucial training area. Due to variable workloads, we need our team to perform multiple functions, which we see as an opportunity. Instead of hiring for specific functions from outside, we prefer to offer internal opportunities. Encouraging mechanical and electrical engineers to shed their narrow focus and become versatile machine engineers has been one of our cross-functional successes.

Another example are Somesh and Vijay, who joined us as drivers in the early 2000s. With training in language and digital literacy, their careers soared. Today, they manage a wide range of administrative functions, from overseeing the company guest house in the city to organising the annual party and handling bank formalities. You can always count on them to deliver.

Attracting and Retaining Talent

The machine tool industry thrives on the passion of those who love machines. As a millennial, I deeply respect the dedication, sacrifice, and emotion that early machine builders poured into their work. However, we must adopt strategies that align with modern times and market conditions to attract and retain talent today.

Young professionals entering the machine tool industry look forward to the opportunity to learn something new every day. However, competitive salary packages are equally important. Industry veterans often criticize the emphasis younger generations place on compensation, blaming the software industry for distorting the job market. But I see these as excuses. The software industry has set high standards in terms of working conditions, and as a technology provider to the manufacturing sector, the machine tool industry should aim to set new benchmarks, too.

Engineering in machine tools is more challenging than coding or testing in software, and our pay scales should reflect that. Over the past few years, Grind Master has worked to align its compensation with tech industry standards. Our company has rewarded good performance with substantial raises, introduced variable pay based on both company and individual achievements, and recognised breakthrough R&D work with special rewards.

During the peak of the Covid pandemic, financial uncertainty forced us to pause salary increments. However, we made up for it the following year by offering double increments. This raise was well-deserved—everyone worked hard on cost reductions and improvements during that challenging period. Our philosophy of fostering growth and development for everyone associated with the company is evident in many of our policies and decisions.

Work-Life Balance

The Covid pandemic shifted priorities for many, as people experienced the value of spending quality time with their families. They now want to be present for their loved ones and pursue personal hobbies. For a while, younger engineers had been asking for a five-day workweek. Given the manufacturing industry standard of six days, we hesitated for years, but eventually, we took the plunge.

Implementing this change came with challenges and lessons. Project planning had to become more precise, as we lost an entire working day in the week. We tightened leave policies and enforced stricter rules on unplanned absences. This shift required a cultural change—employees needed to work with full dedication and professionalism during those five days. They had to earn that extra day off. The transformation has benefited everyone. Previously, people would take unexpected leaves to handle personal tasks, disrupting the team's workflow. Now, with Saturdays off, such disruptions are minimised. Grind Master also encourages employees to plan week-long vacations, making it a norm for everyone to take a family vacation once a quarter.

The five-day workweek has inspired many employees to pursue hobbies and engage in social work. The Grind Master GO Club now boasts several half marathoners and two full marathoners, with enthusiasts like Manoj Borkhade and Abhijeet Kamble leading the charge. A group of employees has formed a cricket club, playing at a turf reserved by the company on weekends. Some team members have even started growing vegetables on the premises, proudly sharing their produce with colleagues. Others enjoy cricket, table tennis, or badminton during lunch breaks or after work.

Shweta Nanajkar, who recently joined Grind Master as a safety officer from an MNC, shares her experience: *"As a married woman, managing everything with just one day off was incredibly challenging. The relentless pace left little time for personal pursuits, family, or social engagements. The prospect of 52 additional days off each year is invaluable. My son is overjoyed at the thought of a Saturday off every week. At Grind Master, there's a clear emphasis on quality work over quantity."* Tushar Joshi, our IT and ISMS manager, echoes these sentiments: *"Grind Master is the only manufacturing company that offers even shop floor employees a five-day workweek. I've attended every parent-teacher meeting at my child's school, something I missed out on in my previous job."*

Celebrating Successes and Failures

High motivation levels within our team drive innovation and invention. As we introduced a culture of intellectual property awareness, we encouraged patents to be filed in the name of the contributing team members. Venkatesh Kulkarni led the way in process research, Deepak Mohite in design, Akshay Bhat and Debanjan Dhar in machine learning, and Prajwal Mhaske and Sudeep Khadse in robotic processes. Their names will forever stand as inventors on granted patents, marking their contributions to technological progress. Other team members, like Monoj Maiti and Onkar Kulkarni, have published papers on subjects ranging from robotics to sustainability in machine tools. Innovation today is a collaborative process, where engineers brainstorm and piece together the puzzle that leads to breakthrough solutions.

Celebrating successes is essential, but celebrating honest failures is even more critical. At Grind Master, we encourage experimentation, even if it leads to mistakes. Accepting the consequences and moving forward is part of the process. Among failures, we find the seeds of success. In our quarterly award program, one person is selected to speak about their failure—detailing the root cause and the actions taken to resolve it.

The Grind Master Family: Common Aspirations

At Grind Master, we set high-performance benchmarks and demand excellence from our team. This expectation is met with positivity and is resolve 100% of the time, fueled by a deep sense of trust. This trust, built over decades by Milind and reinforced by me, ensures that we always act in the best interest of our team. I would never let this trust down. Working intensely in teams to deliver projects naturally fosters deep interpersonal relationships, creating lifelong friendships within our team.

In 1990, when the company was small and cohesive, outside influences attempted to disrupt our unity by encouraging the formation of a union. Milind, believing himself to be the best union leader, called a meeting with the team members and their families. He explained that managers and workers are not on opposite sides of the table ; but on the same side in order to satisfy the customer who ultimately pays everybody's salary. He initiated the Foodgrain Purchase Scheme to ensure that every family had a year's supply of quality wheat and rice and remain food-secure in an event of disruption. The company purchased these grains in bulk, reducing costs, and deducted the value as an advance from employees' salaries over the year. This initiative provided significant security for workers' families who had migrated from villages to the city. The Foodgrain Purchase Scheme continues today, expanding to include other commodities.

Trust builds trustworthiness. In the late 1990s, the company placed a deposit as collateral in a bank, allowing employees to access quick personal loans. To date, out of hundreds of loans, only one has defaulted.

We reinforce this trust by treating everyone with respect, without making distinctions between technicians and staff, except as required by government regulations. In meetings, a technician often has more to contribute than his seniors — and he is listened to.

Our family has grown over the years. Grind Master's annual family get-togethers began in the 1990s with small, intimate gatherings over dinner. As we grew, we moved to larger outdoor venues with interesting themes, making these events cherished by families. Over the years, we've watched our team members' families grow, with children graduating from school and college and pursuing exciting careers.

Some of these children have joined Grind Master. Manish Unhale, a senior controls engineer, is the son of Unhale Kaka, who once served as a security guard. Trustworthy and calm like his father, Manish brings a determined focus to every task.

Our team members often share valuable advice with one another. Lolewar, for example, once approached Milind for a loan to buy a motorcycle. At the time, he commuted by bicycle. Milind suggested he first invest in a house, explaining that real estate appreciates while vehicles depreciate. Lolewar, along with Pawade and Ekshinge, followed this advice and built houses. A few years later, they were able to purchase motorcycles and cars without needing advances.

The Covid Crisis and Inclusivity

During times of crisis, concern for family comes first. The Covid-19 pandemic struck in 2020, and fortunately, we had pulled our team out of China just in time. We devised a plan to emerge from the pandemic stronger, focusing on building people's skills and abilities during the lockdown. We designed a series of online programmes to keep our team engaged and purposeful during the extended lockdown. Novel competitions, like the Art from Waste challenge and Push ups challenge brought enthusiasm amidst the grim scenario. Additionally, a group of employees managed the company-sponsored grain distribution program, delivering over 1,000 ration parcels to the needy in the early weeks of the lockdown, when help was most needed. A team of engineers, guided by Milind, even built a prototype ventilator, though it ultimately proved unfeasible for medical use.

The second wave of Covid-19 hit hard. Partnering with the Red Cross, Grind Master established a vaccination center at the Railway Station MIDC. Our maintenance engineer, Sachin Durgist, managed the center, vaccinating over 2,000 people in a month. During this wave, many of our team members fell seriously ill.

Our CFO, Ravindra Gokhale, faced a life-threatening situation with multiple complications. Gokhale had joined us as a senior accounts manager and pursued his CA certification while working here. With a 'always up for a challenge' attitude, he expanded his role into general administration and later set up a corporate team to manage international businesses in China, Europe, and the USA. After contracting Covid-19, Gokhale experienced severe complications and lost consciousness one night. Milind received the call at 2.30 am and immediately organised help. Sandip and Mahesh rushed Gokhale to the hospital and arranged treatment. After several tense days, he recovered and returned to work. Recently, Gokhale was appointed as an additional director, marking the first time this position has been given to a non-family member.

During the peak of the crisis, Sandip, Somesh, Vijay, Manoj, and Gorakh worked tirelessly to ensure no one lacked medication, often working through the night to secure essential supplies. Nearly all of us made it through the pandemic—except one. Ritesh Nokwal, our international business development manager, fought the Covid virus for over a month before succumbing. We grieved his loss as a family and continue to honour his memory as we build on the partnerships he initiated.

Common Aspirations

I often reflect on the financial assistance we provide to our team and wonder why it is necessary for individuals who have been dedicated to Grind Master for years. A family works towards common aspirations, and our company shares a unified vision. As we make strides towards our goals, the organisation's capabilities improve with every passing year. But it is not enough to have a goal for the business alone; we must also aspire to enhance the lives of the employees and their families.

If Grind Master aims to become a global technology leader, then our team members should see significant improvements in their quality of life. This includes not only intangible benefits like engagement, work-life balance, and a strong sense of family but also tangible economic growth. I challenge the organisation to build the capabilities that will enable us to raise minimum wages, ensuring everyone benefits from the company's growth and success.

Indians often face a mental block—a lingering colonial hangover. We sometimes struggle to see ourselves as among the world's best. Many Indians tend to downplay the achievements of fellow citizens and hold a mental image that anything 'foreign' is inherently superior.

Our shared aspiration is to break free from this mindset.

Everyone at our company embraces the values of passion, trustworthiness, innovation, and expertise, and we all strive for excellence. We aim to build competence like superheroes.

Har Har Mahadev!

"

Relinquish your attachment to the known, step into the unknown and you will step into the field of all possibilities

Deepak Chopra

08

GOING GLOBAL

Supplying machines to a global market has long been a cherished vision for Grind Master. Our early exports reached diverse markets like Russia and Malaysia in 1996 Initially, we exported basic metal-finishing machines—low-value products that fell short of the European market's high standards.

EMO, the hub of the global machine tool industry, is a grand event showcasing the world's latest developments. Grind Master's first participation in EMO in 2005 was a milestone for our small but growing company. However, we faced a challenge when a Dutch company, Timesavers, claimed our brand name 'Grind Master' conflicted with their trademark 'Grinding Master'.

Though Timesavers was a potential competitor, Milind saw them as a possible business partner. Despite the name conflict, we participated in EMO 2005 and 2007 under the name 'MK International'. Although we couldn't use our real brand name, this exposure introduced us to international markets. Over time, discussions with Timesavers led to a strong business partnership that continues even today. By 2013, Timesavers allowed us to participate in the European market as Grind Master, recognising that our products complemented rather than competed with theirs.

My first experience at EMO in 2007 left me feeling like an outsider. Comparing IMTEX to EMO revealed the confidence and pride the European machine tool industry had in its technology. They branded themselves as a technology industry rather than just part of the manufacturing sector. Their booths showcased machines like racing cars, a stark contrast to the less evolved Indian machine tool builders, including Grind Master.

Between 2009 and 2015, we gained confidence in building high-quality machines. Collaborations improved our workmanship, and our NANOFINISH machine range reached a level of refinement suitable for global markets. Our strong reference list in China placed us among elite superfinishing machine suppliers. The global market responded positively after Grind Master's participation in EMO 2013, 2015, and 2017.

Initially, our German competitors dismissed us, skeptical that an Indian company could build complex, high-quality machines. However, after several successful projects in the Indian automotive industry, Grind Master caught their attention. They began to acknowledge that we were doing something right. Projects in China further pitted us against European competition in open tenders. By 2015, our ability to deliver global standards earned Grind Master respect as a worthy competitor. With success in Asian markets, the time seemed right to expand into Europe.

A Disaster in Paris

In 2017, we proudly displayed the French flag alongside the Indian and Chinese flags at exhibitions after acquiring the French machine tool company, SPMS France. Unfortunately, just a few years later, in 2021, the company went bankrupt—a costly misadventure.

Grind Master first encountered SPMS in the Chinese market, competing for projects. Founded by Jacques Pineaut, SPMS catered mainly to the French automotive industry with a strong global reference list. However, SPMS had struggled financially since the 2008 recession. Four former SPMS employees revived the company under the name SMMA, continuing to use the SPMS brand. Despite severe limitations, SPMS delivered quality solutions, thanks to the expertise of their team, particularly Fred and Louis, who managed to produce excellent results despite their constraints.

Adam Norris, an Englishman with extensive sales and business development experience, recognised SPMS's struggles but saw an opportunity for revival through collaboration with Grind Master.

Grind Master had long dreamed of establishing a base in Europe. This dream, however, was driven more by emotion than strategy. We hadn't yet explored markets in America, Japan, or Southeast Asia, but were determined to enter Europe. Europe had many advantages, being a hub for manufacturing technology with strong global exports.

Germany, Italy, and France were traditionally the strongest players, but Italy and France had suffered from recent recessions, leaving Germany as the leading technology hub. We actively sought acquisitions in Europe, and SPMS appeared to offer promising synergies.

We acquired a majority stake in SPMS in January 2017, hoping to build new crankshaft and camshaft machines while using SPMS as a base for expanding Grind Master's product range in Europe. However, both goals proved unattainable. Despite several visits to France in 2017 and 2018, we couldn't transform the mindset or overcome the fierce competition from German companies. The opportunities were few, and our standing did not improve as expected.

Working with the SPMS team also presented challenges. While Fred and Louis supported existing customers, their ability to learn new design and software technologies was limited. Laurent, who handled finance and administration, operated in a manner completely opposite to our way of working. Despite our best efforts, the acquisition ultimately did not yield the results we had hoped for.

Adam Norris played a key role in initiating discussions, and had a strong desire to collaborate with a more established company like Grind Master in sales and marketing. Over time, Adam has truly become a part of the Grind Master family, leading business development efforts in Europe and other international markets.

Unfortunately, Grind Master's initial acquisition strategy was flawed. We structured the deal in a way that funneled all the money into the hands of the four shareholders, leaving nothing for the company. Both Milind and I were confident we could make it work, but our overconfidence cost us dearly. When the Covid-19 pandemic struck, SPMS had no viable future, leading the company to file for voluntary liquidation. This failure left us with valuable lessons and a significant financial loss.

The sting of losing due to overconfidence has taught us prudence, fundamentally reshaping our post-Covid management strategies. Grind Master now proceeds with caution, taking calculated steps. Despite this setback, we have leveraged the knowledge gained from SPMS. Dormant technologies at SPMS, such as new designs for Crankshaft and Camshaft Microfinishing and prototypes for centerless and flat superfinishing machines, have been revived under Grind Master. Moreover, SPMS's customers, particularly in China, have continued their partnerships with Grind Master, recognising the value we offer.

Why Go Global?

Microfinishing and superfinishing technology are highly specialised. It requires significant process knowledge for every solution. Unlike machining SPMs with known processes like turning and milling, the market for NANOFINISH machines in any single region is limited. To grow and mitigate risks, expanding into multiple regions became essential for the company. After our successes in India and China and the lessons from our French expansion, we remained committed to entering new markets.

Our push into these challenging markets was driven by passionate veterans, each with ties to India. Selling specialised technology in developed countries is no easy task, and positioning an Indian company as a technology leader requires both conviction and experience. We have been fortunate to have dedicated partners who proudly represented Grind Master in countries like Germany, Japan, the USA, Mexico, Thailand, and beyond. Their efforts not only built our reputation globally but also pushed us to continuously improve our offerings.

Technology solutions for Germany

A recent example of Grind Master's global impact was a custom-built machine for steering system components, designed for a major American EV manufacturer. This 12-ton machine was urgently needed in Germany, and we managed to deliver it swiftly, flying it from Mumbai to Frankfurt. The machine now operates at unprecedented speed and efficiency, showcasing our ability to meet high demands.

In 2017, Helmut Neufang introduced us to MVO, a company near Stuttgart, Germany, which had recently joined the GMH Group. MVO produced steering rack bars on a massive scale, with takt times of 12-20 seconds, a stark contrast to the 45-90 seconds we were accustomed to in India. During a shop floor visit, it became clear that our initial proposals wouldn't suffice. Dr. Vieweg, a key figure at MVO, emphasised the high-performance standards they required from our first machine. He was direct but also supportive, offering valuable insights.

MVO had previously worked with a German manufacturer but was dissatisfied with their service and unwillingness to customise machines. Grind Master, known for its flexibility in designing solutions that optimise manufacturing processes, took on the challenge of delivering a new concept machine. This situation exemplifies the challenges we face in advanced markets—where a product we believe is well-developed may fall short. We consistently choose to innovate and upgrade, even when unforeseen technical challenges arise and project costs exceed estimates.

MVO urgently needed the machine. While international projects typically take 8-10 months, MVO pushed Grind Master to design and build a complex, custom machine under five months. Milind and I have different operational management styles. Although the company had transitioned to a gated project management system, some projects required a different approach. I recognised that while our project management team could deliver challenging projects within reasonable timelines, MVO's demands called for Milind's 'war room' approach. This approach involves close monitoring and day-to-day management with overlapping steps in design, prototyping, and building.

Milind's task force operates like soldiers in battle, working round the clock. It's common for a problem identified in the evening to be solved by the next morning. There's no 'sleeping over problems'—solutions are often designed late at night, manufactured overnight, and implemented the next day. This is how we completed the first MVO project in just five months—a true miracle.

The new design of the 'steering rack bar superfinishing machine' introduced several innovative concepts and technologies. While the machine achieved the estimated 20-second takt time, it required significant improvements, particularly in the robustness of the part transfer systems. Dr. Vieweg acknowledged our tremendous first effort but highlighted the need for further enhancements. We made some of these updates on site, but we also admitted that the next machine would require a completely new handling concept. Developing the second machine in 2022 and a third in 2023 has been a journey of collaborative improvements. We scrutinised every inefficiency in the earlier machines and solved them with engineering advancements.

Building a close relationship with a precision component manufacturer in the heart of Germany's automotive industry is a source of pride for Grind Master. Our machines at MVO are now used to produce components for major German automotive manufacturers. The image of the machine being rolled onto the aircraft remains vivid in my mind, as Helmut, his son Lucas, and I share a drink in their garden in Saarland.

We made it—Made in India, for Germany.

Automation that is reliable and robust

For years, part transfer systems for superfinishing had been a persistent challenge for Grind Master. As the demand grew for internal transfer systems that automate the entire process from loading to unloading, Grind Master implemented the solutions.

The crankshaft microfinishing machines used an external gantry system integrated into the machine's control system, which proved robust. The crankshaft microfinishing machines used an external gantry system integrated into the machine's control system, which proved robust. However, our other solution, a pneumatic shuttle transfer system, faced operational challenges. On paper, this system appeared promising—economical, fast, and attractive for machines with 15-20 second takt times. In practice, however, it led to more downtimes.

Machine tools are workhorses in high-volume production, so we upgraded all customer machines with the more reliable gantry transfer solution. A senior manager commented, "We invested more in automation on the new machine, but its ultimate productivity is much better than the earlier one." This experience taught us that delivering a stable and reliable solution justifies the higher cost for discerning buyers.

Technology solutions for Japan

Japan is one of the toughest markets for exporting machinery. While Japanese machines are used globally, only a few foreign machines make it into Japan. A mix of factors contributes to this—Japan's advanced machinery technology, the language barrier, and a strong sense of nationalism. So why attempt it? Because it's a challenge worth pursuing.

Grind Master's five-year journey to supply machines to the Japanese automotive industry took us through India, Thailand, and China, and it is a struggle that continues. Leading this effort is Ishida San, a wise and experienced figure reminiscent of Yoda from Star Wars. Having worked in India for NTC Japan, Ishida San had heard about

Grind Master machines performing well in India and China. During his first visit to our NANOFINISH unit, his keen eye pointed out several areas for improvement.

We had been searching for the right person to help us navigate Southeast Asia, and after multiple visits to Thailand, Indonesia, and Malaysia, it became clear that Japanese automotive dominance in these markets meant decisions were made at headquarters in Japan. We needed a voice in Japan, and Ishida San, though retired and based in Bangkok, believed in our potential. He knew that succeeding in Japan would require perseverance, but he also recognised our capability and openness to feedback.

The Japanese automotive industry has played a crucial role in shaping Indian manufacturing. Companies like Maruti Suzuki and Toyota brought Japanese manufacturing culture to India, training countless people in concepts like 5S and Kaizen. Japanese companies in India helped Indian machine tool builders meet their stringent requirements, and we have experienced this approach firsthand. We also supplied machines to numerous Japanese companies in China, creating a strong reference list.

The Japanese approach to change is methodical and deliberate, advancing step by step. Our most successful partnership in Thailand has been with Siam Compressor (SCI), a Mitsubishi Electric Group company. SCI, which builds scroll and rotary compressors, initially used a stone process for finishing eccentric shafts, yielding unsatisfactory results. We saw the opportunity to upgrade SCI to the highly reliable microfinishing process. After visiting Mitsubishi HQ in Japan, Grind Master's Process Research Lab conducted tests, and SCI validated the results. The first machine was delivered in 2018.

As SCI produced a variety of parts, they needed a more flexible machine. Although it would be bigger and more expensive, SCI opted for the more sophisticated flexible CNC machine, and they haven't looked back ever since. Grind Master delivered one machine after another, with minor improvements each time, in the past few years. In 2023, we developed a specialised deburring machine for precision plates of rotary compressors, replacing the Japanese machines. Despite being more expensive and occupying more space, our machine was selected for its sophistication and process improvements.

Ishida San always smiles when we talk about Nissan. References from Renault Nissan India and Dongfeng Nissan were key to securing a meeting at Nissan Powertrain Thailand (NPT). Like most automakers, Nissan traditionally set up dedicated lines with high-volume capacity and required precise finish specifications for crankshafts. However, the plant in Thailand was intended for lower capacity. Japanese machines used in other plants featured only multi-station dedicated machines. Grind Master, with its extensive experience in Tier-1 crankshaft production, developed a highly flexible model over the years. This made it an ideal fit for NPT, and our machine was selected. The versatile machine showcased the power of innovative technology over conventional solutions, paving the way for further opportunities with Nissan.

Nissan Japan developed a new engine platform with entirely new components. Would these require microfinishing? Grind Master's Process Research Lab developed prototype parts, which were accepted. This ability to develop the process was a key factor in being selected as a supplier for the Nissan plant near Tochigi. Delivering machines to Nissan Japan was a different challenge altogether.

Built in 2020, they had a major impact on defining a higher benchmark in Grind Master's quality mission, setting a new standard for processes. Engineering the machine to Japanese standards required deep learning in electricals, safety, and fluid circuits. Monoj Maiti and Nilesh Kathar, young engineers with three years of experience from our graduate engineers' programme, spearheaded these improvements and delivered. We knew we had to raise the build standard even higher.

Ensuring a dry floor by testing the machine on brown paper and using foam sheets to prevent scratches were just some of the measures taken. Machines with many sensors, diagnostics, and sophisticated elements require excellent software. Our machine software technology had been gradually improving, and Debanjan Dhar, another graduate from our programme, developed NANOSMART, a state-of-the-art software. This system was well received by Nissan and has since earned accolades from various users globally and in India.

Commissioning the first machine for Nissan in Japan was a learning experience. Working under Japan's strict safety rules taught us a lot about their methodology and systems. Ours was the only non-Japanese machine in the entire factory.

When the Covid-19 pandemic hit, global travel came to a halt. Our second machine in Japan, destined for Mazda's factory in Hiroshima, had to be commissioned with the support of a Japanese service team. Our machines were specialised and complex, far different from machining centers or grinders, and local service contractors lacked the necessary skills and experience. However, we had no choice.

Radhakrishna Barde took over international service and, together with Milind, coined the philosophy: "sweat on the shop floor—don't bleed at the site." Barde worked closely with the Japanese service team, training them as best he could online and later remotely guiding them through the installation. It took much longer to complete, but we succeeded, though at a tremendous cost. We knew that paying Japanese engineers for the project was financially unviable and we could have invoked force majeure in our contract with Mazda. Yet, that thought was fleeting. We were committed to doing whatever it took.

The high costs of the Mazda installation reverberated through our management discussions. Global travel restrictions highlighted the fact that only our team could install our machines. The choice was clear: innovate or give up international business. We unanimously decided to develop 'plug and play' machines, leading to a series of upgrades.

Machine engineering now considers how the machine will be unpacked and installed. A picture speaks a thousand words, and videos speak a thousand pictures—creating mock installation videos for every part of the process has enabled us to train technicians in any country.

The proof of success came through subsequent rapid installations in Japan. Selected for our technology and process research, our machines now operate in the most challenging market—Japan. We achieved what several European companies attempted and gave up on and what most Indian or Chinese companies wouldn't even consider.

We did it—Made in India, for Japan.

Ritesh was one of our most dedicated champions in international markets. His efforts in America and Asia, and the partnerships he helped build, continue to transform our business. Although he witnessed the delivery of our first machines in Mexico and Japan, he tragically passed away during the second wave of Covid-19. His legacy inspires us to carry on.

2003 © Building the first Microfinishing machines - a determined team

2018 © Microfinishing Machines for Crankshafts are quite complex. Over 2000 engineered bits and pieces coming together to perform a mission critical function

2013 © Microfinishing Machines Building area fills with projects for Chinese Automotive industry

2014 © Milind receiving the Emerging India Award

2015 © Exhibiting in CIMT China

2015 © Milind speaking at Big Boss on a Marathi News channel

2017 © Imtex - Launching a machine with Mr. Shailesh Sheth and Mr. Trilochan Singh Sahney gracing the occasion.

2014 © Inclusion - Grind Master family participates in Branding

2017 © Grind Master GO - a Cycling and running club at one of the events

2024 © Bringing a culture of enduring excellence to the fast growing Marathwada region - Sameer delivers a talk at an HR Event in the city.

2018 © Afforestation projects - visiting fast growing forests is a joy for the Kelkars. Shown here is a few months old Native Miyawaki Dense forest at Grind Master Waluj campus.

“

This is the essence of science: Ask an impertinent question, and you are on the way to a pertinent answer

Jacob Bronowski,
The Ascent of Man

09

INNOVATE OR DIE

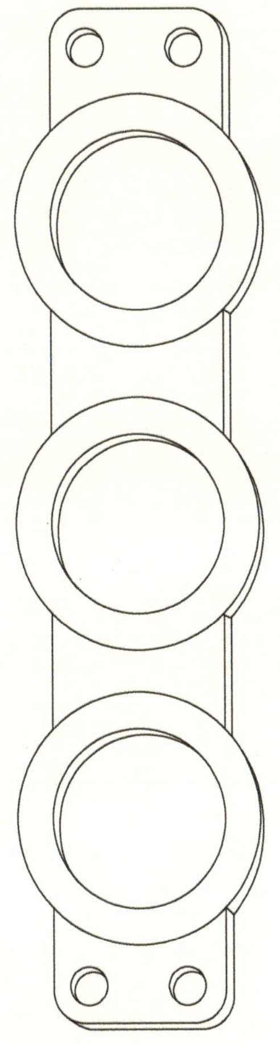

The electric vehicle (EV) was once a buzzword, but discussions around it have been ongoing in the international automotive world for years. While we focused on advancing crankshaft and camshaft microfinishing in India and China, a critical realisation emerged: the internal combustion engine faces the risk of obsolescence. Recognising this challenge, Grind Master crafted a long-term plan to ensure resilience.

Our strategy focussed on expanding our product range. We invested in developing the ROBOFINISH business, which is detailed in our chapters on robotics, along with heavy hydraulics and bearing superfinishing. The message is clear—innovate or die.

Innovating benchmark technologies for hydraulic cylinders

Heavy hydraulic cylinders are essential for various applications, including earthmovers, aerospace, pallet trucks, and forklifts. These cylinders endure harsh conditions and require long-lasting, corrosion-resistant surfaces. Achieving such durability demands high-quality surface coatings, which in turn rely on precisely finished surfaces.

Grind Master entered the heavy hydraulics finishing market in the early 2000s, developing machines like superfinishing systems, centerless belt grinders, and centerless finishing systems. Each machine serves a different production process, reflecting the diverse needs of the industry. What ultimately determines corrosion resistance performance is a combination. We see an opportunity to innovate and set a new industry benchmark. We've dedicated ourselves to this goal.

Initially, we built a few machines for the limited Indian market. However, the Chinese market operates on an entirely different scale. When SANY, a major Chinese earthmover manufacturer, decided to establish a mega-factory for producing hydraulic cylinders internally, they aimed to enhance quality and chose the best machines for the job. The project required ten machines in its first phase, all part of a fully automated cylinder manufacturing facility—the first of its kind. The vision was ambitious, and realising it meant pushing engineering boundaries and getting it right the first time. Although risky, this project was essential for de-risking Grind Master's business.

In the pursuit of breakthroughs, taking calculated risks and making them work is key. Entering into the largest contract in our company's history was one such bold move.

While we developed robust designs, reliable processes, and advanced software, our front-end engineering team validated concepts in the lab before releasing them for production. Seeing the machines lined up on the floor was impressive, and securing a follow-up contract for ten more machines was the cherry on top. In just two years, we had delivered more machines for this application in China than we had in India over 15 years.

Process research drives progress

Process research has played a crucial role in our success, leading to the development of new products. For instance, a major Japanese joint venture in India wanted to validate Grind Master's superfinishing results—a technology they hadn't previously attempted.

After a Japanese engineer visited us and confirmed the effectiveness of our methods, he thanked us for our collaboration. This partnership changed a manufacturing process, showcasing the impact of our knowledge and technology.

Performance upgrades drive this process research. In earth-moving equipment, for example, hydraulic cylinders once had a one-year warranty, but the benchmark has gradually risen to five years. The highest specifications come from specialised hydraulics used in aerospace and construction.

An American engineering company that custom-builds high-end hydraulic cylinders – used in spacecraft, aviation, and bridge stabilisers – provides warranties exceeding 25 years. Their requirements for surface finishes are ten times finer than those of any other hydraulic cylinder manufacturer. Our process research pushed the limits, achieving roughness values as low as 10 nanometers on large parts. Delivering this machine and seeing it go into production was a proud moment, highlighting our ability to export high-technology products to advanced customers. Grind Master were selected as a solution developer because of our R&D capabilities.

Remanufacturing for a Circular Economy

Hydraulic cylinders often require reconditioning after years of service, having sustained damage in harsh environments. This process typically involves makeshift machines, like lathes, and manual labor. Caterpillar's REMAN facility at Carter Machinery aimed to ensure that rebuilt cylinders matched the quality of new ones, necessitating an automated process. Refurbishing components is more challenging than making new ones due to variable input.

Grind Master designed and delivered a special machine—the first of its kind – that includes adaptive grinding to remove the chrome layer and superfinishing to achieve the required finish. This automatic piston rod remanufacturing system was a game-changer.

Across the spectrum of companies we've worked with, hydraulic cylinder piston rod manufacturing varies widely. Each company experiments with methods to improve corrosion resistance and extend warranty periods. A global 'best practice' has yet to emerge. However, Grind Master is poised to set a new benchmark in this domain. With deep process knowledge, we're on a difficult but promising journey to generate research and demonstrate the best processes. This step is crucial in our vision to become a global technology leader, creating a reference point for manufacturing methodologies worldwide.

Catching up and leapfrogging

Microfinishing and superfinishing were invented in the 1940s. Grind Master quickly mastered these techniques and adapted to new demands, always believing that we could become technology leaders. The next generation of manufacturing requirements has given us the chance to leapfrog the development cycle. We've embraced this challenge with boldness and maturity.

Ballscrews, which convert rotary motion into precise linear motion, are critical components in machine tool slides and steering systems. Their performance—whether in terms of noise, efficiency, or lifespan—depends heavily on surface finishing. Experts now agree that superfinishing can significantly improve ballscrew performance, especially in machine tools and automotive steering systems. However, achieving a surface roughness of Ra 0.1 microns on a screw's profiled surface seemed impossible—not just for us, but also for the Europeans and Japanese.

The challenge of finishing screw profiles required a series of innovative solutions. We combined unique tooling, modified abrasive media, and developed a control methodology that allowed the machine to follow the screw's contours without damaging it. The result was our globally patented NANOSCREW technology, invented by Venkatesh Kulkarni, Milind Kelkar, and Sameer Kelkar. This technology gives Grind Master a unique edge. Our first machine using this process was commissioned by a leading Taiwanese machine tool ballscrew manufacturer, marking a significant advancement in precision components.

We believe our solution is superior to alternative methods and should become the future standard for ballscrew finishing. This will be our 'S = K log W' moment. (S = K log W is the formula with which Boltzmann is known. Refer chapter on Ascent of Man for details).

Collaborative developments towards Atmanirbhar

Bearings—whether cylindrical roller, taper roller, or ball groove—are essential for high-speed motion across various industries, from automotive to home appliances. Every bearing requires precise grinding and superfinishing, and German and Japanese machine builders have long led this field. Most high-quality bearings made in India are still superfinished on imported machines. This technology clearly needs to be indigenised – Atmanirbhar.

In 2017, we acquired basic technology from SPMS France and developed superfinishing with films for pin-type parts. Varroc became our first customer for this machine, but they faced a challenge. As an ancillary supplier to Bajaj Auto, Varroc had to follow a drawing that specified a 'stone lapping process'.

Although stone lapping and film superfinishing achieve similar results, film superfinishing offers better consistency and requires less maintenance. We demonstrated this to Bajaj engineers, who studied the process and approved the change. The success of our centerless superfinishing for crank pins opened doors for other pin-type applications, leading to improved designs and more machine deliveries. Our ability to work with both stone and film processes adds versatility to our solutions.

One of the most critical machines in bearing manufacturing is the superfinishing of raceways—the tracks on which moving elements roll at high speeds. These tracks come in various shapes and sizes, with cylindrical, taper, and circular grooves being the most common. To succeed in this field, we had to step out of our comfort zone and develop stone superfinishing.

NBI, a Spanish bearing company specialising in medium to large bearings for earthmoving equipment, expanded a plant in India and considered buying Indian machines. It's rare for a European company to take such a risk, but dynamic director Aditya Chindalia and CEO Marion Radu led this mission. NBI worked with Micromatic Grinding, and introduced Grind Master as a potential superfinishing developer. NBI's team visited us, and despite our lack of experience in raceway machines, they believed in our engineering ability. Their valuable inputs helped us deliver a machine that performs well. This project has been a true collaborative effort.

R&D and collaborative innovation

Conducting R&D for an entirely new product range can be expensive and time-consuming. Grind Master has consistently invested in R&D, generating breakthrough innovations. Recognising machine tools as a cornerstone of manufacturing, the Indian government supports machine builders through initiatives like the DSIR scheme for internal R&D units. We've benefited from this support, which has spurred further research. Additionally, the government funds industry-academia partnerships for research. We participated in one such project with IIT Bombay and MHRD under the UAY scheme. Although this project faced limitations and didn't result in a commercial product, it taught us valuable lessons.

Academia excels in core research, process modelling, and analytics, while machine tool makers specialise in design and construction. Recognising these strengths is key to successful collaborations.

IIT Madras has established the Advanced Manufacturing Technology Development Center (AMTDC), which works closely with several machine tool builders. Founded by Prof. Ramesh Babu and led by dynamic research engineers, AMTDC has delivered excellent results. Despite our initial reluctance to join another government-funded project, Prof. Babu convinced us of the merits. In hindsight, our hesitation seems foolish. We simply needed to find a way to collaborate effectively with academia.

In 2022, we received approval for an applied project with IIT Madras. Together, we are developing a highly specialised bearing spherical raceway machine. The resulting intellectual property will be jointly owned, allowing Grind Master to commercialise it. This project accelerates development, achieving in three years what would normally take eight to ten. The IIT Madras team, led by Principal Research Engineer R. Srikanth, works closely with Grind Master's team, led by Deepak Mohite. While Grind Master builds prototypes, IIT Madras focuses on process modelling and machine learning. This collaboration brings academic rigour and scientific insights to our engineers, drastically improving our capabilities.

The machine developed under this project will be showcased at IMTEX 2025, demonstrating the strength of industry-academia collaboration with world-class products and technologies.

Together, we can achieve remarkable things!

Process innovation

Metal finishing evolves rapidly, often appearing in research papers and not in textbooks. Processes like polishing, finishing, lapping, superfinishing, microfinishing, external honing, paper lapping, and buffing are sometimes used interchangeably in the industry. At the core of our business is process innovation. Surface finish–texture, roughness, and fine geometry–significantly impacts component performance. This realisation drives our pursuit of new challenges and solutions.

At Grind Master, process development is about both 'know how' and, more importantly, 'know why'. Collaborating with partners in abrasives and machine building, we learned that applying this knowledge to Indian manufacturing conditions required a unique approach. For example, the abrasive process used by VSM for hardware and sanitary fittings in Europe didn't work well in India. Understanding how an abrasive performs under specific conditions makes process optimisation a matter of customisation. Material composition and input quality are key factors, and the guidelines from our partners are just the starting point. This challenge of discovering the best method attracted Milind, Mohini, and our team of process engineers.

Our Process Research Lab is the hub of innovation at Grind Master. Each year, we conduct over 250 application development tests, and over time, we have demonstrated solutions for more than 5,000 different components worldwide. Manufacturers approach us with their finishing challenges, sparking our research. Each experiment is a learning opportunity. The processes we develop are valuable to many manufacturers, and those willing to invest in the research have a vested interest in the results. Recently, several research projects have been funded with financial assistance from customer partners.

Front-End Engineering (FEE), as we call it, is a critical R&D activity that assures both our manufacturing partners and Grind Master that the proposed solutions will work under specific conditions. Successful collaborations with companies like John Deere Foundry USA, Bradken Foundry Australia, Magotteaux Foundry Belgium, and Pragati Automation India showcase the effectiveness of this approach.

Venkatesh Kulkarni, our lead process development engineer, plays a crucial role in process research. Hailing from Beed district and with experience as an assembly and service engineer, his grasp of processes and his ability to explore new methods have driven significant advancements. The Kelkar family remains closely involved in these activities, with Milind and I focusing on key new processes and specifications, while Mohini connects the lab to new market applications.

When a Japanese company asked, "What happens if we superfinish a sports car engine part to very fine parameters?" it sparked a research partnership. Grind Master created prototypes with finishes as fine as 10 nm (nanometer). Producing such samples for product testing is a core part of our Process Research Lab's work. Recent innovations in superfinishing for turret rings, microfinishing for electric vehicle motor shafts, and fine microfinishing for compressor shafts have led to upgraded component specifications and improved performance.

Process research is now merging with controls and software. Traditionally, metrology equipment validated processes, but with more robust metrology devices and increased computing power, process and condition monitoring are becoming integral to the machine.

This presents an opportunity for us to leapfrog in technology, which is now a focus area. Two of our young engineers, Debanjan Dhar and Akshay Bhat, have worked with me to patent machine learning applications in superfinishing and belt grinding. The initial results are promising—reducing cycle times by up to 30% and ensuring consistent output even with variable input. These technologies represent a new paradigm in finishing.

Building an innovative organisation

Innovation is in our DNA at Grind Master. We stay ahead of the competition by developing new products and methods, with as much as 30% of our revenue generated from innovations within the past five years. Maintaining this momentum requires a culture of innovation within the organisation. Over time, we've identified key drivers that make Grind Master an innovative company:

- Providing space and freedom to explore and ideate, breaking down hierarchies
- Ensuring clarity about the organisation's vision and strategic direction
- Continuously motivating and inspiring people
- Overcoming the fear of failure
- Acknowledging ideas that don't work quickly—Fast to Fail
- Absorbing new technologies through training
- Exposing our team to the outside world

Audacious endeavours, supported by a growing maturity in structuring developmental projects, yield better results. Our focus on finishing and deburring is deep and requires full dedication. Discerning customers have guided us along the way, and international projects have challenged us with their performance demands and varied process specifications. The global manufacturing industry often leads Indian manufacturing by a few years. To innovate, we must confront challenges head-on, wherever they appear.

"If you fail, never give up because F.A.I.L.. means "First Attempt In Learning" - End is not the end, if fact E.N.D. means "Effort Never Dies" - If you get No as an answer, remember N.O. means "Next Opportunity". So, Let's be positive"

APJ Abdul Kalam

10

EXPERIMENTS IN ROBOTICS

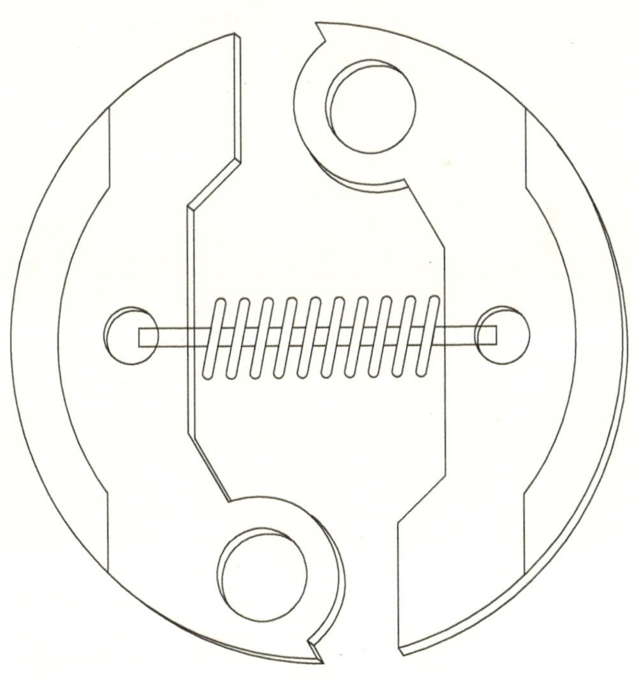

Robotics has long been recognised as a next-generation technology in manufacturing. My introduction to robotics began during my engineering studies, and I gained practical experience with industrial robotics as an intern at Fanuc India. This journey continued through my master's thesis at the University of California, Berkeley, where I worked on robotic vision systems, and later at Güdel Switzerland, focusing on press automation robots and high-precision gantry drilling systems for aerospace parts. These experiences prepared me to bring robotics to Grind Master.

Robotics deployment in India has gradually gained momentum, with around 6,000 robots introduced annually. The automotive industry has led this trend, particularly in robotic welding and machine tending. However, there was a gap in applying robotics to grinding, finishing, and deburring applications. We saw an opportunity to carve out a niche in this space.

We started with a small team, successfully executing projects like robotic pouring and machine tending. These early efforts helped us build a foundation in project execution, primarily through system integration. Robot manufacturers encouraged Indian machine builders to become system partners, and we collaborated with ABB, KUKA, and Fanuc to provide turnkey solutions. These projects taught us valuable lessons, particularly in managing integration challenges.

One significant hurdle was overcoming the negative perception of robotic automation among labour unions, who viewed robots as job threats rather than tools that could improve quality, productivity, and safety. In such cases, success required strong commitment from both the customer's management and our team. Our first customers, companies belonging to the Bhogale family, successfully deployed automation across their businesses, demonstrating the benefits of this partnership.

Our technology development efforts focused on applying Grind Master's expertise in grinding to robotics for complex geometries. This began with robotic front axle beam grinding, a project for Bharat Forge that marked a generational shift from the

Linishing SPM built for the same application in the early 1990s. Under the guidance of Mr. Raju Kalyani, who emphasised the importance of fixturing and firm clamping. Grinding operations that remove up to 2-3mm of material require robust engineering to handle the significant process forces. Over the years, we refined this solution, delivering more than 10 machines to 5 FAB makers globally.

We also explored robotic polishing and finishing, areas where we already had a strong process understanding. There was considerable interest in automating the polishing of complex parts, such as motorcycle fuel tanks and sanitary fittings. While automatic processes can produce excellent finishes, they often result in a different appearance than manual polishing. Moreover, robots in these operations aren't much faster than humans. Although we had the right technologies, low wage costs in India and a lack of safety awareness limited our ability to scale these solutions. In the early years, we built a few robotic polishing systems for bent tube polishing and stainless steel fabrication, but we knew we would need to wait for the market to catch up.

Through our experiments, we realised that to succeed as a robotic solutions provider, we needed to specialise in specific applications that were also economically viable in the Indian context.

A Compelling Problem

In May 2012, I visited a typical dirty fettling shop in a foundry in Kolhapur. The scene was chaotic—sparks flying, heavy dust in the air, and over a hundred workers grinding castings with various tools. The environment was hazardous, with risks of injuries, white finger syndrome, and lung disorders. The shop floor manager lamented the difficulty of finding workers for such gruelling jobs, while the foundry owner expressed frustration with the younger generation's reluctance to work hard. This environment reminded me of the manufacturing workshop at IIT Bombay, where we were required to fettle or grind extra material from castings as part of our lab work. I hated it, and here were people doing it day in and day out. This was a problem worth solving. An automated solution could transform the lives of these workers.

A transformative solution for aluminium foundries

Mr. Munjal, Managing Director of Rockman Auto, emphasised the importance of simplicity in our approach. By simplifying the machine and reducing costs, we could focus on tasks where robots outperformed humans while accepting that certain complicated operations would remain manual. This balance of technology and economics was key.

In 2013, we formed a dedicated robotics team to explore robotic deflashing and grinding in foundries. It was tough going. Mahesh understood that closing deals for custom-built machines required patience and determination. It was a process of introducing the concept to more and more customers and staying positive with every opportunity. After several attempts with unfeasible solutions based on European models, we struggled to develop concepts that would work in the Indian context, where wage rates were dramatically lower than in developed countries.

However, after an insightful discussion with Mr. Munjal, Rockman Auto purchased three machines in 2013 and later expanded to over 25 machines for alloy wheel deflashing. This was one of the most successful deployments of robotic deflashing in the cost-conscious two-wheeler industry. Other companies took a different approach, focusing on automatic deflashing for export customers willing to pay for robotic automation. We delivered complete turnkey solutions integrating with pressure die-casting machines, automating the entire line. This approach proved efficient, with systems delivered to companies like Sundaram Clayton and Alicon.

Yet, as a machine builder, I had concerns about certain aspects of this approach. The compromises on safety and reliability for short-term benefits troubled me. Wire mesh enclosures couldn't adequately protect operators from heavy machining operations. The lack of safety awareness and the industry's unwillingness to invest in these 'luxuries' led us to gradually pull back from this sector, choosing to work only with specific companies that prioritised safety and long-term reliability.

Changing lives in ferrous foundry

Non-ferrous castings, typically made in metallic molds, are relatively easy to handle. They are lightweight, with low flash levels, and the material is easily machinable. However, grinding ferrous castings presents a much tougher challenge. These castings are heavier, often weighing between 100-250 kg, and the grinding process is more complex. Flash on ferrous castings, by definition, is uncontrolled and inconsistent from one casting to the next. Since castings are produced through a 'near net shape' process, there can be significant variations in their size and shape—sometimes by several millimeters. These challenges are even more pronounced in sand mold-produced castings, such as cast iron, compared to metal mold-produced castings.

Successfully applying robotics to these types of castings requires advanced technologies that combine force control, compliant tools, and process modifications. Unfortunately, many installations fail due to a lack of understanding of the process requirements and the correct techniques, leaving them unproductive.

My first exposure to ferrous foundries, during a visit to Saroj Industries with my family friend, Mr. Madhav Gokhale, was eye-opening. Mr. Jadhav, recognising that we were new to the field, patiently shared his thoughts for a solution based on European videos. At the time, I proposed a machine that, in hindsight, would have been unworkable. Luckily, Saroj Industries didn't place an order, and we realised we needed a different approach than the one we used for aluminium.

Mr. Tyeb, responsible for setting up a greenfield foundry for Amtek Auto, suggested a simple yet powerful idea: use more power. This insight led us to develop a viable solution using heavy-duty robots, high-power grinding spindles, and newly developed electroplated diamond wheels. Although financial problems at Amtek prevented us from completing this breakthrough order, we successfully created the first indigenous iron casting grinding machine.

Subsequent machines took this solution into the production environment for foundries like Zanvar Group, Kumar Pumps, and Dunung. The first-generation Grind Master ROBOFINISH machines for ferrous castings were basic but functional, and we developed key technologies like adaptive grinding during their commissioning.

By 2016, our second-generation machines were even better. Our reputation in the Indian foundry industry grew, with successful installations producing castings. The power levels in these machines increased significantly—iron casting applications jumped from 3-4 kW to over 15 kW, while aluminium applications rose from 300-500 W to 5-10 kW. Naturally, performance improved, and we saw faster, more efficient results.

As our revenues from robotics grew rapidly, we recognised even more potential in the foundry sector and robotic automation in general. Our company aggressively pursued revenue expansion, and robotics became a major growth driver. However, this pursuit led us down a path of unnecessary diversions.

Taking Detours - Another misadventure

Grind Master created a new business unit, Group 4, to explore non-foundry applications, such as robotic sculpting and machining, robotic education cells, robotic 3D printing, and collaborations with the public sector.

However, working with public sector undertakings (PSUs) proved challenging. Bureaucratic systems, internal politics, and slow decision-making processes made it difficult to achieve technological advancements. Changes in key officers disrupted continuity, and the environment was far from conducive to innovation. In specialised equipment, the proposal itself requires substantial expertise, years of experience, and carefully collected data. Unfortunately, public sector tenders often disregard this effort, allowing competitors to simply agree to everything that we put up in our proposal.

Our focus on too many technology developments spread our engineering and research resources too thin. While we managed to create basic proof-of-concept projects for enthusiastic industries, many of these solutions were not scalable. Grind Master has always been known as an expert in niche domains, but our robotics business was straying too far from this core value. The business was becoming too diversified, and rapid revenue growth wasn't backed by strong margins and cash flow.

Robotics Talent Management

Robotics is a relatively new discipline, and finding and retaining qualified engineers in this field is challenging, especially in Aurangabad. Our robotics team at Grind Master was almost always made up of fresh graduates, whom we trained from scratch in robotics and machine building. These young engineers were talented and delivered impressive results.

However, stability within the team was always an issue. A robotics engineer typically becomes proficient in basic robot programming within 1-2 years, at which point they are often recruited by other robotic automation companies. Quick job changes are common in this field, and the niche technology at Grind Master requires time to learn and master. An engineer trained in finishing, for example, cannot easily be replaced by someone with experience in welding or handling.

Consequently, while our trained engineers were in high demand elsewhere, it was challenging to find replacements with the necessary skills. Additionally, many robotic engineers seemed unwilling to stay in any role for more than a couple of years. We also encountered a lack of professionalism in areas such as communication, reporting, and responsibility. In some cases, this even devolved into unethical behaviour, which shocked us as management.

One particularly low point involved a case of 'Jugaad Automation' (name changed). What began as a suspicion of unethical conduct escalated into a full-blown scam. Three young engineers from Grind Master formed their own company and delivered services to our customers while still employed by us. To do this, they stole valuable data, including technology and commercial information. These engineers had been promising employees with bright futures at

Grind Master, yet they conspired in a way that was both shocking and damaging. As a result of their actions, we lost credibility with several customers, and team morale plummeted. When confronted with the evidence, the three engineers could only offer weak excuses. We eventually resorted to legal action and relented on humanitarian grounds only when the three agreed not to transgress in the future.

These incidents marked a period of low morale. We had to scrutinise many employees, conduct interviews, and impose restrictions on access to information. This process may have been disturbing or even humiliating for some, but fortunately, most of the Grind Master team understood the gravity of the situation. They accepted the challenges and moved forward, helping the company recover from this difficult period.

Break Point

When my mentor and friend, Rudolf Gudel, visited India, he was excited to see our robotic applications in action. But, as a sharp strategist, he asked, "Did you consider that the foundry industry is quite primitive to deploy high technology?" His skepticism didn't deter us; we pushed forward with our efforts.

Robotic system integration in India is challenging. Many solution providers, especially in welding and handling, work with razor-thin margins. Manufacturing companies constantly seek alternatives, mixing and matching solutions from previous projects. Intellectual property rights often take a backseat. While robot manufacturers and key technology suppliers are well-protected, system integrators, who are crucial in delivering successful solutions, face the most significant risks and receive the smallest margins.

The ROBOFINISH business was my brainchild, a startup I brought into the company. The responsibility to analyse and fix it rested squarely on my shoulders. Like many automation ventures, innovative solution-building often struggles financially, and the robotics group at Grind Master was no exception. Profits were slim, and cash flow was tight.

Initially, we set prices low to introduce the product to the market, but these prices were unsustainable. While European and American system integrators charged three to four times as much for similar solutions, the Indian market wasn't willing to pay more. Compromises—whether driven by customer specifications or internal cost pressures—sometimes led to unsuccessful solutions. We were committed to making every solution work, but this often came at a high cost.

The manufacturing industry, particularly in India, has a poor understanding of robotic solutions. Many senior managers and foundry owners have unrealistic expectations of what robots can do, often imagining them as magical machines straight out of a movie. This gap in awareness is a significant challenge.

Transforming manufacturing methods requires strong management, backed by excellent technology change management. Unfortunately, most companies fall short in this critical preparation, which includes the mindset and approach needed to deploy automation successfully. In a typical robotic automation project in a foundry, too many people get involved—none with the necessary expertise or experience to implement the solution. There is no single project manager, and various departments—operations, maintenance, tooling, and engineering—make conflicting demands at different stages, ignoring previously agreed-upon terms. Under these conditions, keeping the project on track becomes nearly impossible.

This initial phase of robotics at Grind Master has been an adventure, a journey into uncharted territories where we delivered some solutions despite the odds. The rest of the company supported us through the financial losses. But now, we were at a break point. It was time to make strategic decisions to move the ROBOFINISH business forward:

1. Focus on robotic grinding in foundries.
2. Implement hands-on, tight management.
3. Build a strong core team.

By specialising in robotic grinding for foundries, we could develop the expertise needed to transform an internal startup into a mature business. This niche focus would leave a meaningful impact on an industry desperate for change.

"We are nature's unique experiment to make the rational intelligence prove itself sounder than the reflex. Knowledge is our destiny" ... Tim Redford reviewing 'The Ascent of Man'

11

THE RED PILL

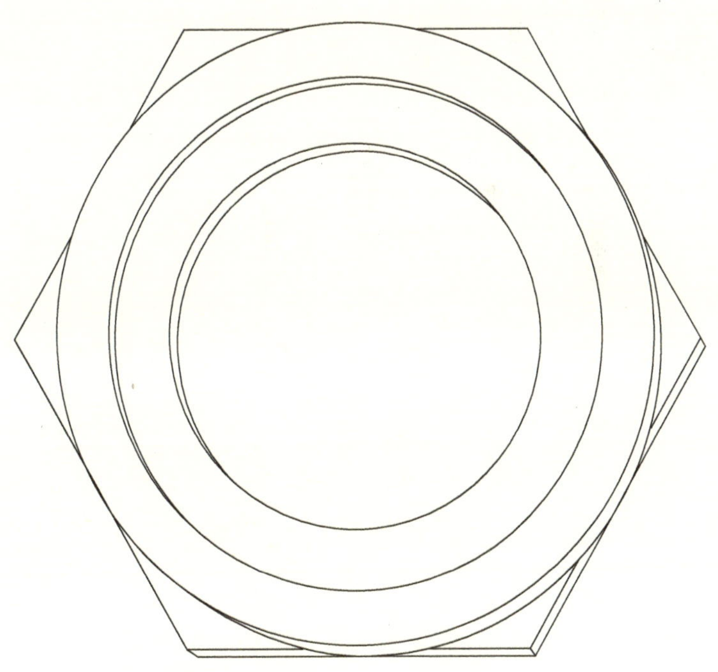

In the popular sci-fi film *The Matrix,* Morpheus offers Neo a choice between two pills. The blue pill represents returning to the world as it is while the red pill symbolises diving into the unknown to see how deep the rabbit hole goes. At Grind Master, we chose the red pill.

We consciously reduced the size of the business by being selective about projects, deep diving into wonderland and building technology in a specific domain. This was an audacious strategy based on exploration in America.

When we developed robotic grinding machines for iron castings in Indian foundries, I initially believed that automation must already dominate this operation in developed countries, given their higher wage costs and stronger emphasis on health and safety. So, I was surprised when a consultant for John Deere approached us, seeking robotic auto grinding solutions for large agricultural castings. They were exploring multiple options, particularly in Europe. Though our technology wasn't fully refined, it was moving in the right direction, and we were eager to develop custom-built solutions. This mindset led to a contract for conducting a Front-End Engineering study. A container full of castings was shipped to India for testing, and we built a powerful demonstration system, developing several new technologies.

In the spring of 2019, I drove to Iowa. The snow had yet to melt, and I felt nervous in the cold. Fortunately, a video package of the tests had arrived just in time. Over 10 foundrymen gathered and applauded as they watched the breathtaking footage of robots performing violent cutting and grinding actions. I knew we had created something to be proud of.

American foundries operated differently. The 'Chip and Grind' process was a major bottleneck, pushing foundries to extremes, including shipping castings to Mexico or using prison labour. Given the wage costs, various business models could emerge in developed countries.

This first exposure to international markets provided key insights that reshaped our approach to the ROBOFINISH business. With our entry into the global market, a new business model began to take shape. We were producing several economic robotic machines each year, but the average value of those built for the international market was much higher. If we could excel in specific niche applications and earn a strong international reputation, we could transform the business into a mix of Indian and international projects. With less reliance on the Indian market, we could become more selective, choosing only the best projects. International business would bring high-value projects with good margins, but to achieve this, we needed to dive deep into technology and build a refined solution that could be considered a breakthrough on the global stage.

Achieving this required a major restructuring, shifting our focus from operations to research and development. While I had guided the ROBOFINISH team, managers from machine-building or automation backgrounds had led it. However, this new business model demanded a unique combination of both. The transition called for a different approach.

'Generation 3' machines

Software developers often say that Version 1 is a proof of concept, Version 2 is for extensive testing (sometimes called Beta), and Version 3 is the one that truly works well. Over the years, we built machines proving that robotic grinding could work. But could we advance to Generation 3—a machine that truly excelled?

Some international opportunities were already on the table when I returned from America in 2019. While I was glad to gain traction in the international market, I remained skeptical of our capabilities. We struggled to deliver a fully functional machine, but we weren't alone—others faced similar challenges! I learned that other systems purchased by foundries also had commissioning, teething, and long-term issues. Solving these problems presented an opportunity. Could we approach our solutions differently?

Most integrators built robotic solutions as 'cells,' constructing the automation at their premises for testing and later reassembling the entire cell at the customer site. This method was inefficient and prone to quality issues on site. Foundry floors often lacked proper preparation, and poor chip and dust management led to significant maintenance problems. Most importantly, grinding and finishing are machining operations, and the stability of the concrete affects process accuracy. In developing our Generation 1 and 2 solutions, we had thought like system integrators. Now, it was time to think like machine builders, which set us apart. The Generation 3 machine took shape with these considerations in mind during a long flight and crystallised in the months that followed.

Building a breakthrough machine is a rewarding experience, especially with a discerning and collaborative partner. Elgi Foundry in Coimbatore, led by Mr. Subhash Ramdos, was such a partner. With a keen eye for detail and an understanding of machine building, their suggestions were instrumental in creating a robust design. Dust is a major enemy of machine longevity, and in robotic grinding machines, the abrasive dust from castings accumulates quickly. Within just 3-4 hours of production, a few millimeters of fine dust covers the entire machining area. Protecting every single element inside the machining envelope was a key focus. Elgi has been one of the best users of our machine, and after several years of operation, the system still looks as good as new.

The Generation 3 machines brought significant improvements in casting quality. Unfortunately, few foundries truly value such improvements. Captive foundries, which produce both the casting and the end product, are more discerning than supplier foundries. Kumar Pumps, a foundry near Vijayawada, appreciated the upgraded models, which were much faster and more reliable. They continued to purchase machines every year.

Kirloskar Ferrous (KFIL), one of India's large supplier foundries, successfully deployed robotic grinding using multiple machines from European companies. Led by the ever-enthusiastic Mr. Gumaste, their team understood the limitations and challenges. They clearly judged the Generation 3 machine design as superior to the alternatives available, and we built several machines for their foundries in Hospet and Solapur.

The Indian foundry served as a test bed for our developments. With key discerning buyers, we fine-tuned our technology, preparing it for the international stage. Confidently, we participated in CASTEXPO and GIFA in 2019, showcasing our technology to the foundry world. The key partnerships we formed at these exhibitions would go on to transform the ROBOFINISH business in the following years.

Explorations in Mexico

Grind Master's first international project took place in Mexico with Blackhawk. Ritesh, our Business Development Manager, visited Mexico alongside our channel partner, Guillermo. It was Ritesh's first visit to a foundry, and I assumed it would be just an introductory meeting. However, we ended up closing a deal for two machines! Guillermo, who was 80 years old, brought tremendous enthusiasm and had a strong rapport with the customer. The Foundry Director, Patricio Gill, believed in Grind Master's capability to deliver.

We faced the daunting task of building a new, more powerful machine than any we had created before. Our engineering wasn't up to the mark, and the project took much longer than expected. As the inspection date approached, we were far from ready. In a state of panic, Ritesh called me back from a tour. It was a wake-up call. This project represented a golden opportunity to turn around our business, and we were on the brink of missing it.

Amol Ghule, Sudeep Khadse, and I worked around the clock. I even wrote some of the key algorithms myself. We couldn't afford to miss the deadline. We pulled at least three all-nighters—something I hadn't experienced since my days at IIT Bombay! Fortunately, we passed the inspection.

Rodrigo from Blackhawk knew we would face challenges getting the machines online at their production facility, but he also trusted that we would do whatever it took. Amol and Sudeep spent almost a year in Monterrey, deploying programmes and retraining the Blackhawk team. During my visit, I saw both the challenges and the opportunities in solving them.

Mexico turned out to be a fascinating market—open to experimentation like India, but with slightly higher wage costs (about 3-4 times those in India). Without a strong local machine tool or automation industry, Mexico heavily relied on imports. People from developed countries often carried biases against Mexicans, which might have made them more comfortable working with us Indians. Or perhaps it was our shared sense of humour or love of spicy food that made us click. Either way, the ROBOFINISH business quickly gained traction in Mexico.

In 2018, on the day of the World Cup soccer semifinal between Mexico and Sweden, Ritesh and I visited Forja de Monterrey. We had a perfect solution to grind the parting lines of front axle beams. The plant director, Mr. Moncayo, welcomed us in, and we found him and his senior engineers, including Gustavo Braga, watching the match. Beer bottles were on the table, and we joined in, cheering for Mexico. It was a close game that ended with the right team winning. Soon after, we finalised the order. Moncayo wanted the best equipment for his factory and had heard about our credentials. The videos we showed him demonstrated that we had the perfect solution. We signed a handwritten MOU on the spot. Viva Mexico!

The next order, with Nemak Mexico, was much harder to secure. However, the willingness of Mexican manufacturing engineers to develop new technology played a key role. Nemak had primarily purchased German and Italian equipment to de-gate and de-flash automotive die castings, such as cylinder heads and blocks. But the larger castings they were producing for EV structural parts presented new challenges. Our adaptive technologies offered a better solution. We conducted a Front-End Engineering (FEE) study with Nemak in 2020 and built and delivered the machine in 2021.

Partnering with the Mining Industry Foundry

At the GIFA trade show, we showcased robotic grinding on a large cylinder block. Our understanding of large castings was about to change. Arpit Srivastava from Bradken Australia approached us to discuss mining industry applications, including grinding large mill liner castings.

These castings were enormous—up to 4 meters in diameter and 6 tons in weight. Large castings may look like their drawings, but once loaded onto a fixture, their inconsistencies become apparent. The only constant in large castings is variation. Bradken had been trying to develop an automatic solution for not only grinding the flash but also generating the final geometry these castings required. The castings were made from a special, very hard steel that made cast iron seem like butter by comparison. Earlier projects had failed in 2012 and 2018. Could we succeed where others had not?

This was a specific niche, and if we could crack it, we would have a globally unique solution. We dove into research and development, creating a proof of concept and demonstrating it. Our methodology worked, but would Bradken commit? The machine would be complex. Bradken was clearly in a desperate situation—they needed to move towards automatic grinding, especially in their Canadian foundry. High wage costs and safety concerns were major drivers. Robotic grinding would significantly improve the quality of their castings.

The Bradken Canada team was enthusiastic about moving forward. This would be the largest machine ROBOFINISH had ever built. Numerous challenges arose during the engineering and construction phases, requiring all the energy and innovation of our team over nearly two years. The Front-End Engineering study had only demonstrated proof of concept—developing a foolproof solution required several new technologies:

1. Grinding hard steel with a new superabrasive
2. Generating coplanarity with a patented machine learning software
3. Keeping the casting cool
4. Programming flexibility with proprietary offline software

The Bradken Canada team worked closely with us in a true partnership. Both companies were deeply invested in the solution. The machine was delivered in 2022, and we were contracted to build four more machines for different applications in Canada, China, India, and Australia. Building complex machines for the mining industry has since become a focus of our business strategy at ROBOFINISH.

A Unique Technical Collaboration

In the niche foundry industry, specific companies provide a range of systems—sand management, furnaces, shot blasting equipment, molding machines, and die casting machines. These companies know the foundry well, but Grind Master was an outsider to this business. Collaborating with a foundry equipment company made perfect sense.

Joe Ponterri from Sinto America exclaimed, "This is a breakthrough," after witnessing what ROBOFINISH could achieve. Roberts Sinto Corporation (RSC) had already been working on CNC grinding machines for small castings, and the addition of our robotic range complemented their product portfolio. We forged an agreement in the middle of the Covid-19 pandemic, launching a collaborative effort.

Led by Michael Halsband, the RSC team was introducing IOT, Digitalisation, and Robotic solutions into the American market. As expected from a Japanese company, RSC took a cautious approach, ensuring the solution's validity without disrupting existing business relationships. This cautious stance pushed us to evolve the technology further, especially for challenging applications.

One such challenge involved large aluminium castings, weighing over a ton, for the semiconductor industry. Producing these complex castings requires even more intricate engineered gating, with over 50% gating in many cases. The RSC team was amazed when we confidently said we could handle this with robots. I knew we could figure it out.

Building the international business was key, and large casting solutions were our specialty. This project developed in parallel with the Bradken machine, and many of the solutions were similar. Seeing the actual castings in person was crucial. Vivek Gatade, who had previously installed machines in Mexico and the US, led the project on-site, conducting extensive R&D with our inputs. We faced many challenges and learned valuable lessons, but we passed the test.

Challenges in the Foundry Business

Our goal was to partner with foundries to bring about a transformation and improve human lives, but it didn't always work out. Robotics is a new high-tech discipline. The automotive industry has the competence to deploy robots, and foundries with in-house CNC machine shops or technologically oriented management were able to deploy robotic machines. However, others who desired to do so couldn't pull off the transformation.

One example involves a buyer from Bengal. Let's call him A. He visited Grind Master's facility and finalised an order for five machines to grind castings. These machines weren't complicated—our Generation 3 RCP series was fully capable of handling complex grinding operations. We quickly built and delivered the first two machines, but the foundry wasn't prepared for automatic grinding. The castings kept changing, requiring constant reprogramming. They lacked stable, skilled manpower to operate the machines and couldn't retain CNC or robot-trained staff.

The next two machines arrived at the factory but suffered rain damage as they were stored outdoors. Despite these setbacks, A ordered 12 more robots from ABB, which were delivered to Grind Master for integration. Today, the four machines lie idle, and a fifth built at Grind Master has been liquidated. The 12 robots remain at Grind Master, waiting for a legal case decision so we can sell them to recover our dues. This situation is a case of poor planning, poor management, and an utter waste of resources.

Another example involves a reputed automotive OEM that ordered automatic deburring machines for their supplier facility. Overconfident and aggressive, they placed an order for four machines for a process that had been done manually. The first two machines were delivered and commissioned, but the supplier never put them into production due to unresolved issues with the OEM. This inertia and unwillingness to adopt a technology they hadn't directly invested in are classic examples of poor vendor support activities.

Robotic finishing machine users are still immature, and there is a long way to go. Managing automation is not automatic—social, cultural, and economic factors pose significant challenges.

ROBOFINISH: A Breakthrough Technology

The last few years have been eventful. Starting from a troubled robotics business, we have built a reputation for unique technologies in the foundry industry. Our deep focus on robotic grinding technology has resulted in several patents, copyrighted software, and registered designs. Our audacious projects, particularly for exotic materials, have led to breakthrough technologies that we are proud of.

Young engineers like Prajwal Mhaske and Akshay Kole have risen to the challenge, learning and developing in demanding situations. Sohail Shaikh has worked closely with customers as partners and has been leading the ROBOFINISH unit since mid-2023, with me taking on a mentoring role. The Sinto collaboration has delivered successful projects in the US and Mexico, and our business with Bradken is set to grow. Our experience in the mining industry foundries will be particularly relevant. The stage is set to expand the ROBOFINISH business line to more foundry markets.

I recently visited foundries in Germany with a partner. Usually a closed market favouring European-made solutions, the foundries in South and East Germany welcomed our approach for large steel castings. We clearly have something special to offer.

The foundry industry needs modernisation. Casting cleaning is one of the most labour-intensive and dangerous operations, making it difficult to automate. ROBOFINISH technology has successfully tackled this challenge, enabling foundries to leapfrog from Industry 2.0 to Industry 4.0. This is just the beginning of an industry-wide transformation. The vision of a fully automated grinding shop, where operators work safely in a clean environment and castings are handled with care and pride, is becoming a reality.

"

I can do things you cannot, you can do things I cannot; together we can do great things."

Mother Teresa

12

FORGING PARTNERSHIPS: BUILDING A GLOBAL LEGACY

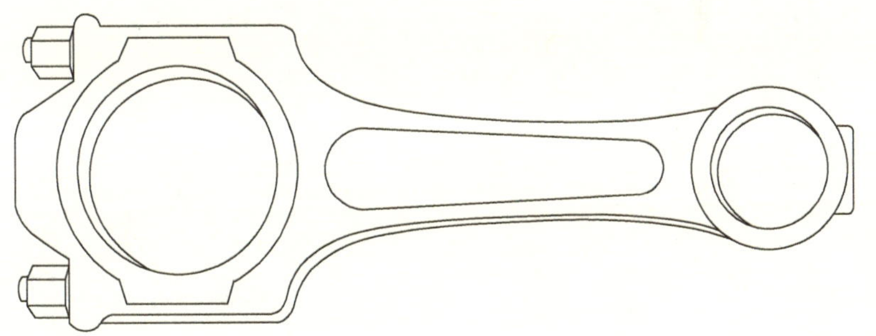

Grind Master has thrived by forging powerful collaborations with international partners. These partnerships have been instrumental in delivering complete solutions to customers—encompassing the machine, process, and tools. Automatic finishing, a new domain, required continuous search for the right tools, leading to strategic alliances with companies like VSM for coated abrasives, Fujistar for film-backed abrasives, and Lippert for polishing tools. By collaborating with machine builders in Europe and America, Grind Master gained invaluable exposure to the global machine tool business. Partnerships like those with IMPCO USA for microfinishing and Timesavers Netherlands for belt finishing illustrate this approach.

Partnering with VSM for coated abrasives

Grind Master's partnership with VSM (Vereinigte Schmirgel- und Maschinen-Fabriken AG) started during a crisis project where initial cooperation with another supplier fell short. VSM's Export Manager, Mr. Gunther, stepped in with solutions and samples, helping Grind Master succeed in several applications. He shared his philosophy, "Abrasives are indefinite by nature, and there's no fixed theory. Sharing our experiences will help us both learn a lot." This open exchange of knowledge led to more opportunities, including a speaking engagement for Grind Master at a technical event in Australia, further expanding its presence in the Asia Pacific region.

The collaboration with VSM was initially driven by the business with Jaquar India, a manufacturer of high-quality sanitary ware. Jaquar produces large quantities of faucets, finishing them with a mix of manual and automatic European machines. For ensuring a superior finish on complex faucet shapes, a flexible product was essential—and VSM had developed this niche solution. The significant improvement in the quality of the faucets sealed the deal, and Jaquar has continued to use the same material for nearly 30 years.

Beyond specialised products, VSM's quality was a key differentiator. Their highly regulated manufacturing process ensures consistency in abrasive grain size, which is crucial for automatic machine use. Any inconsistency could lead to visible scratch marks, considered defects. VSM's methodology and work culture are rooted in precision.

Mohini recalls Dr. Flory of VSM as a pivotal mentor in sales. His guidance during sales reviews, goal-setting, and team management left a lasting impact. During his first visit to India, he remarked, "Machine tools and abrasives cannot be sold by the same person. Sales teams need clear objectives." This insight led to the creation of a separate Abrasives and Spares business vertical at Grind Master.

In 2001, VSM demonstrated a conversion unit in Milton Keynes, England, showing how processes like cutting, slitting, joining, and curing belts in specific sizes were relatively straightforward. Milind took this knowledge and built the necessary equipment for an in-house conversion facility at a fraction of the market cost. This enabled Grind Master to purchase jumbo rolls and convert them into customer-specific forms, optimising both delivery times and costs. Only raw materials needed to be stocked, allowing for just-in-time production. VSM went above and beyond to support the development of the Indian market.

DS (D. Srinivasan), a key figure in Grind Master's Abrasives business, humorously remarked, "My blood test shows there is abrasive grain flowing in my veins and arteries." Now retired, DS was a South Indian who settled comfortably in Delhi and earned immense respect in the market. He was an authority on coated abrasives, with a unique talent for explaining grains, backing, and grinding parameters to workers and supervisors. His extensive experience in manufacturing quality and application development made him a champion of abrasive sales. DS's connections helped establish Grind Master Abrasives in the market, and many customers have remained loyal for over 25 years.

A dedicated abrasives sales team was built around Mr. Shrikant Dhande, who led the unit and grew the business multifold over 20 years. Dhande highlights key achievements in coated abrasives: "Our focus on providing complete solutions drove us to support customers by developing ideal process sequences for their products, minimising cost per piece and maximising productivity. The expertise of our application team in achieving this is a major factor in our success. Notable examples include finishing processes for hydraulic piston rods and tubes, where we guaranteed the required output finish, even on third-party machines. An application for a strategic PSU was also crucial—meeting the requirements brought tremendous satisfaction, as it directly contributed to the nation. Our customers appreciate our efforts to minimise their end-per-piece cost through trials and documentation of various abrasives and parameters."

One operator's feedback was particularly rewarding: "Ye belt Cadbury chocolate ke jaisa sabe accha hai" (this belt, similar to the Cadbury chocolate, is the best)

Establishing a Superfinishing Legacy with Film-backed Abrasives

Mark Sterner from 3M had been a mentor and guide to Grind Master in the superfinishing business. However, the relationship with 3M weakened after a management change, forcing Grind Master to seek alternatives to continue the film business. Over time, the relationship with 3M was restored, and we continue to use 3M film for specific customers, such as the Chinese automotive industry, which prefers 3M products.

NACHI Fujikoshi, an IMPCO licensee in Japan, was using a microfinishing film made by Sankyo Fujistar. A visit to Fujistar in 2005 initiated cooperation between the companies. Despite language barriers, the relationship has remained highly professional, and the product quality has been consistently excellent. As the automotive market in India grew, with both Indian and multinational companies, Grind Master supplied machines and films for various applications, including crankshafts, camshafts, transmission parts, pumps, hydraulic cylinders, and rotogravure cylinders.

Microfinishing and superfinishing are mission-critical operations for part quality, so customers are cautious about any process changes. This caution worked to our advantage in the Indian market. Since the microfinishing machines were often installed with Fuji film, it became the obvious choice for most customers to continue using it. We also supported cost optimisation through our process optimisation approach.

The abrasives business at Grind Master has complemented the machine business. Abrasives are needed year-round, which helps maintain customer relationships. Many new applications, such as roll grinding and finishing, have been initiated within the abrasives group. Offering complete solutions with highly synergistic components under one umbrella has created a powerful mix, providing stability to the organisation.

A Joint Venture for Polishing with Lippert Osborn

Grind Master's association with Lippert Germany began with deburring and finishing components using Liprox wheels. Recognising a need for high-quality polishing wheels and compounds for automatic machines, the two companies initiated a joint venture, resulting in the formation of Lippert Unipol India. Despite challenges, such as the initial complications with travel and logistics, the partnership thrived. The venture focused on providing specialised wheels and compounds, often supporting Grind Master's machines.

Eventually, Lippert was acquired by Osborn USA, leading to a divergence in interests. While Osborn aimed to expand in India, Grind Master focused on microfinishing, prompting a mutual decision to part ways. Grind Master sold its shares but continued to support the transition. The close relationship with Osborn's leadership even extended to personal friendships, underscoring the strong bonds forged through this collaboration.

Complementary Technology: Partnership with Timesavers

Grind Master's partnership with Timesavers Holland began at EMO 2005, when the two companies realised they could complement each other's product lines. While Grind Master focused on conveyorised belt grinding and deburring machines, Timesavers specialised in wide belt sanding machines. This partnership enabled Grind Master to sell Timesavers' products in the Indian market, resulting in over 200 machines sold across various sectors, from aerospace to laser cutting workshops.

The collaboration with Timesavers provided Grind Master valuable insights into product-driven approaches, learning from

Timesavers' rigorous design and production methodologies. When Timesavers challenged Grind Master to build a batch of manual sanding machines, Grind Master rose to the occasion, refining their processes and ultimately delivering high-quality machines that met European standards.

This partnership continues to evolve, with the joint development of a 300mm wide machine co-designed and manufactured by Grind Master, set to be sold by Timesavers worldwide. The overwhelming response at Euroblech 2023 marked a new chapter in this collaboration, demonstrating the success of their combined expertise.

IMPCO and Grind Master: A Force in Microfinishing

Grind Master's collaboration with IMPCO played a pivotal role in its success in India and China. By supplying components, assemblies, and machines, Grind Master gave IMPCO a competitive edge in America and Europe. Together, they secured one of the biggest contracts in their history: General Motors' global order for 16 microfinishing machines to factories in the USA, Mexico, Korea, and Germany. With IMPCO's presence in America and Grind Master's strength in Asia, they formed a robust team ready to serve the global automotive industry. Several of these machines were fully built at Grind Master, while others were completed with components supplied for final assembly at IMPCO.

Martin Nagel, Global Controls Projects Leader for General Motors, praised Grind Master after inspecting the first machine: "Your facility is excellent, and your team is a delight to work with. I look forward to our continued partnership." It seemed IMPCO and Grind Master were on the path to becoming global leaders in Microfinishing technology. But the story took a different turn.

IMPCO's owners, seeking retirement, decided to hand over the company to Neuteq, their UK collaboration partner. Though disappointed, Grind Master was not surprised. The deep collaboration that had once won major contracts began to fade. Grind Master, proud of its independently developed technologies, entered the European and American markets without violating the agreement with IMPCO. However, IMPCO's management changes led to weaker communication and distrust between the former strong partners. This uncertainty partly motivated Grind Master to acquire SPMS, a company with its own crankshaft and camshaft microfinishing technology.

After years of friction, the companies are again working together from 2024. The future of the collaboration is dependent on how each partner charts its course in a very volatile automotive manufacturing environment. The transition to EVs brings both threats and opportunities to the businesses.

The Journey of Collaboration: Paths in the Forest

Collaborations often begin like dating, where both parties see potential in each other—complementary skills, products, technologies, or market access. What starts as a casual encounter at an exhibition can evolve into cooperation over time. However, whether the partnership flourishes or fades depends on various factors, such as the success of initial projects and market forces. For every successful collaboration, many attempts lead to dead ends. Like paths in a forest, you need to walk the trail to discover where it leads.

Inspired by the success with IMPCO, Balance Engineering (BE) in Troy, Michigan, sought a similar partnership with Grind Master for crankshaft balancing machines. Together with BE, Grind Master co-developed a new flexible machine design for the Asian market. Balancing, with its complex science of mathematics, signal analysis, and dynamics, became an area of expertise under the guidance of Steve Pierce, who mentored the Grind Master team. The first machines delivered outstanding results, with BE's WIN CBI Balancing instrumentation system at their core. This black box boasted ten times better guage repeatability and twenty times better linearity, marking it as a masterpiece of its time. The collaboration thrived, with successful projects suggesting a strong future.

However, the path took another unexpected turn. BE a part of Micropoise, was acquired by AMETEK, a large corporation. The once-bustling BE factory in Troy, with over 50 engineers in 2012, dwindled to just four employees by 2017. The key technology, WIN CBI, was slowly phased out, leaving only essential spare parts. The people involved in this business remember the 'good old days' when they built great machines together. Their stories remind us that machine building is more than just a job—it's their life. The light in their eyes when they speak about developing the WIN CBI and their disappointment at its decline teach valuable lessons. Machine tool businesses are unique and should be run by machine builders who understand their ethos. Bringing in large corporations or private equity without alignment can lead to problems. BE, as a competitive American entity with high-tech products, is now a thing of the past—a sad end to a promising journey.

Gear Chamfering and Deburring: A Collaborative Success

Grind Master's gear chamfering and deburring method, inspired by a German machine, offers one way to tackle the task. Another method, which gained popularity due to its consistent and strong results, is the forming/rolling method pioneered by the Italian company Samputensili (SAMP). Recognised as a quality gear machine manufacturer, SAMP discontinued its SCT3 gear chamfering and deburring model in 2008 due to economic reasons. However, the demand for this machine remained strong, especially in India.

Grind Master and SAMP discussed a collaboration: Grind Master would build and sell the machine in India, while SAMP would handle global sales. This win-win situation revived a successful product. Carlo Amandola, a long-term SAMP advocate, played a key role in pushing the collaboration forward. After launching the machine at IMTEX 2015, several units were sold over the next few years, including joint projects for automotive facilities in Europe and America. These projects exposed Grind Master to the rigorous automotive build standards in Europe, preparing the team for the exacting requirements of deliveries to Germany and Japan.

But once again, the path took a surprising turn when SAMP declared bankruptcy just months after a strong showing at EMO 2019. By 2023, SAMP had been acquired by EMAG, a strong German company. Despite the setbacks, there is hope that the partnership will continue to build successful machines together.

Manufacturing Partners: The Backbone of Quality

A machine is only as good as its components, and Grind Master's success owes much to its manufacturing partners. These suppliers contribute cutting-edge expertise, producing accurate sheet metal work for enclosures, heavy fabrications for machine bases, and critical castings. Many of these vendors possess advanced capabilities that can be horizontally deployed in other industries. They also offer valuable suggestions and insights to Grind Master's engineering team. One vendor reflects on the relationship, saying, "When I started this business, Grind Master was my first customer. They believed in my abilities even when I lacked a full infrastructure. Now, I have a good setup and produce machine bases. The hand-holding from Grind Master engineers, including top management, has been invaluable."

While costs have risen over the years, the collaboration has kept overall project costs under control through value engineering contributions from vendors. Commercially, transactions with Grind Master have always been smooth, with timely payments. Technically, the work can be challenging, but the collaborative approach ensures that quality standards are met.

To enhance machining capabilities, Grind Master nurtured a network of machined part vendors in and around Aurangabad. Initially, Grind Master funded many vendors to buy their first machines. Over the years, these workshops have grown, creating an ecosystem that other machine builders in Aurangabad can now leverage.

Technology Partners: Driving Innovation

The machine tool industry thrives on products built by technology providers. High-precision components like LM rails and ballscrews have transformed machine design and construction. Motors, pneumatics, hydraulics, and advanced electronics have simplified motions and control systems, while sensors add value by monitoring machines and making them error-proof. Japanese and European product companies have played a key role in advancing Indian machine tool and automation building.

CNC technology was introduced to India by pioneers like Fanuc and Siemens. Early CNC machines in India, built around 1990, were boutique solutions with lead times of 8-10 months. Mr. Gomtesh Ekhande from Fanuc India recalls Grind Master's first CNC project: a 1-axis superfinishing machine. Fanuc's close hand-holding during deployment gave Grind Master the confidence that CNC technology would work well for specialised machines like superfinishing and microfinishing. This experience helped Fanuc India apply similar solutions for other special-purpose machines. Over the years, the strong partnership between Grind Master and Fanuc has only deepened.

Japanese electronic products, known for their robustness, have proven critical in developing countries where power supply quality is inconsistent. Mitsubishi Electric Automation has been a trusted partner of Grind Master since 2006, providing reliable automation products like PLCs, HMIs, Servo Drives, and motors. Rakesh Patil from Mitsubishi notes, "Grind Master's applications are always specialised, pushing us to go deeper into our framework." Together, we have built pioneering applications.

Siemens and Rockwell have also been key partners in advanced electronics, contributing to several significant projects. Fluid systems—such as coolant filtration, pneumatics, hydraulics, lubrication, and dust collection—depend on technology from experts in these domains.

Festo is one of Grind Master's most frequent visitors, with an application engineer on-site at least once a week. Their innovative products and support have made working with Festo a learning experience for Grind Master's engineering team.

Hydraulics, a complex field, has benefited from the expertise of Mr. Lakhani from Fluid Logic Systems in Gujarat. A veteran with a passion for hydraulics, Lakhani took on projects as personal challenges, contributing significantly to Grind Master's understanding of the field.

Many products are essential for machine building, and localising these components is key to competitiveness in terms of cost and delivery times. Compared to China's machine-building industry, India still imports a significant amount of material. However, several recent initiatives aim to increase domestic production of these components in India.

The automation business required a completely new set of partners. Large rotary machining tables used in the foundry industry were a critical element, where we partnered with FIBRO. SETCO has been a reliable partner for high-speed robotic grinding spindles. Robots are also key components in these solutions. "Robots have traditionally been used in hazardous, monotonous areas. While welding and handling systems have evolved over the years, grinding and finishing applications are still considered very challenging. Grind Master is one of the most successful companies pushing the limits of what robots can do. We are proud to associate with Grind Master," says Subrata Karmakar, head of ABB Robotics India.

Grind Master has enjoyed productive partnerships with ABB, KUKA, and Fanuc since embarking on ROBOFINISH, building solutions with high-quality robots. As a robotics engineer, I observed that these three brands are clear leaders. KUKA robots are mechanically robust, Fanuc robots are electronically reliable, and ABB offers a wide range of robots along with strong simulation and programming software. (The above opinion is personal.)

The machine tool industry in India is a small world—an ecosystem filled with veterans and young professionals deeply embedded in machine building, whether as manufacturers, suppliers, or buyers. There are many overlaps, and people often move between roles. The IMTEX exhibition is a hub where all these individuals come together. A dinner at the show feels like a gathering of old and new friends. The deep interpersonal relationships built over the years with fascinating people forging their own paths in this fast-growing field are some of the most exciting aspects of being in this business.

Trusted Partners in the Manufacturing Industry

Machine tools are the foundation of manufacturing, requiring complex engineering across mechanical, electrical, control systems, and software. The Indian machine tool industry stands out among developing countries like Mexico, Brazil, and Indonesia, which lack strong machine tool industries. Grind Master, as a maker of specialised custom-built machines, occupies a niche within this industry. However, the Indian manufacturing sector still imports over 50% of its machine tool requirements.

To develop specialised solutions domestically, the traditional 'buyer-supplier' relationship in manufacturing must evolve into long-lasting partnerships. End-user feedback is essential for building and refining effective solutions. Many solutions and processes are 'co-evolved' with support from end users, and we deeply respect and value this spirit of partnership, which has consistently led to breakthrough solutions. The 'Make in India' initiative is possible because of such developments.

The mindset of 'customer is king' needs to shift to 'customer as a partner.' Machine purchasing should mature into building equitable relationships. Unfortunately, the Indian machine tool industry has often viewed itself more as a service industry than a technology-driven one. This inequitable dynamic is disturbing, especially for a second-generation millennial entrepreneur like myself. Bright young engineers are often demotivated when they encounter this reality. As a technocrat passionate about engineering, I find it unacceptable. In contrast, the software industry has been more successful in forging equitable relationships with its customers.

At Grind Master, we've been fortunate to have excellent, long-lasting partnerships. From our beginnings, innovation has always been a response to the demands of the manufacturing industry. We've worked with various sectors—from the cookware industry on buffing machines to the forging industry on belt grinding, and the tubes and bars industry on finishing and grinding. Later, we collaborated with the automotive and hydraulics industries on microfinishing and deburring, and most recently, with the foundry industry on robotics products.

Our partners and the individuals we've worked with are integral to our story. The formation of these partnerships can be divided into four phases:

Phase 1: 1984-1998 - Replacing manually performed conventional operations in finishing

This phase involved pioneering customers who wanted to replace manual buffing, polishing, and belt grinding with low-cost automation. The motivations were a mix of productivity, safety, and quality. Imported machinery was available to a limited extent and was prohibitively expensive. Industries like cookware and forging recognised Grind Master's ability to innovate and provide solutions at a fraction of the cost. Partners from this period supported us extensively, sometimes even contributing to design engineering. However, despite being the main beneficiaries, they could have been more considerate in offering better pricing and terms. We continued working with discerning customers, particularly in the foundry and forge industries, which, like our robotics products, were driven by similar objectives.

Phase 2: 1996-2009 - Striving for quality in the Indian automotive industry

During this phase, superfinishing, microfinishing, and deburring became increasingly significant in the Indian automotive industry. While a large percentage of machines were still imported, there were distinct efforts to indigenise several processes. Pioneering partners such as Netalkar Group, Precision Camshafts Limited, and Bharat Forge trusted Grind Master to develop critical machines for volume production lines. Their guidance helped us improve machine quality and reliability.

Phase 3: 2010-2022 - Partnering with the global automotive industry

The Chinese automotive industry demanded higher machine quality and finer finishing specifications. Although language barriers limited our interactions with Chinese industry partners, we formed several meaningful relationships that guided our work. Multinational corporations in India began trusting our machines only after we had built a strong reference list in China. Partnerships with Japanese companies, in particular, played a pivotal role in our development. Our reputation for process development and machine customisation attracted partners from developed countries like Japan and Germany.

Phase 4: 2019-2024 - Advanced technology development partners

Strategic industries, such as aerospace, mining, construction machinery, and energy have highly specialised requirements that demand advanced engineering. Grind Master has been identified as a capable partner for co-developing solutions to challenging problems—whether generating geometry over large castings, achieving the finest finishes for long-lasting cylinders, or finishing exotic materials. These projects have been executed with a true spirit of partnership, and we continue to pursue meaningful collaborations in areas like precision machinery components and bearings.

Overcoming Stumbling Blocks

Our approach to working with customers has evolved over the years. As engineers gain more experience in a specific application, they become increasingly confident in their technology. This confidence can sometimes come across as assertiveness, which earlier customers may not be used to. Having influenced the initial developments in a particular field, this phase of the relationship needs to be handled carefully by both parties, with sensitivity and an open mind.

There have been instances where trust has broken down, but in most cases, it has been restored through renewed cooperation between senior management. The automotive industry, at some point, started the practice of withholding a portion of the payment for a machine until installation and commissioning were complete. This retention practice, which can range from 5% to 30% of the payment, has become standard across the machine tool and automation industries, with various buyers demanding it. However, this term is quite one-sided. It is solely at the buyer's discretion to define what 'installation and commissioning' mean. We've encountered situations where companies expect the machine to produce parts for over a year before declaring the commissioning complete. In my opinion, this term is draconian and unnecessary.

Most machinery businesses rely on repeat orders from existing customers. Reputation is largely based on word of mouth, and defaulting on warranty or support results in an immediate negative brand image. Purchasing capital goods is not like buying a commodity; it's an investment in equipment that the buyer will use for 10–15 years. This retention practice hinders the development of a good relationship and the proper maintenance of equipment over its lifetime.

I came face to face with this reality after 2014 when I took on a larger role in managing the company. We often had discussions about collecting payments from customers where the machine had been installed long ago, and regular production was running, yet our payment was still held up. Using software to interlock the machines seemed like a logical solution to me. This would also enable us to monitor the machine's production count and trigger a health check of the system.

Initially, there was reluctance, but I adopted a polite and transparent approach with customers, sending clear communication via email and displaying warning messages on the machine's HMI. The warning and alarm counts were set to ensure that sufficient production had been run on the machine before any action was taken. There were a few instances of upset customer calls. One that stands out involved a very senior manager at a leading company. I was quite nervous—a young technocrat representing a medium-scale company, facing an accomplished manufacturing industry veteran. Despite warnings that I might ruin a reputation built over 25 years, I persisted. To my relief, he was calm and not angry. He asked me to explain the entire situation, and after listening attentively, he said, "This could have gotten you into big trouble. I understand you have a grievance, and I assure you that it will be resolved shortly. Please start the machine immediately, and in the future, if there is a situation like this, please bring it up to me." The issue was fully resolved and we did not have to resort to this ever again. The spirit of partnership must always involve two-way communication, mutual respect, and the ability to respond to each other's issues.

To date, there is only one major automotive—with whom we do not have a retention clause. We are fully paid upon the delivery of the machine. Our team is more motivated to continue providing excellent support and service beyond the installation and commissioning period. The trust and respect shown by a large-scale manufacturing buyer have inspired its medium-scale supplier. We continue to build new machines, retool for model changes, remanufacture old machines, train new operators, debug machine problems, and solve challenges with a genuine smile.

I believe that more mature capital purchase policies will go a long way in building mutually beneficial partnerships. Both manufacturing engineering and commercial purchasing teams need to be involved in the process. Short-term cost savings may result in long-term losses. Investment in a machine only pays off if it works well throughout its lifespan. There are a couple of capital purchase policies that are particularly detrimental to the spirit of partnership:

1. Tender/Bid/L1: Does anyone select their personal car through a bidding process, choosing the lowest bidder? Automotives are differentiated products, and machine tools and specialised machines are even more so. An apple-to-apple comparison between two custom-built machines is simply not possible. We have politely refrained from participating in any auction or bidding situation.
2. Application of Penalty Clauses: Machine delivery timings are important, yet when purchasing specialised equipment, there must be an understanding that delivery depends on several factors. Custom-built machines are designed after the order is received, and design approval is done jointly with the buyer, which can take time. Finally, machine testing depends on component availability. In most cases, penalty clauses are more of a deterrent, preventing the machine builder from delaying the project. However, we have had several instances where penalties were levied without just cause, with purchasing teams viewing this as a way to squeeze money out of a medium-scale machine supplier as a 'cost-saving' measure.

At Crossroads

One incident that caused significant turmoil for both organisations involved the acquisition of a foundry by an automotive supplier. The foundry was a medium-sized, family-run operation. Their fettling shop resembled a war zone, with over 200 manual grinders working amidst noise, dust, and sparks. A young family member was eager to implement robotics and ordered three machines during the Covid crisis. We built all the machines, only to discover that the foundry lacked the resources to pay for them, leading to several months of delays. The last machine was delivered after 18 months in storage, only after we accepted a distress settlement. The young man at the foundry then began tinkering with the machines, causing a series of failures.

At this point, Grind Master had installed over 30 machines in the foundry using similar technology and was confident the machines were not being used correctly. Instead of partnering with Grind Master to drive internal transformation, the new management opted for punitive measures, blacklisting us as a supplier across its group companies. Due to longstanding relationships, some senior leaders with close ties helped resolve the situation after a six-month embargo. The solutions we applied on-site were known to us all along:

1. Demonstrating to the foundry how the machines should be operated by visiting successful users.
2. Modifying part programmes according to machine capability.
3. Controlling input quality.
4. Improving machine maintenance, including better air supply.

As a partner, I would have been happy to support this process, but I was forced to do so under pressure. The embargo was humiliating for Grind Master, and especially for me. The ROBOFINISH business was my creation, and the breakdown in this long-cherished, over 30-year-old partnership was a personal blow. It also strained my relationship with Milind. This was a generational clash: an older veteran, experienced in life's ups and downs, wanting to resolve the situation amicably, versus a younger person with high technical competence in the relevant technology. We clashed in arguments almost weekly for over six months.

In July 2022, I was with my newborn son Shiroy in the NICU. I was under immense pressure, managing large, complex robotics projects on the shop floor, guiding the team around the clock, and caring for my family. In the midst of this, a stressful discussion about the situation at the foundry took place. While I maintained my composure, something deep inside me shifted. It was a transformative moment.

I hope that one day we can look back at this entire episode as a source of great learning. We continue to build machines for the automotive group, and as valued partners, they have profoundly influenced Grind Master. With a legacy of relationships dating back to when Mohini designed machines, this situation has had a significant impact on me. While we continue to work for other units, I must draw a line when the company is humiliated. We no longer feel motivated to work for the foundry and have closed all business transactions. This is the only customer I have ever refused to work with in my career.

Owning Risk

Metal finishing is a subjective field, especially decorative finishing. Beauty is in the eye of the beholder, and so are polishing results. Automatic polishing is not the same as manual polishing. While one could argue that consistency is better, one could also say that it looks and feels different from the established norm.

Superfinishing and microfinishing are engineering processes, where both input and output are defined objectively and measured using well-defined standards. None of our projects in this space have encountered the same issues faced in metal finishing. Supplying machines for buffing and belt grinding has always been challenging, particularly in defining the requirements. First-time developments are inherently uncertain. In developed countries, it is generally accepted that new technologies may not achieve 100% of the wishlist. However, some Indian customers have been less receptive to this, leading to occasional project failures.

One particular instance that comes to mind is the fuel tank weld grinding for a major automotive OEM. It was a new development: automatic belt grinding of the weld line on a fuel tank, followed by finishing to blend the grinding with the surrounding material. The goal was to completely automate a manual process. A fairly complex machine managed to succeed up to 80%, eliminating four out of five manual operations, leaving only a final finishing step for an operator. Despite our efforts, this last step could not be fully automated. As the customer was not entirely satisfied with the machine, Grind Master took responsibility, recalled the machine, and repaid the full amount.

There have been a few such recalls in the past, usually involving some subjective element. Metal finishing still relies heavily on manual work. We believe that for the manufacturing industry to transition towards automation, an acceptance of 80% automation and 20% manual work is a necessary starting point. By improving input quality, objectively defining and accepting finish results, and implementing process improvements, manufacturing can leapfrog towards global standards in this area.

The Future of Manufacturing Partnerships

The demands of a global industry partner base have spurred innovations. Partnerships developed during this period have provided opportunities to leapfrog in technology. Moving beyond the 'first time in India' tag, Grind Master has been involved in several 'first time in the world' developments. These advancements within the organisation have been largely appreciated.

Grind Master has distinguished itself in the manufacturing industry as a beacon of excellence and innovation. In an industry known for producing decent quality at low costs, and often focusing on frugal engineering, a company that envisions and succeeds in building top-end products, exporting the majority of its turnover, is considered special.

The future belongs to collaborations and partnerships. The era of the 'sole expert' is over. Collaborative developments are essential for progress, and those who recognise and nurture partnerships will thrive. Over the years, Grind Master has developed a deep understanding of what makes partnerships work: equitability, understanding, and a shared commitment. Successful partnerships have withstood the test of time.

Grind Master is ready for strategic global partnerships.

Introducing Grind Master, the Brand

Grind Master's philosophy has always differed from that of traditional machine tool companies, which approach the market with standard products designed for mass production. From the beginning, Grind Master was a solution-driven company. To describe our business approach, we coined the terms 'Ideas, Solutions, Results,' which were later refined to:

- Innovative Ideas
- Complete Solutions
- Guaranteed Results

In the 1990s, special-purpose machine makers typically did not invest in branding, relying instead on word-of-mouth and references. Grind Master, however, wanted to project its capabilities more assertively. The first logo, an oval with the name inside, was conceptualised by Shirish Jogdeo.

Becoming Brand-aware: A Rebranding Exercise

A brand is an identity—a flag that each of our team members carries with them at all times. It is not only an external projection but also an internal awareness of who we are. The inconsistency in our usage of the logo, name, and colour scheme reflected a lack of brand awareness within our organisation. We needed a rebranding exercise.

Ashwini, the founder of Elephant Design, led this activity. The rebranding exercise articulated our core values—Passionate, Innovative, Trustworthy, Expertise—and our motto, Absolute Engineering. This was a consolidation of 30 years of evolution. The spirit of partnership was encapsulated in the new logo, GM. The colours red, signifying passion, and grey, representing innovation, trustworthiness, and expertise, became defining characteristics. The brand handbook provided guidance on various other aspects.

This was a pivotal moment for Grind Master as it emerged from the garage into the international arena.

Ashwini's vision of branding brought a new level of understanding and appreciation for the brand. Ashwini noted, "A corporate brand must be inside-out–articulating the core of a company in words. We were on a quest to discover what makes this company tick. The professionalism in the Kelkar family was evident–there was a deep work ethic, a commitment to live by the brand. Further interactions with the Grind Master team revealed a pride in technology solutions. There were no hollow promises. The words 'Absolute Engineering' best describe the core."

The entire Grind Master family is part of the brand. The branding activity raised a question for everyone: What should each person do differently? The rollout of this exercise began at the company's annual day party, where employees and their families were introduced to the brand in Marathi and Hindi, reflecting the inclusiveness of the exercise.

Beyond Vision and Mission

Grind Master is now ready to assert itself as a technology leader on the global stage, marching shoulder to shoulder with global players. What began in a garage is becoming a global enterprise. There has been a realisation of additional core values: 'Inclusiveness' and 'Sustainability'.

The 'Purpose' of the organisation is its foundation. Grind Master exists from the passion to innovate unique solutions and create an Indian brand that's recognised globally for its technology. We are a true contributor to 'Make in India' and 'Atmanirbhar Bharat', a reliable partner to the manufacturing industry, and creators of a culture of enduring excellence built on 'Absolute Engineering'. We are leading the way towards 'Net Zero' with deep commitment.

The brand will continue to evolve, reflecting this sense of purpose that goes far beyond financial motives–a purpose that is a compelling drive for the organisation.

"If you want to walk fast, walk alone. But if you want to walk far, walk together."

Ratan Tata

13

FAMILY IN THE BUSINESS: THE GUIDING BEACON

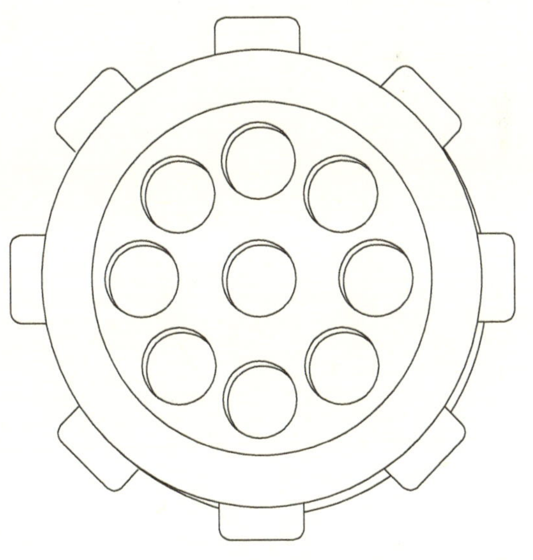

"Coming together is the beginning.
Keeping together is progress.
Working together is success."
- Henry Ford / Edward Everett Hale

Appa had an adventurous streak in him. A 'Dabangg' of sorts, Milind enjoyed the freedom the Kelkar kids were afforded to the fullest. Whether playing insane games like tag on the banyan tree, engaging in brawls after cricket matches, taking on school bullies, or cycling and hiking long distances, Appa and Ajji were relaxed parents. Once, Milind and a friend ended up in a lock-up for pranking a policeman. After getting them out of the police station, Appa commented with a smile, "The prank was good."

Mohini's parents, whom I referred to as Ajoba (grandfather) and Bhoorajji (grandmother), were also well-educated. Lata Phadke (Bhoorajji) was a graduate, Raghunath Phadke (Ajoba) was an excellent civil engineer. Being in government service, the family moved often. Ajoba was a very upright and honest officer who never engaged in anything remotely dishonest. He carried his integrity in his pocket, in the form of a resignation letter, ready to be submitted immediately if anything untoward was asked of him.

The family background had a deep influence on Milind and Mohini. Finding a passion and pursuing excellence was valued more than simply earning money or gaining power. When Milind and Mohini discovered their purpose in life—making automatic machines—the family strongly supported them.

Milind and Mohini had no background in running a business and learned the fundamentals as they went along. It's remarkable that, despite the risks taken early on through various projects, the company has never been in the red. Perhaps it was just common sense to run a machine business: estimate the costs, ensure the machine proposal covers all costs, overheads, and a small margin, work on controlling costs during engineering, build and deliver the machine well, and absorb any additional costs to ensure the machine works when put into production. If the engineering is done correctly, this cycle earns money if the customer pays a decent price.

If a decent price isn't possible, don't do that business. It's really simple. Even today, we run our operations on this basic framework. We are engineers, not businessmen. We know how to engineer specialised machines, but building complex business models isn't our game. Stick to basics in business, and move to advancements in engineering and technology!

Money was needed to make machines, and building good machines would naturally earn money as a byproduct. Perhaps this is why, even today, when a wealth manager discusses where to invest funds, our usual reply is to put it in a safe place, de-risk as much as possible by diversifying safe investments, and let it 'RIP' (Rest in Peace). Most finance people don't understand this approach.

Perhaps this simplicity and clarity of thought allowed Mohini and Milind to enjoy both work and family time in the early years. It was an adventure, not a struggle. They worked hard in the factory during the day and spent time with family in the evenings and on weekends. They followed the mantra 'eat well, play well, sleep well, study well'.

The financial and emotional stability the Kelkar family provided gave the entrepreneurs the freedom to evolve without any shackles. In the early years, there wasn't much income, but that was okay. Material possessions like houses or cars were never an important issue. The family provided a strong foundation at home, which became a launchpad for both Mohini and Milind. In her speech at the FII Foundation Award, Mohini mentioned that her in-laws treated her not as a daughter but as a son, embracing her ambitions.

By 1992, it was clear that the Kelkar technocrats were firmly established as special-purpose machine builders. The formation of the company in new premises was a proud moment for the family. The house was rebuilt, adding a second floor while keeping Ajji's garden intact. There was also a special space left beside the house to play cricket. While teaching me to bat and bowl, Milind reconnected with a game he had played in school and college. This probably inspired him to take up more serious cricket, playing for the Nirlep team for several years.

Later, when a batch of young graduate engineers and cricketers, including Ashish, Samad, and Mahesh, joined the company, Grind Master had an 11-member team, despite having barely 30-40 employees. I remember cheering as a child at the industrial tournament. Even though they didn't win often, the team returned happy, having played their hearts out and giving tough fights to much larger company teams. This image and spirit of the game stayed with me.

Milind's friends who were like family all returned to Aurangabad after various experiences in India and abroad. In particular, Ram and Mukund Bhogale were running various industries. Their business style contrasted somewhat with the Kelkars'. Ram knew how to effectively take along a group of family members and friends, delegating responsibility and instilling business ownership in younger siblings, cousins, and relations. Many members of the Bhogale family were involved in the various businesses, a tradition that continues in the third generation of the family today.

Except for Ketan Kaka, other family members weren't directly involved in the business. This was deliberate—Milind was wary of personal relationships being affected by working together and wanted to keep the factory professional. This was probably why, even though a number of cousins and nephews did a brief stint at Grind Master as a stepping stone in their careers, it was never considered to include them in the company's management. Sanjay Pethe, a cousin from Chennai, was an excellent mechanical engineer and designer who also ran an SPM business. The cousins joining forces could have potentially given the united company stronger managerial and engineering bandwidth, but Milind thought it best for both of them to keep their autonomy.

As the company grew, professionals with expertise in their fields joined the business. One of the key areas in machine building is assembly and testing. The company's reputation for delivering results to customers depends on this. Milind naturally kept a close hand on this function and indeed enjoyed his time on the shop floor, being the man of tough moments, micro-managing multiple activities to get development to work. Recruiting experienced machine builders from Bajaj Machine Tool Division made a tremendous difference to the way the company was managed—Nilesh Pathak, Prashant Yeole, Santosh Patil, and Radhakrishna Barde are now business leaders in the company. Along with some home-grown leaders like Mahesh Sahasrabuddhe, Shrikant Dhande, Ravindra Gokhale, and Deepak Mohite, the management team today is strong and experienced.

In 2004, the company celebrated its 20th anniversary. Recent collaborations with IMPCO, Timesavers, and VSM, a joint venture with Lippert, and an expanding business marked a turning point. Building microfinishing machines allowed Milind, for the first time, to stop worrying about cash flow. There was a brand-new building next to the previous one, with a nice office.

Another momentous occasion that year was something the Kelkar-Phadke and Grind Master families celebrated with gusto—Ajji-Appa and Ajoba-Bhoorajii, both sets of grandparents, were celebrating their 50th wedding anniversary. A gathering of relatives and friends was organised at the Grind Master premises. Milind never believed in ceremonies to mark the opening of new facilities. We start construction just like that and simply move into new premises once they are ready. Occasions like this serve the purpose of inviting well-wishers over. It was a proud moment for the entire family.

Ajji from Pune summarised in a poem, "With determination and hard work, a business has been established. A dream has been realised. Today, in this factory, both of them have made their home."

Mai Ajji (Milind's grandmother) visited the factory after a long time and was speechless, finding it unbelievable that her engineer-grandson had achieved so much! Ajji narrated the story of the mouse who fell into a bucket of milk and struggled and swam so hard that he turned it into butter and walked out proud. There were tears in her eyes as she softly said the last words, "Minya ne cheez kele" (Milind has made something valuable out of an opportunity).

Numerous other relatives, who until then had only heard about the venture and had been encouraging throughout, saw and touched Grind Master for the first time. The company was really like a family member. Many of them commented that Milind and Mohini gave birth to twins in 1984—Sameer, the son, and Grind Master, the daughter. I was in my second year at IIT Bombay that year and felt, for the first time, an unspoken expectation of taking on the mantle in the next few years.

Appa: The Stable Roots of the Grind Master Tree

Dinkar Balbhim Kelkar, known as Appa, made Aurangabad his home in 1958. He visited, fell in love, and settled there, establishing a reputed practice as a chartered accountant. Appa attended college in Pune, met Ajji in her village, Saswad, and fell in love. Despite some resistance from the family, the couple married and moved to Aurangabad in 1958. Milind was born in Saswad but grew up in the Osmanpura area of town, among a gang of friends that went on to become extended family.

Appa's practice was interesting as a business. Appa first made friends and then sometimes did business. Known for his friendliness, humour, and calm demeanour, his ever-present smile hid a tough resolve. There was a precarious time in 1979 when he struggled with recurring migraines. It became a real issue as he became non-functional for a time, but Appa persisted and was able to overcome it, returning to work and eventually establishing a healthy work-life balance.

Working with a diverse range of people, including educational institutions, as well as sugar mills and industries, Appa's clients became lifelong friends. He often walked in just to chat, tell a joke, or share sweets, without any business talk. He believed in the philosophy of 'Service before self,' which was reflected in his actions. A calm man, I have rarely seen him angry or upset, and he never held a grudge. He avoided confrontation and always found ways to dissolve tension with kindness and humour.

He had a unique relationship with his clients. A famous story in the Aurangabad community involved a businessperson who had the opportunity to acquire a significant order but couldn't secure a bank guarantee. Appa quietly made arrangements, securing the guarantee from his own savings, and simply informed the businessperson to proceed with the order. He didn't ask for any formal agreements or anything in return, believing that helping others would bring good karma.

Ajji managed the home with a firm hand, always making sure it was a warm, welcoming place for guests. Whether it was the smell of her famous sabudana khichdi or her hosting expertise, everyone who visited felt at ease. As children, we often saw our house filled with people, each enjoying themselves without a care in the world.

Appa and Ajji's home was a true melting pot, where friends, family, and clients all came together, forming an extended family.

Grooming the Next Generation

Being part of a joint family – four generations under one roof – with parents who lived and breathed machines, I was unconsciously mentored into becoming a second-generation entrepreneur. My first exposure to working in the company came while building a science project in Class 9. Afsar Bhai, a technician at Grind Master, showed me how to cut wood, nail it together, and make small shafts. Later, we attempted to wind copper wire around the shaft using a hand drill. The experience was enjoyable. After several iterations, the dynamo worked—lighting up a small bulb. I continued working with Afsar for a month to build a larger version, converting an exercise cycle borrowed from a family friend into a generator that could power a house mixer. The milkshake produced by this contraption during my school's science exhibition was indeed sweet. This project inspired me to pursue Mechanical Engineering, and I worked hard for two years to crack the IIT JEE, the gateway to this prestigious college.

During my senior secondary years at Nath Valley, I was clear about pursuing Engineering. For this, I needed to excel in Physics, Chemistry, and Mathematics. I was always decent at English, having developed a habit of reading daily. The fifth subject needed to be something easy. Since Electronics was not an elective at Nath Valley and I was afraid of Biology, I chose Business Administration—little knowing that I would be a natural at it! Despite not really studying for the exams, I topped the class by writing common-sense business answers. It turned out that learning about business organisation from my parents was more than enough.

After graduating from IIT Bombay with a silver medal, I wondered whether I should join Grind Master, take up a consultancy job, or pursue further education. I had completed a couple of internships with the company during summer vacations. Brief interviews with consultancy firms during campus recruitment confirmed that I was probably not suited for a big corporation. Milind immediately ruled out my joining Grind Master, saying, "You must learn and travel. Explore first. The doors of Grind Master are open."

I was passionate about robotics and controls, and, inspired by Prof. Shashikanth Suryanarayanan, I accepted a fellowship at the University of California, Berkeley. I did get cold feet on the day I was to fly to the US, but Milind took me for a walk, motivating me to continue on the chosen path. He also gave me some warnings about American culture and advice on avoiding certain things. Joining the university's cycling and hiking clubs even before completing my course registration was a great motivator!

After the initial apprehensions, Berkeley became a game changer for me. I fell deeply in love with robotics and controls applied to mechanisms. Working on projects like 'Vision-Guided Robotics for High-Precision Motions' and 'Adaptive Control for Robots' in Prof. Tomizuka's lab, I had the opportunity to engage in real, industry-oriented research. The masters thesis at Berkeley is almost like a mini-PhD, and I had to come up with a genuinely new idea to defend my work. This was the essence of postgraduate studies—excellence in research. The culture at Berkeley—open-minded, liberal, and full of chaos and energy—deeply influenced me.

Milind visited me once and was impressed by the deep technology I was working on. I often thought about Grind Master, wondering what it would be like to join the growing business. After ruling out continuing with a PhD programme, I considered working in a technology role at an international company to delve deeper into applied technology. I was unsure about moving to Japan to join robotics and controls companies, but a chance encounter led me to Gudel Switzerland, a manufacturer of high-precision machine components and a provider of sophisticated automation solutions.

Dominique, my research mentor, guided me through various projects to develop new robotic mechanisms and optimise existing kinematics, introducing me to machine control software development. Within two years, I had become a seasoned machine engineer, combining mechanical, controls, and software engineering aspects. I was enjoying life in Europe, with lots of outdoor activities and plenty of time to read and study a plethora of subjects.

A big rock from home on my table reminded me how territorial I was. That basalt-quartz piece was an instant connection to my roots and remained on my desk. It was a strong magnet—a daily reflection of who I was. Milind visited me in Langenthal once, and I proudly showed him the Gantry Tau Robot I had worked on. It was a specialised system conceptualised to drill accurate holes in composite material for aircraft. The kinematics and dynamics of the parallel link manipulator were complex, and I had developed and deployed the entire software to run it. During this project,

I developed a passion for building machines. I was pleased to tell him, "I too am a machine builder," and that I wanted to return to Grind Master to lead the business.

Milind was impressed by the project and by the fact that Gudel had entrusted such a task to a fresh graduate. Over the years, Milind had transformed from being a father to a friend. Before leaving for an expedition in the Himalayas, I had indicated that I intended to propose to Natasha. Therefore, he wasn't surprised when I broke the news that we were engaged, having exchanged Tibetan rings on the top of Thorung La Pass. Natasha had been a close friend for several years. During trips back from the US and Switzerland, we bonded over our love for mountains and backpacking. Close friends probably knew before I did that I was head over heels in love. Mai Ajji was blushing with joy upon finding that her great-grandson was continuing the family tradition of love marriages. Ajji had suspected that something was up. With her blessings came a clear directive—"Get married soon, and considering my health, do it in the house." Unfortunately, we lost two generations of our family in quick succession in 2011. We emerged from mourning deeply loved ones with our marriage in August 2011. As per Ajji's wish, it was a small, intimate ceremony in the garden, under the trees that Ajji and Appa had planted and nurtured over the years.

Rudolf Gudel

A chance encounter: Milind and Rudolf met on a flight from Mumbai to Zurich. Gudel Switzerland was a well-known name in gantry automation, supplying several turnkey projects, including crankshaft lines in India. Rudolf invited me to interview with them. The Alps were a big attraction for me, and I was fascinated by the idea of living and working so close to the mountains. I arrived in the small town of Langenthal for the interview. Rudolf drew up a contract on a whiteboard, and within a month, I was back in Switzerland, working in R&D at Gudel.

Rudolf invited me for a hike with him in the Jura Mountains. It was winter, and there was a lot of snow. I assumed that the nearly 60-year-old hadn't planned a big hike. However, we ended up walking for over six hours in knee-deep snow. During the walk, our conversation covered a wide range of subjects. Rudolf's first job had been in an energy plant in Western Australia, where he enjoyed his time in the bush. After returning to Switzerland, as his ageing father wanted to hand over the business, Rudolf applied his acute intuition to the precision components business, transforming it into a global technology house for gantry automation.

"At the base of my business is a deep knowledge of producing very good racks and pinions. It is important to do the one thing that matters really, really well." This was one of many wise words he shared with me during our hikes together in the Jura and the Alps. I fell in love with Jura and with the man who showed me this beautiful wilderness as his home. Rudolf became my mentor, philosopher, guide, and friend.

One day, I was surprised to see Rudolf approach my desk with a bulky object in a bag. He opened it and placed a big rock—about 20 kg—on my desk. I instantly recognised it as being from Bandijai. Rudolf had been to India and said, "You must be homesick, so I brought you a piece of your land."

Inducting a Millennial

Kahlil Gibran writes in 'The Prophet' - On Children:

- Your children are not your children.
- They are the sons and daughters of Life's longing for itself.
- They come through you but not from you,
- And though they are with you, yet they belong not to you.
- You may give them your love but not your thoughts,
- For they have their own thoughts.

- You may house their bodies but not their souls,
- For their souls dwell in the house of tomorrow, which you cannot visit, not even in your dreams.
- You may strive to be like them, but seek not to make them like you.
- For life goes not backward nor tarries with yesterday.

I joined Grind Master in September 2010, during the success celebrations of the first machine for China. It was an exciting time—the right moment. The platform had been set to take the company to international markets. The moment of pivot for Grind Master was also a moment for the Kelkar family to work together to break through into a new avatar. During the early years, Ketan, Milind, and Mohini all mentored me in their respective areas of expertise. While information and advice were freely available, it was left to me to figure out my own way. I may have rocked the boat somewhat with my different ideas, but this was accepted.

Designated as an R&D engineer, I worked on introducing robotics technology, updating the control software framework, and understanding the wide range of finishing technologies. Milind gave me some interesting assignments, including setting up offices. Later, I was introduced to business development in China, making visits and contributing to what became our most important market in the coming years. I took on the responsibility of running the METALFINISH business unit in the absence of a senior manager—a dive into the dark that taught me a great deal.

Fresh from a more structured, disciplined culture at Gudel, I was eager to impose the same on our team at Grind Master. I was quickly put in my place by Milind. The experienced hands-on shop floor team worked tirelessly, often in chaotic, unplanned conditions. I had much to learn. It was here that I deeply understood the critical importance of 'the human factor.' Machine tools are precision products—machines that are themselves designed and built to close tolerances in a controlled environment. Although most processes are automated, a wide range of human actions and skills is involved. It is crucial to recognise, develop, and value this human factor.

One aspect of the human factor at Grind Master is the special sense of 'ownership' among the team. In general, people were not afraid of making mistakes; rather, they saw them as learning opportunities. This was a strong factor that contributed to our entrepreneurial culture, along with the ability to bounce back from difficult times. This same human factor created a unique relationship with our customers—a sense of loyalty and trust that helped us create strong partnerships.

I slowly started introducing changes in a subtle manner, driving the company to become more process-driven while valuing creativity. This is when Ketan and I worked together more closely. He had built the entire systems department with a couple of engineers. Ketan prefers to ponder, reflect, and debate ideas before taking action. Milind is the opposite—a doer, always trying new things, with a knack for thinking on his feet. I would like to believe that I was a bridge between the two, balancing action with thinking.

Building the Organisation

> *"Visionary companies are so clear about what they stand for and what they're trying to achieve that they simply don't have room for those unwilling or unable to fit their exacting standards."*

- Jim Collins, 'Built to Last: Successful Habits of Visionary Companies'

Milind and Mohini created a strong work ethic—Grind Master has always been a family business managed professionally by the family. This was rooted in a simple rule: 'Science Prevails,' a principle we follow to this day. It was always understood that personal finances must be kept separate from business money, with no diversion of funds between the two.

Over the years, the organisation has evolved. The journey towards building a strong, visionary organisation began with a vision workshop. We needed a mentor to guide us, and Mr. Shailesh Sheth, considered a guru by many in the machine tool industry, stepped into this role. A veteran machine builder with vast experience in managing and guiding companies, Mr. Sheth's counsel over a couple of years was invaluable at this critical juncture in our development. While our branding exercise defined who we were, Mr. Sheth's vision-and-mission exercise clarified where we wanted to go. Up to this point, the company had grown by trying many different things and seizing opportunities as they arose, while generally adhering to basic principles. The vision-and-mission exercise aimed to provide more focused direction and form an action plan to achieve our goals.

We started by documenting 'The Grind Master Way' in a handbook. This was a major project, during which every 'It's always done this way' was debated and revised, sometimes multiple times. Organisation structure was also part of the plan. Becoming more professional, with senior management members taking on clear responsibilities, was clearly needed. Activities in NANOFINISH and METALFINISH were generally guided by Milind and Mohini, respectively, while Robotics was left to me. The directors stepped back, taking on more strategic and mentoring roles, and allowed the team to take charge of operations. We established a real organisation structure for the first time, defining business units—each with a clear head.

A key introduction during this period was a robust reporting system, including a Management Information System (MIS) to monitor various activities on a monthly and quarterly basis. This also gave managers a sense of responsibility for their deliverables. Moving managers from an 'effort-oriented' to a 'result-oriented' mindset was a key shift for our homegrown engineers who had transitioned into management roles. Our monthly review system now brings accountability and serves as a platform to brainstorm, decide, and communicate tactics and key action items for the coming month. This is a core method of managing the business today.

As Milind and Mohini had more time to focus on other areas, the company ventured into interesting new directions. Milind concentrated on NANOFINISH research, leading to a surge in global patents and breakthrough innovations after 2017. Mohini dedicated time to marketing and business development, introducing Grind Master to several new markets, including Japan, Thailand, and

Germany. Through platforms like CII, CMIA, and later IMTMA, she became more connected with the industry, marking a new phase in her evolving personality as a businesswoman.

Managers in a family-owned, professionally-run organisation gradually adapt to the family ethos, with their personal values undergoing a transformation. Like branches of a tree, they draw their core values from the roots. This process takes time, and hiring senior professionals externally often doesn't work unless there is a values match. At one point, I was keen on bringing in ready-made managers, focusing on communication skills and leadership experience. However, without a strong background in specialised machine building and metal finishing, newcomers could only scratch the surface. In our process technology-oriented field, effective leadership comes from the ability to perform well as an engineer. Milind never said "I told you so," but would always discuss the next steps. He introduced me to the concept of 'sunk cost'—understanding the past without letting it dictate the future. We concluded that it was better to guide homegrown engineers and managers into leadership roles.

As the organisation developed, we built various cross-functional committees to ensure the horizontal deployment of best practices. Functions like materials, engineering, execution, and Make for World guide operations across the organisation, bringing all business units to a common platform and implementing improvements learned in one part of the business elsewhere. Additional committees maintain systems like QMS, EHS, 5S, and ISMS, ensuring our progress in adhering to and improving industry standards is sustainable. Each committee is led by a functional head.

While we share a few core principles—passion for machine building, an inclination towards specialised technology development, and a vision to make Grind Master a global technology leader—our management approaches are very different. Over the years, I observed Milind and Mohini's methods and developed my own.

Milind is a leader who works from the front, always taking charge of situations. This approach inspires people but also limits his ability to delegate and guide from the back. I learned to put myself in the front by being faster than him in responding to situations – an extremely demanding task!

Mohini, on the other hand, holds people accountable, ensuring they stayed on track. While her intentions and thinking were aligned with what I believed to be the right direction, our approach of communicating has been widely different.

Both Milind and Mohini had not drafted clear goals for senior management, including me. I was CEO in 2016 but I didn't have a clear mandate. I had to imagine what an owner would expect from a highly paid CEO and build my work around those expectations. Involving some senior management members in board meetings was a significant step in making structured strategic decisions and ensuring their full support in implementing them.

I recall a board meeting at the end of FY2018-19—it was the year of the highest revenues for the company. Yet, the figures hid some concerning signs. The working capital required to run the business was at an all-time high, as were receivables and inventory. Profitability percentages were down, and headcount was up. We had been adding too many unskilled and incompetent people, and several business units were not too profitable. We took these early signs seriously and decided to act. There was a need for sharp, astute management during these transitional years. I took it upon myself to improve the financial results.

We initiated multiple improvement projects, including execution streamlining, design standardisation, cost reduction on the operations side, and astute sales management – such as receivables control and pricing improvements. Gradually, we improved results each year. Our financials remained strong during the Covid years and have become better than ever since. Moreover, the policies implemented jointly in FY2019-20 are now championed by the managers leading them. Prashant Yeole, appointed COO in 2021, has taken the lead in improving operations, with several initiatives every year.

During these years, I took the lead in conceptualising, defining, and guiding policies. Various people across the organisation had to start shouldering responsibility and being accountable for results rather than efforts. When pushed in this direction, the team rose to the challenge, with tight implementation following. The directors had grown the business by micromanaging the team, often spoon-feeding people on what, how, when, and why to do things. I started defining expectations that required the team to figure out tactics and actions based on strategies. Since the team had more experience and knowledge, this transition, though challenging, worked out, with most people rising to the challenge.

Over the last 3-4 years, Grind Master has undergone a drastic restructuring of the team, with fewer employees in supporting or assistant roles and more people taking direct responsibility. This transformation is likely to continue. From a family-owned, family-managed business, we are becoming a family-owned, professionally managed company.

Milind and Mohini nurtured the company through much more adverse conditions than those I was handed. They were fortunate to have a son who shares their passion for machine building. While Grind Master was like a daughter to Milind and Mohini, to me, it is an entity with a DNA of its own, shaped by its history and people. Being a steward of the legacy that the name represents is a great responsibility, one I take seriously.

Work-Life Balance

We've built a good life for ourselves in Aurangabad. The honest reason for returning from Switzerland was that I could live much better at home. Here, I have the work-life balance I need, with short commutes, a strong support system, and a close social circle. The mountains have always felt like home to me. Trekking, mountain biking, and trail running are integral parts of my life, allowing me to explore the hills. Aurangabad's surrounding hills offer plenty of opportunities for exploration, and I spend many mornings and almost all weekends outdoors, finding new spots.

Natasha and I had our daughter, Almitra, in 2016, during a time when we were both working at a breakneck pace to grow our respective businesses. I was on international tours for 7-10 days each month and missed a lot of time with her. Then, in 2022, our son Shiroy was born prematurely by two months, and we spent over a month in the NICU with him. That experience triggered a personal transformation. The fragility of life in that hospital environment and watching our 1.2 kg baby grow through his early struggles had a deep, profound impact on us. After we came home from the hospital, I wondered if I was the father of Shiroy or the other way around. Sameer Shiroy Kelkar!

The deep reflections that the emotional time in.the hospital afforded me led me to gain more clarity about the many goals that I wanted to reach. I thought deeply about the changes that the management of Grind Master would undergo in the coming years. I wanted to spend more time with my family and pursue goals in travel, study, afforestation, and wildlife conservation. I wished to continue to provide thought leadership and strategy to the company and offer a new vision, but I wanted to step back from babysitting the company. I wondered if my sister would manage independently without the firm grip of the hand that's always held her tightly? As all these questions swirled in my mind, I believed that the strong DNA of Grind Master would take it to new heights. We had a passionate, dedicated, and trustworthy team. My vision for the future was to build a strong institution that is family-owned and professionally managed with capable professionals.

Zen and the Art of Mountain Wandering

Mountain wandering is a way of life. Many of my excursions are solo, providing countless Zen moments for introspection. I used to wonder what it would be like to wake up every morning, day after day, week after week, and month after month with a new pass to cross, a new valley to explore, and a new river to camp by. Then I asked myself: Would I be at home in the mountains, or would I run away like an unwelcome guest?

This quest led me to a life-changing experience in the Himalayas in 2010, on a trek from Nepal to Ladakh, covering over 2,500 km and 26 high passes over 150 days. Some sections were well-known, while others were semi-expeditions. Traversing numerous valleys, sometimes alone and sometimes with friends, I discovered that each region had a different topography, flora, fauna, and culture, each with a distinct message. There was always a sense of wonder about what the next journey would hold.

The experiences were vast and enriching, from getting engaged to Natasha on Thorung La to being robbed at knifepoint in the Pindari Valley. On these mountains, I made lifelong friends among porters, horsemen, and sadhus and led a protest to secure necessary permissions. Guided by a local shepherd, I once toiled up a mountain for an entire day, only to hear him say, "Sirji, we climbed the wrong mountain." I learned to accept and relish uncertainty, and embraced the joy of living in the moment.

The monsoon initially brought fear and discomfort, but within a week, I began to appreciate its beauty. The freshness in the air, the burst of flowers in the high meadows, and the play of clouds and sunshine revealed extraordinary sights. In the Milam Valley, the clouds played hide and seek with the mountains for a week as I waited for Nanda Devi to reveal herself.

Eventually, as our supplies dwindled, I began the hike out via the Ralam Pass. Climbing to the col in the early morning, the world was shrouded in cold darkness, but a light shone on the Goddess of Kumaon. I felt as if I was in her sanctum. As the glorious sunrise colours spread across the dark sky, I felt the eternal beauty flow through me. Immersed in the tremendous panorama around me, I was also immersed in the Devi. This was destiny.

That journey made me feel at home, deeply in love, and at one with the mountains. The Himalayas became a part of my life—ridges that represented my past and valleys that symbolised my future. As autumn approached in September, crossing the Digar La into Nubra, I left the Himalayas behind and faced the Karakoram ahead. Meeting a 76-year-old shepherd in the high meadows made me wonder: Is this what I was born to do?

I started the journey as a city slicker and ended it as someone else. The transformation was complete—and irreversible. I've felt at home in the mountains ever since. The lessons I've learned in the mountains have been invaluable in my professional life as a technocrat. The ability to take calculated risks and live through the consequences, to be light and flexible in seizing opportunities, and to organise and lead a team into the VUCA (Volatility, Uncertainty, Complexity, Ambiguity) world of the Himalayas are things that can never be taught in school.

Exploration is a game of wandering, of stepping into the unknown, finding new paths, embracing uncertainty, and trusting your instincts. We would be a deadly boring species if we never wanted to get lost. Exploration drives innovation and helps us find our true selves. In one world, I eat, sleep, and dream of machines; in another, I explore meadows, valleys, and ridges. Going into the wild brings me Zen, allowing me to touch my real self. I explore both worlds—one through engineering and technology, and the other through wet, mucky trails and stark, dry landscapes. By becoming part of nature and discovering your true inner self, you blaze your own trail. Be a child at play, exploring the unknown, with achievements as by-products, attaining a state of bliss, becoming Zen!

“

What I am most proud about is not the making of steel or trucks but our social concern

JRD Tata

14

TOWARDS SUSTAINABILITY AND SOCIAL RESPONSIBILITY

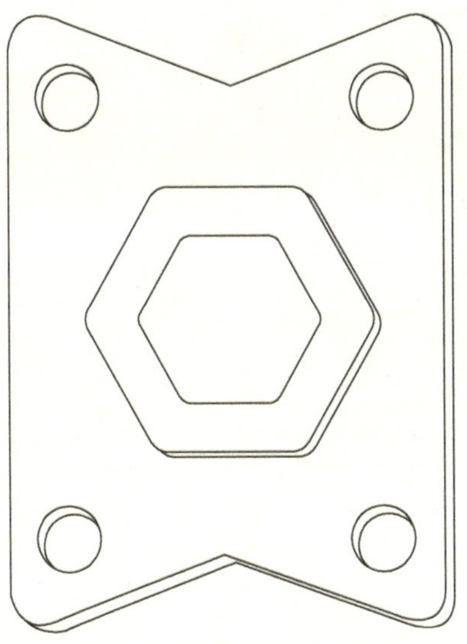

In June 2013, Natasha and I were huddled in a tent in a valley leading to the Bhawa Pass in Kinnaur District, Himachal Pradesh. The rain was relentless, soaking our tent. We had been forced to retreat from the Bhawa Pass base camp after over two feet of snow fell in just three days. Having traversed the Bhawa Pass a few times before, I knew the way well. The weather in June in the western Himalayas was usually stable, with the monsoon arriving in July. Occasional storms might last a day, but this was different.

We packed our heavy, wet sacks and descended to a meadow, where the snowfall had turned to sleet. We decided to continue further down to Kafnu village. The path led through forest and gorge country, where beautiful streams had transformed into wild torrents. Each crossing became a challenge. Wooden bridges built by local shepherds had been washed away. Holding hands and balancing with our sticks, we faced the raging, muddy waters. At one point, where two streams met, creating a triangular patch of land, we crossed one stream with great difficulty. The second, however, had become a mudslide, bringing down rocks and mud from the ravine above. The unstable mud made crossing impossible. We had to wait for the slide to stabilise, which could take a day, yet going back was not an option. We pitched our tent in the triangle, burned some wet, smoky wood, and huddled together, hoping the streams wouldn't break their banks and sweep us away at night. Every thunderclap made us shudder, and each flash of lightning illuminated our frightened faces.

Climate change brings more uncertainty, with unseasonal and stronger storms. We were experiencing it firsthand. Despite all our technological advancements, the vulnerability of our species was undeniable. Fortunately, the rain eased somewhat the next day, and the mudslide stabilised. We struggled our way to Kafnu village and found refuge in a friend's welcoming home. Warming ourselves by the fireplace, we learned of the devastation over the past few days, with Kedarnath in Uttarakhand being the most severely affected.

Bandijai

Appa had always been attached to land, yearning for a piece of earth like the one in Konkan that he had left behind in his childhood. The memory of land lost in Jalgaon after the family land laws changed lingered. In 1984, despite not owning a car and relying on a Lambretta scooter, he took the plunge and bought a 28-acre plot, naming it Bandijai Ban after his village in Sindhudurg district. Appa and Ajji conducted countless experiments in farming, water conservation, animal husbandry, and forestry there. Years of hard work transformed the dry, semi-desert into a green haven teeming with life. Walking in the shade of the forest, feeling the breeze over the grassland, and listening to the stream's gurgle, there is a deep sense of gratitude for the legacy they left behind. Sacred groves (Devrai), ancient forests protected by village communities, are passed down through generations. They tie generations together, nourishing them. Bandijai Ban is such a place—a gift of love to future generations, to creatures big and small, to the wild.

Milind and Ketan also shared a deep connection with land and farming. Ketan contributed to Bandijai's development by building a collection of medicinal plants. Milind and his close friends invested in a beautiful site in Shulibhanjan, developing a teak farm there. Originally intended to provide income after 15-20 years, it has now been over 30 years, and over 5,000 teak trees stand strong in the valley. The forest's beauty has long since overshadowed its economic purpose. Both Bandijai and Shulibhanjan were rocky, scrubby land—not ideal for farming. In 2003, Milind bought fertile farmland near Nakshatrawadi, located in the Kham river basin. Pursued more out of passion than profit, the farm has yielded sugarcane, turmeric, sweet lime, hurda, and various vegetables over the years. Salim, the enterprising farmer working on the land, also practices poultry and goat rearing.

I recall conversations in the old bungalow—Appa, Ajji, Ketan, and Milind each had their own theories about growing things, each convinced their latest idea was the best. They continued their experiments, gaining experience and enjoying the thrill of seeing seeds grow. The journey continues today.

During the Covid lockdowns, I resolved to move to Bandijai as soon as possible. We moved into Prithvi, our home in the forest, with gorgeous views of sunrise and sunset. It is an idyllic location with trees, grassland, rocky scrubland, and a small stream. We have pets—10 dogs, 5 roosters, and hens. The wild creatures are here, too—snakes, hares, peacocks, civet cats, jungle cats, monitor lizards, and porcupines. It is a home to return to, where our kids are growing up close to nature.

Milind, Natasha, and I now jointly steward the Bandijai land, planting many rare and endangered varieties of trees with newer techniques in afforestation. Milind applies innovative engineering methods to plant, maintain, and monitor the forests. All pilot projects are conducted here, making it a hub of experimentation. We have also set up a nursery for jungle trees and shrubs that are not stocked by commercial nurseries. I feel Appa and Ajji smiling down on us, pleased that we have inherited their legacy well and continued what they would have wanted.

CSR and PSR: Corporate and Personal Social Responsibility

Grind Master is committed to operating and growing its business in a socially responsible way, with a vision to be an environmentally friendly corporate citizen. Ensuring sustainable and inclusive growth is in our DNA. Our CSR approach reflects our core values of innovation, expertise, passion, and trustworthiness towards society and the environment. We strive to apply absolute engineering to CSR projects and create meaningful change in our environment.

Grind Master has supported various social causes over the years. Notable contributions include donations to schools run by Hedgewar Trust (Omkar Balwadi), a home for the mentally challenged (Navkshitij), and girl education initiatives (Udyan Shalini Foundation). Supporting the Savitribai Phule Mahila Ekatma Samaj Mandal (SPMESM) to improve women's health in low-income areas has had a tremendous, measurable impact. Additionally, we have supported engineering education by funding and guiding competitions such as Robocon, Baja, Supra, and Tifan for local engineering colleges, including Deogiri, MIT, and GECA, giving students exposure to practical engineering.

To expand the scale of activities, especially in nature conservation and afforestation, the Kelkar family formed the Bandijai Trust. This trust supports various organisations, including Jansahyog and WE for Environment, in creating forests through citizen engagement.

CARPE - EcoSattva: Solving Civic Challenges

Natasha Zarine and Gauri Mirashi share a passion for solving civic challenges. Addressing problems like solid waste management (SWM) in cities requires strong implementation of systems like segregation at source and decentralised waste management. Mentored by Almitra Patel, the grandmother of Solid Waste Management (SWM), they started CARPE - EcoSattva, a hybrid organisation that makes a significant impact in solid waste management, afforestation, and river rejuvenation. Milind's advice was clear: if you believe you can solve the problem, start a venture and take it on. Based out of the Grind Master building, their organisation has grown significantly.

Initially, Grind Master supported pilot projects in SWM at the colony and ward levels. Later, CARPE received funding from Bajaj Auto to implement SWM across the city. With an impact in over 20 cities in Maharashtra and consultancy projects with McKinsey in Bali (Indonesia) and Buenos Aires (Argentina), the BOTRAM model of SWM used by EcoSattva is recognised as the way forward for cities.

EcoSattva pioneered the Miyawaki dense forest method in the Marathwada region, customising it for local conditions. Their professionalism, planning, and execution with a "do what it takes" approach have led to the nurturing of over 500,000 trees across the district, with projects in Kerala and Ludhiana. In recent years, EcoSattva has innovated further, developing the Labyrinth Dense Forest method, which is as effective as the Miyawaki method while eliminating drawbacks like over-density and allowing trees to grow fully.

CARPE and Grind Master also launched the Prakriti Research Fellowship programme to support research in nature conservation, wildlife, and ecosystems by individuals and small organisations. Over the past five years, more than 18 projects and 13 fellows from across India have received seed funding. This year the fellowship has expanded with over 12 projects supported.

CARPE-EcoSattva is best known for its Kham River rejuvenation project in partnership with the Municipal Corporation, Cantonment Board, and Varroc. This project, envisioned by Varroc founder Mr. Tarang Jain, involves building public spaces along the riverbanks, restoring heritage structures, and engaging citizens with the river. Recognised by the World Resources Institute (WRI), this project continues to gain strength. Grind Master is proud to join Varroc as an industry partner in this endeavour. The Kham river rejuvenation project recently won International awards by WRI Ross Foundation in New York and St. Andrews University in Scotland.

The GREEN AURANGABAD MISSION (GAM)

Afforestation was a subject of deep interest. The Kelkar family had been in various farming and plantation activities over the years. Over 5000 trees in Bandijai, and 3000 trees at Shulibhanjan (teak farm/forest) already stood tall from years of nurturing. Grind Master attempted to experiment with native tree plantation in the Daulatabad ghat hillside, realizing that a proper method and dedicated organization was required for making this a success at a scale.

Partnering with CARPE-Ecosattva for bringing in best practices and knowledge led to the formation of the Green Aurangabad Mission (GAM) that has been the flagship activity for Grind Master ever since. The Daulatabad Hill eco restoration site was first nurtured into success. During this process it was realized that the hard rocky soils in the Marathwada region were very hardy conditions. While trees planted in fertile farm lands could survive, afforestation projects had very poor results due to the conditions.

Dr. Akira Miyawaki, a Japanese professor, evolved a methodology to grow DENSE FORESTS. Originally designed for city forests in industrialized Japan, the 'Miyawaki' method had been adopted to Indian conditions by Bangalore based Afforest, who conducted training programs. Further adapting the Miyawaki method with tree mix available in the Aurangabad region, first pilot projects of this novel technique at Bandijai and Grind Master Waluj campus were a tremendous success. The growth of the trees was unbelievable - a

1 year forest would be already so dense and impenetrable. Within 3 years it was independent of maintenance (watering). The Miyawaki method - based on intense soil preparation, close planting of trees and shrubs mimicking the rain forest, and maintenance including mulching and watering, delivers 10 times faster growth and 30 times denser forest than conventional methods. Botanical Engineering applied to give a solid methodology.

Under the GAM we supported Miyawaki Forest Pilots to demonstrate the method - building 2000 sq ft to 4000 sq ft forest patches in city areas. Some of the pilots were in Government land - including Police Commissioners office, ITI Aurangabad Campus, MIT College Hostel campus, while others were in Private / NGO land - including Sai Baba Temple campus, Astha Foundation campus. Every single one of them was a success - with over 95% survival rate.

GREEN SCHOOLS MISSION

The success of the pilots of Afforestation encouraged scaling up - in form of the Green Schools Mission (GSM), a collaborative project with Zilla Parishad, Forest Department, Ecosattva and Grind Master. The objective of the project was to build Native Dense Forests in 100 Zilla Parishad Schools across the district. Each forest would be 2000 sq ft with over 600 trees of 45-50 native varieties. The plantations were done in 2020. The survival rate after 3 years has been over 90%, and most of the forests have grown fast and are independent. The earliest forests under the scheme were planted before the Covid crisis, and have been pulled through the hot and stressful summer of 2020. While the credit for initiating the program goes to Zilla Parishad CEO Pavneet Kaur and Mangesh Gondawale and Ecosattva team led by Natasha and Gauri, the real heroes on the ground are the teachers.

Natasha and I cycled to see our forests often. ZPPS Nadikathvasti, located beautifully by the banks of the Kham river as it approaches Jayakwadi dam. With only 40 students mainly from nearby hutments it is a small school. Misal Sir gave us a hearty welcome as we rolled into the campus. Somehow the fatigue simply vanished as we met the enthusiastic team managing the schools here. The forest here was planted in August 2020. In a school that does not have electric connection, the teachers had somehow ensured that the forest got water through a harsh summer. Misal Sir explained 'the village is a close knit community' and everybody supports a good cause. We indeed knew this was the case. We had supported the nearby Bramhagavhan school in building Toilets. The support had been given subject to the village doing better at solid waste management. Once again the teachers had proved their zeal for bringing about a change, going door to door, explaining segregation at source, enabling composting at a household level and setting up a dry waste recycling center for the village. We could also see the village Gram panchayat really coming together to bring about this transformation. A vision of self sufficient Indian villages built by strong cooperative bonds emerged out of our visits to Bramhagavhan.

During my cycling tours to visit various dense forests across the Aurangabad District I was hit by the enormity of the rural landscape, and the humongous challenges it presents in various administrative functions including education. There is practically a village every 3-4 kms, and Zilla Parishad runs a school in every village. It even runs schools in small settlements outside villages where there can be as few as 20-30 students. In August 2020 amidst a heavy downpour I reached such a school at Wakodwadi. Around 20 kids were getting the saplings out of a tractor. The area to be planted had been prepared in the earlier - digging, getting coco peat, rice husk, manure and other ingredients was managed by the school teacher under the advise of an experts like Siddharth from Ecosattva. The saplings were carefully organized. Soon we were all in the mud completing the plantation.

Malkar Sir, from ZPPS Tadpimpalgaon explained that the students had been really surprised to see a full forest before/after covid lockdown. What they had seen as small saplings had converted into an impenetrable jungle when they came back. Magic ! With the vegetation came numerous birds, bees and insects. The kids were keen to learn about the trees. Most of them had some use in traditional practice - including medicinal ones.

Deshmukh Sir, of ZPPS Ghanori, explained that many of the students from school continue farming and other rural occupations. His school is full of posters of interesting fundae that leave much to ponder about. Discussions with him always inspire several ideas and projects. The school is nestled in the beautiful esoteric hills north of Aurangabad. Being on eroded slopes the land is rocky. Due to this the area preparation consisted of digging upto 4.5 ft instead of the normal 3ft, explained Deshmukh Sir. The efforts have created a showcase forest - something visited by many people as an example of success in adverse conditions. Having seen their earlier determination to succeed I believe anything is possible.

Every visit to the Zilla Parishad Schools over the years has been inspiring. In 2024 we have launched GSM2 - a sequel to the first successful project. A further 100 schools across the district will build forests under this novel partnership project. Zilla Parishad CEO Vikash Meena flagged off the scheme expressing confidence in the model being developed and demonstrated in the process.

Remanufacturing

Manufacturing inherently involves the use of natural resources, such as steel and energy, to convert raw materials into machines. This process inevitably leads to emissions. That's why we need to find ways to minimise emissions and offset what cannot be avoided. Traditionally, this follows a linear model of resource usage, culminating in waste at the product's end of life. We are doing our part to offset this impact through solar energy usage, afforestation projects, and energy efficiency measures. But is there a way to fundamentally change how we do business?

Ajay Phatak, our mentor for the Sustainability Mission, challenged our team to explore ideas and solutions to this crucial problem. After extensive discussions and brainstorming on various business models, we concluded that common approaches such as 'Solution as a Service' and 'Extended Producer Responsibility' (EPR) or machine buy-back were not suitable for us. Instead, we found that the 'Remanufacturing' methodology was the right fit. Inspired by industry leaders like Caterpillar (one of the world's biggest construction machinery manufacturers) and Cummins (one of the world's leading heavy diesel engine manufacturers), we launched our own Remanufacturing programme.

Remanufacturing is defined as 'the rebuilding of a product to the specifications of the original manufactured product using a combination of reused, repaired, and new parts.' A machine tool comprises a wide variety of materials, including:

1. Steel and aluminium
2. Motors, gearboxes, and cylinders, each made from various materials, and
3. Electronics

Most of the elements used in a machine tool have a long life if properly maintained.

The life of a machine tool is typically between 5 and 10 years due to:

1. Technological obsolescence and
2. Product obsolescence

One common solution used by the manufacturing industry to address these issues is to 'refurbish' or 'recondition' the machines. Reconditioning is usually an on-site activity that involves cleaning, repairing or replacing worn-out or damaged parts, oiling, and fastening to make the machines functional again. However, there are some inherent limitations to the refurbishing process for machine tools:

1. It must be conducted with the available resources on site.
2. Only limited upgrades and modifications can be implemented.
3. It extends machine life by just a few years, until the next refurbishing is required.

A refurbished machine does not offer the same performance or longevity as a new machine. Over time, the mechanisms continue to deteriorate, increasing the frequency and severity of failures. This unpredictability is unaffordable in mass manufacturing. Remanufacturing takes things to the next level.

Remanufacturing is now a core part of our business model, providing a win-win situation. Remanufactured products are:

1. As good as new, with warranties and an expected lifespan comparable to a new product.
2. Contemporary, incorporating necessary technological upgrades.
3. Economical, offering substantial cost savings to the end user.
4. Sustainable, reusing a significant percentage of the original raw materials.

The process of remanufacturing is inherently different from both manufacturing and refurbishing. It must incorporate the scalability and consistency of manufacturing while also reusing materials. Grind Master formed a cross-functional team to apply the principles of remanufacturing and create a systematic approach to deliver consistent results. This strategic and systematic approach led us to formulate our own phased project implementation plan.

A remanufactured machine undergoes the same engineering reviews, part quality checks, assembly, testing, delivery, and commissioning as a new machine. Both the customer and Grind Master meet some of their sustainability goals. Remanufacturing has thus proven to be a highly feasible business model for custom-built specialised machinery such as finishing machines. Integrating remanufacturing into our business model can contribute to a sustainable circular economy in capital goods, including machinery. However, there is still a long way to go in bringing about this transformation. Challenges include:

1. Machine tool manufacturers' willingness to explore and adopt this model
2. Customer acceptance of remanufactured products, and
3. The need for systems, methodologies, and standards for remanufacturing across the industry.

Defining Sustainability for a Machine Builder

"We envision becoming a net-zero company by 2030, with sustainability as a core value."

We set this goal in 2023, but it took nearly a year to fully understand what it entails. Achieving net zero by offsetting and reducing Scope 1, Scope 2, and Scope 3 emissions is not easy. Scope 1, which represents fuel burned, is not a major contributor. Scope 2, mainly representing electricity bills, is somewhat larger. The forests we have planted so far have been sufficient to offset Scope 1 and 2 emissions.

However, Scope 3 emissions are more complex and revealing. These are indirect emissions caused by upstream and downstream activities. As a machine builder, we purchase many materials—steel, aluminium, electronics, motors, etc. Each of these purchases carries an 'embodied' energy cost. After several months of work, we developed a calculation methodology for our embodied energy usage. Adding other Scope 3 factors, including travel emissions and capital goods purchases, resulted in a daunting number—almost 15 times our Scope 2 emissions. This represents a significant challenge that the entire manufacturing industry, particularly the machine tool industry, will face in the coming years in the drive towards net zero.

Towards Net Zero: Defining Sustainability as a Core Value

Using sustainable methods and innovations has always been part of our culture. Several measures on our campus demonstrate eco-friendly technologies. Our sewage treatment plant (STP) uses the 'Constructed Wetland' methodology, a novel technique piloted by Ashwin Paranjape from Pune. These STPs have been maintenance-free, delivering consistent results. Moreover, they resemble gardens, creating pleasant environments. Our STP at the Waluj premises, in particular, is a beautiful area where I often conduct outdoor meetings. The treated water is reused for gardening.

Marathwada is a drought-prone region, so cautious water use is crucial. We have integrated water harvesting into all our buildings. A solar roof generates over 60% of our energy needs. We recycle waste, with segregated waste collection across our offices and manufacturing areas.

Our team engages in various activities, including spot-cleanup drives, afforestation efforts, and the Kham riverside cleanup. Many family members also participate in upcycling activities, using waste materials to create useful products. Our administration team ensures that no event generates waste, such as single-use cutlery and packets. Ideas for reducing our environmental footprint—like using bamboo as a renewable material or replacing aluminium with steel—are just a few examples. A cross-functional committee (which I lead) oversees all sustainability activities with a monthly review meeting.

The drive towards sustainability in our company was inspired by books like 'Doughnut Economics' by Kate Raworth. Discussions with Almitra Patel further cemented the idea that we must set ambitious goals and do whatever it takes to achieve them. We are committed to reaching net zero by 2030.

Remanufacturing is a growing business model for Grind Master. In over 15 projects executed, we have saved more than 75 tonnes of material. Our customers, Shanghai General Motors and Maruti Suzuki, were among the first to partner with us in this venture. Many more companies, including Bajaj Motors, Precision Camshafts, and Changan Automotive, have recognised the value of this approach. We envision significant growth in this business, contributing up to 20%-25% of our revenues by 2030.

Since much of our emissions come from purchased materials, we have started to encourage a green supply chain—preferring suppliers who have sustainability built into their business model, from manufacturing to operations to end-of-life management. Many of our technology partners, such as Fanuc, Mitsubishi, and Siemens, have also defined net zero missions. This is a very positive initiative by market leaders, and we hope others will follow suit, adopting aggressive timelines to meet the same goals.

Our passion for afforestation now has a new, ambitious goal – 1 million trees by 2030. We estimate that this many trees will be necessary to offset the remainder of our greenhouse gas emissions. Over eight years of the Green Aurangabad Mission, we have planted and nurtured 150,000 trees. Now, our goal is to plant 150,000 trees every year. The task is enormous.

Allocating a significant portion of our yearly revenue was the first step. Fortunately, the Kelkar family is passionate about these efforts, and financial decisions related to sustainability are met with unanimous support in family meetings – 'just do it.' Planting 150,000 trees every year requires large tracts of land—15 to 25 acres annually, depending on the method used.

We have partnered with the zilla parishad, launching the Green Schools Mission 2, and with the CSMC (municipal corporation) for afforestation in the Kham River Rejuvenation project. We continue to seek partnerships for future projects.

Net zero is an urgent goal, and we seek support from our customers in achieving it. Every machine we produce generates an average of 150 tonnes of CO2, requiring 180 trees to be planted to offset this over its lifetime. We hope that our strong partnerships with the manufacturing industry will appreciate this effort and contribute to it.

The Grind Master family pursues the sustainability goal with passion. The Kelkar family is personally involved in several projects, driving them to successful conclusions. A culture and attitude of sustainability are gradually becoming embedded in Grind Master's DNA.

"Man is unique not because he does science, and he is unique not because he does art, but because science and art equally are expressions of his marvellous plasticity of mind. "

Jacob Bronowski,
The Ascent of Man

15

JAGAT BHARI

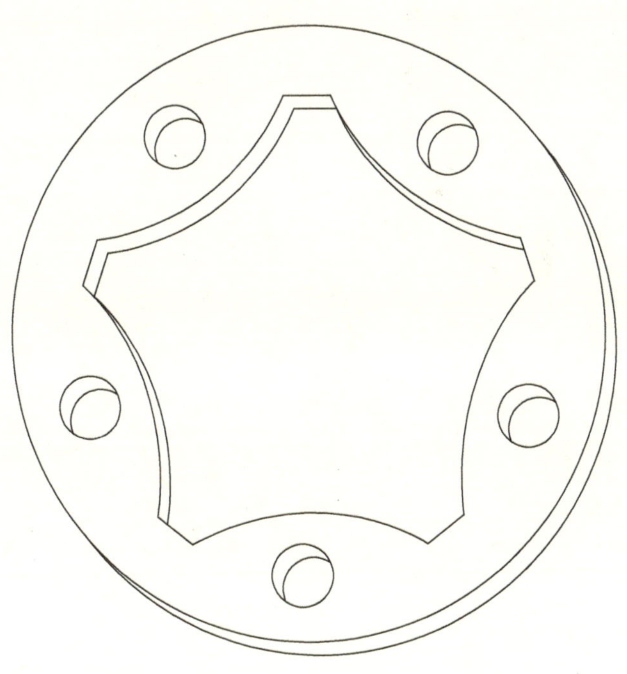

Jagat Bhari

Jagat = in the universe
Bhari = awesome, fantastic

The Marathi phrase 'jagat bhari' encapsulates the vision of Grind Master—a desire to become a global technology leader. Grind Master started in a garage, bootstrapped, with no prior experience in building machines. Driven by a passion to create a novel product that would make a mark, the company has been proudly contributing to 'Make in India' since 1984, long before the concept gained popular traction. Beyond commercial industries like cookware, automotive, earthmoving, foundry, tubes and bars, and general industry, Grind Master has significantly impacted key strategic sectors like aerospace, healthcare, and energy through breakthrough innovations. Developing processes and cost-effective machines has empowered Indian manufacturing, especially in strategic industries. The full development of homegrown technology embodies the true essence of Atmanirbhar.

Grind Master now boasts one of the widest product ranges among its peers. Its high-tech products have found great success in the Chinese manufacturing industry, often recognised as equal to or better than German and Japanese products. The introduction of this technology in developed markets has been promising, with strong partnerships evolving over the years in the automotive industry in Japan and Germany, hydraulics in the US, and the mining industry in Australia. This progression motivates us to take the next leap—'Make for the World'.

We aim to move beyond 'Atmanirbhar Bharat' and create an Indian brand known for its technological prowess globally. Breaking out of the 'low-wage country' mould to become an 'innovation-competent country' aligns with Bharat's emergence as a global leader.

The phrase 'jagat bhari' embodies this aspiration—recognised as awesome universally. But what does it truly mean? A technology leader sets benchmarks. In some niche areas, we have challenged those benchmarks and set new, higher standards. Two prominent examples are ballscrew superfinishing and hydraulic piston rod superfinishing. When we consistently achieve this and become a trusted partner for the most discerning manufacturing companies, including those in developed countries, we can truly say, 'jagat bhari.'

Looking Through the Periscope

In a rapidly evolving technological landscape, we need to stay agile and lean. We must keep our vision open to disruptive challenges and breakthrough opportunities.

Revolutionary advancements in machine learning and artificial intelligence will impact the entire ecosystem that we are part of. Staying ahead of the curve by proactively researching and deploying these concepts in our products will bring tremendous benefits to our customers. Internalising these methods will transform our operations. Upskilling our team to leverage these technologies and become more effective will be crucial.

Environment, health, and safety (EHS) are becoming core values in industry. Over the next decade, the world will unite to tackle some of the planet's most pressing challenges. As a responsible member of this community, we must ensure our entire supply chain is part of the solution. As a technology developer, we must play a transformative role for our customers—helping them reduce environmental impact, including energy consumption, and providing healthier, safer working conditions for their teams.

We must have a transformative effect on everyone who interacts with Grind Master through our commitment to sustainability, inclusiveness, and absolute engineering. Our core values—our DNA—can have a positive impact. Our team, which shares these values, must be empowered to think like entrepreneurs. The 'unboundedness' that has driven the company's progress so far must continue.

The future of our process technology and products is bright. Finer finishing is considered the holy grail for achieving fuel efficiency, noise reduction, and corrosion resistance. Any component in relative motion either already requires a fine finish or soon will. This presents a tremendous opportunity to leapfrog in technology development and set global benchmarks.

Despite the challenging global geopolitical situation, we must strive to expand our global footprint, not only by exporting our technology but also by deepening partnerships through joint ventures. With our experience and approach, we have something unique to offer in these collaborations. Strategic partnerships are the way forward. Strong international collaborations have been Grind Master's strength. A stronger IMPCO-GM partnership will enable global reach, especially in making inroads to America. We continue to seek collaborations with international conglomerates in specialised machines.

Being the Grand Master of One

The rabbit hole goes deep. Any specialised technology is already niche, and becoming better means going deeper. 'God is in the details.' When we dig below what seems to be the final step, we find another wonderland. Producing engineered finishes is a rapidly evolving field. Moving beyond surface roughness into bearing surfaces, and further into specific tribological characteristics, is the next frontier. The technology for generating such surfaces—NANOFINISH—is set to explore the submicron peaks, valleys, and plateaus of a seemingly smooth surface.

The future of Grind Master lies in mastering nanometer accuracies in finishing. Our goal is to explore, research, develop, refine, and deploy finishing technologies that enhance performance across various applications. Focusing on technology products will lead us to this goal. We were never the 'jack of all trades.' The vision pulls us towards becoming not just the 'master of a few' but the 'Grand Master of One'.

Grind Master's brand has evolved from a garage pioneer to a trustworthy partner for Indian manufacturing. As the next-generation entrepreneur, it is my responsibility to lead it into becoming a high-technology company.

A new state-of-the-art integrated facility will soon be established on our beautiful Waluj campus. Amidst 10 acres of forests with jogging tracks, the campus will inspire creativity while enforcing the value of discipline. Reflecting our commitment to sustainability, it will be a global Indian facility.

Process research has always been Grind Master's strength. We have demonstrated that when faced with new challenges, we can innovate faster, better, and simpler solutions. The volatile manufacturing environment, with new materials and technologies, including disruptive EVs, presents a disguised boon—an opportunity to leapfrog. Improved finer finishes are becoming a new industry paradigm. Our Process Research Lab is increasingly focused on developing patentable solutions to these challenges. With strong academic rigour, we will become a formidable R&D centre generating more breakthrough innovations. Innovations in machine learning, deployed in finishing processes, and a new range of intuitive AI-based man-machine interfaces, will imbue our finishing machines with a user experience like never before.

We can and will provide excellent global service. A new model of proactive service, backed by a strong global network, is essential for recognition as an outstanding support provider. Along with promoting remanufacturing of our machines, we are committed to continually improving our support.

Defocus to Focus

There's a lesson from the movie Fight Club: Tyler Durden (played by Brad Pitt) says, "No fear. No distractions." Focus isn't possible without defocus. We have a history of pioneering numerous product lines, all developed with passion, blood, sweat, and tears. Each one has grown into a child with its own potential. But a child doesn't learn to run unless you let go of the guiding hand.

Passing on the Legacy of Economy Products

We offer a wide range of standard machines, including cookware polishing, tube and bar finishing, and basic gear deburring and brushing. These technologies were introduced between 1984 and 1992 and have since established a track record of over 5,000 machines. Known as pioneers in the cookware, tubes, and bars industries, our machines are so well-regarded that buyers often ask competitors for a 'Grind Master equivalent'. These products were novel when introduced but later faced increasing competition, gradually becoming commoditised. However, the robustness of our machines remains a benchmark.

The wide range of these products clutters our corporate shop window, sending confusing signals about our focus and capabilities. Despite this, there is significant potential in these products. Automatic cookware polishing, pioneered over 40 years ago, still has only 15%-20% market penetration. Tubes and bars represent a growing segment with advancing requirements for better machinery. Growing this business requires aggressive marketing and a different approach. A specialist in these industries could better exploit the platform. Grind Master ventured into these product lines when they were novel. The Indian machine tool landscape has since evolved into a vibrant ecosystem, and the market for these solutions has matured. We see a collaboration model where Grind Master hands over its pioneering legacy and robust customer base through technical collaborations. This will bring new vigour and focus to developing these product lines. Our customer base will continue to receive support, with the possibility of better pricing and delivery.

The Coated Abrasives Business

This business was introduced when quality abrasives and application support were hard to find. Over 30 years later, the situation has changed dramatically. Almost all leading coated abrasives manufacturers now have facilities in India, and some have established technology centres conducting R&D here. The supply chain is strong. We've been successful in introducing new methods to the market and have built long-term relationships with customers. However, we no longer bring the technological edge we once did. It's a business whose time for us has passed. We anticipate a graceful exit, handing over our business to partners who can take it further.

The Curious Case of ROBOFINISH

ROBOFINISH technologies began as experimental projects in a high-technology area. We successfully introduced Robotic finishing and polishing, Robotic grinding, Robotic deburring, Robotic deflashing, and Robotic machining across a range of industries. Later, we focused on Robotic grinding for the ferrous foundry, leading us to a niche in the mining industry foundry. Here, we developed a truly unique, highly specialised, and cutting-edge solution. Robotic large steel casting grinding is the product of years of research and is a solution to be proud of, recognised as a global first. It has been a personal *S = K Log W* moment for me, as I was the chief architect of this solution.

ROBOFINISH needs restructuring. There is a global opportunity to upgrade foundries and change lives. Only a few foundries worldwide have modernised fettling shops. Robotic auto grinding is a nascent technology globally. It represents a shift in manufacturing methodology and requires a major transformation in foundries. Implementing this transition needs an automation company steeped in both robotics and foundry operations—understanding the requirements and ways of the foundry to bring about what is needed. Grind Master is simply not cut out for this. I had been coming to this realisation over the years. The moment of final clarity was an incident I narrated in the chapter about Grind Master forging partnerships.

Beyond the foundry business, various other product lines within ROBOFINISH each have potential in their own right. We have been ahead of our time in making various developments, mainly working with first movers in different industries. However, due to low wage costs in India, opportunities to horizontally deploy these solutions have been limited. Across industries, manual operations continue to be the norm, resulting in inconsistent quality and poor health standards. There is significant potential for transformation.

ROBOFINISH is a brand in its own right—with strong current business and substantial future potential. Taking this business forward requires new talent that can dedicate efforts to technology, business development, and operations. The core technologies underlying ROBOFINISH can be 'productised' and brought to the market on a much larger scale, enabling general-purpose integrators to implement solutions, much like handling and welding solutions are implemented today. I envision myself as an advisor to this new entity—the form and structure of which will reveal itself over time.

The Grind Master Way

The transformation outlined is a vision of the next generation, based on ideas that evolved through numerous discussions with the founders and senior management team. Several courageous decisions have been made, driven by the confidence of a team that is undeterred by geography, playing in harsh conditions. Time will reveal the results, but we will play on the front foot. Core values and strategy propel us forward, nimble and ready for any challenges and opportunities. We focus on what matters and proudly pass on what we cherish, continuing to transform the industry.

Each entity is responsible for striving towards its destiny. We believe that it is Grind Master's destiny to carve a name in the story of technology as an innovator. The process of striving towards this makes us 'Jagat Bhari'. The journey is exciting—full of learning, empowerment, pushing limits, and setting new ones, leading to self-realisation. We love moving in this direction, and we will certainly get there.

2017 ◎ Visiting Japan with Ishida San - the Japanese advisor reminiscent of Yoda from Star Wars

2022 ◎ Developing a unique solution for grinding large mining industry casting gives Sameer a thrill.

2023 © Grind Master Chinese engineer Kenny providing support on a machine supplied in the USA - a truly global operation

2024 © Collaboration partners Fujistar meet Grind Master at JIMTOF 2024 in Japan

2009 © Natasha and Sameer

2011 © Rudolf Gudel - friend philosopher and guide to Sameer mentored and inspired the new generation at Grind Master

Family of Machine Builders - Milind, Sameer and Mohini

2023 © The Kelkar family at the Kailash temple in Ellora

2024 © Envisioning a new integrated manufacturing facility - for a global company

16

SUBHASHITA

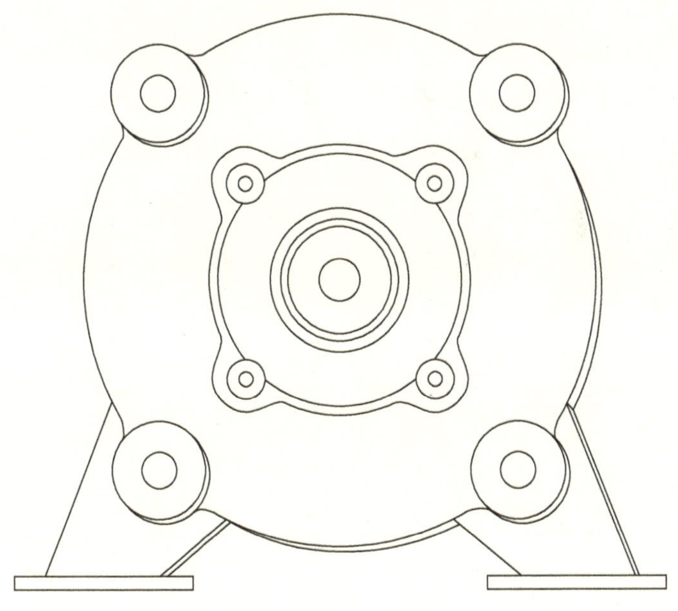

'Subhashita' is a literary term from Sanskrit poems, containing maxims with profound meaning and lessons. 'Su' in Sanskrit means good, and 'bhashita' means well-articulated, generally in one or two lines. 'Subhashitas' carry high intellectual content and are impactful. Many such 'Subhashitas' were selected from the narrative and, when put together, explain what constitutes the very DNA of Grind Master.

- ***"It takes a hundred things right for a machine to work well, and only one thing wrong to make it fail."***
  Sameer Kelkar
- *"Engineering prevails over opinions."*
  Milind Kelkar
- *"It has always been done this way' is unacceptable."*
  Milind Kelkar
- *"The measure of an engineering team's productivity is the accuracy with which they deliver."*
  Sameer Kelkar
- *"If in doubt, build a test."*
  Sameer Kelkar
- *"We are all machine engineers. Our background may be one of the engineering disciplines, but we design a product that works through the good integration of hands and brains."*
  Sameer Kelkar
- *"The devil is in the detail. And so is God."*
  Sameer Kelkar
- *"Use of adjectives is not allowed, except in genuine praise."*
  Milind Kelkar
- *"I was on a machine high for almost a couple of days—a state of innate joy, bliss."*
  Sameer Kelkar
- *"My blood test shows there is abrasive grain flowing in my veins and arteries."*
  DS (D. Srinivasan)

- *"An entrepreneur is one who controls the what, where, how, and when."*
  Milind Kelkar

- *"If the machine works, it is yours. If it does not work, it is ours."*
  Milind Kelkar

- *"Sweat on the assembly floor, do not bleed at the site."*
  Milind Kelkar

- *"A corporate brand must be inside out, articulating the core of the company in words."*
  Ashwini Deshpande (Elephant Design)

- *"Payat bhingri, dokya var barf, tondat sakhar (wheels on the feet, ice on the head, sweetness in the talk)."*
  Mahesh Sahasrabuddhe (#Salesman Mantra)

- *"The one thing we detest is 'jugaad'—which also means gambling, and we are not into that."*
  Milind Kelkar

- *"We cannot improve the whole world, but we can create an island of excellence within our four walls."*
  Milind Kelkar

- *"Every solution has a problem."*
  Milind Kelkar

- *"Mountains are for climbing."*
  Sameer Kelkar

- *"Pinch and Pat—Pinch when inside, knowing that you know nothing; pat yourself when outside, knowing you are better than most others."*
  Milind Kelkar

17

CHRONOLOGY OF EVENTS

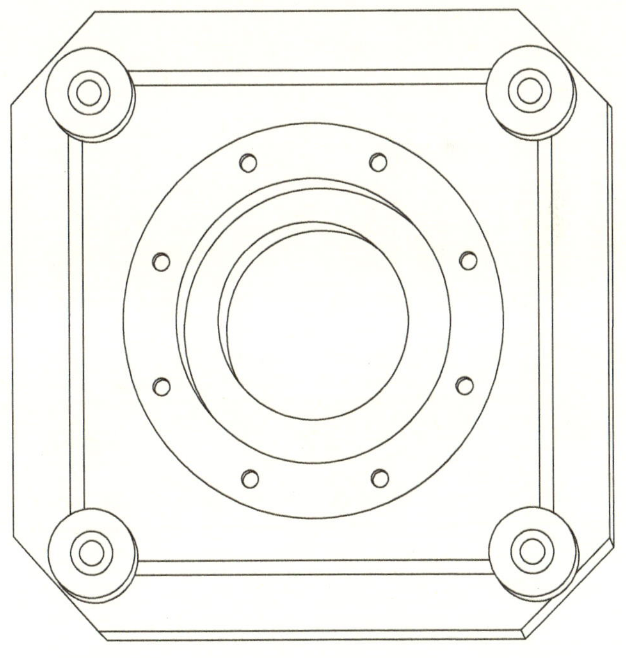

GARAGE OF ENGINEERING MINDS

- **1980-1981:** Milind (1980) and Mohini (1981) graduate from VJTI
- **1984:** Created the design of the buffing machine for Nirlep
- **1984:** Sameer is born
- **1984:** Precision Engineers is born in a garage
- **1985:** Seed separator machine, rotomoulding machine created
- **1986:** Hand tool polishing machines created
- **1986:** Filed patent for automatic edge polishing – No. 164932 of 2 April 1986
- **1987:** Pressure cooker buffing for Hawkins
- **1988:** Cutlery polishing machines created
- **1988:** Received the Parkhe Award by Mahratta Chamber for cookware polishing machine
- **1989:** Grind Master name established and Pvt. Ltd. founded
- **1989:** Rim polishing machine for a leading cycle manufacturer
- **1991:** Received FIE Foundation National Award for contribution to the field of machine tools
- **1991:** Received Parkhe Award for automatic linishing & belt grinding machines
- **1992:** Centreless belt finishing machine for LMW created

1992
2003

BUILDING A SPECIALISED BUSINESS

- **1992:** Established a factory and company at the new premises as Grind Master Machines Pvt Ltd
- **1995:** MK International was formed as a merchant export firm
- **1996:** Decora tubes centreless belt grinding machine created
- **1996:** Exports undertaken to South-East Asia through Accord, Singapore
- **1997:** Collaborated with VSM Germany for coated abrasives
- **1997:** Visit to 3M Technology Center, USA
- **1999:** Ketan Kelkar joins Grind Master
- **2000:** Joint venture with Lippert for buffing wheels and polishing compound
- **2001:** Set up conversion facility to make coated abrasive belts with VSM
- **2001:** Received Best Design Award by CMTI-PMT Trust at IMTEX 2001 for Superfinishing Machine
- **2002:** Expanded the Grind Master facility with a new building

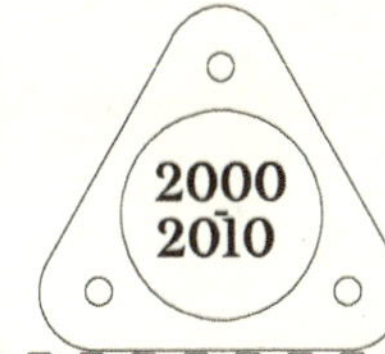

OPERATING AT THE FINISH LINE

- **2002:** Success of several superfinishing machines
- **2003:** Collaborated with IMPCO USA
- **2004:** First crankshaft and camshaft microfinishing machines built for Netalkar Group and Precision Camshafts
- **2004:** 50th wedding anniversary for Senior Kelkar and Phadke
- **2004:** Exports of metal finishing machines to Australia after Milind's presentation at the VSM Sales Conference in Australia
- **2005:** Collaborated with Timesavers Holland
- **2005:** Exported metal finishing machines to Greece
- **2006:** Sameer graduates from IIT Bombay
- **2007:** Building crankshaft microfinishing machines for Bharat Forge
- **2007:** Companywide ERP - AXAPTA executed
- **2008:** Building several crankshaft and camshaft microfinishing machines for Indian automotive companies
- 2009: First machines for Chinese automotive companies - BYD

ENTER THE DRAGON

- **2010:** Sameer Kelkar joins Grind Master
- **2010:** First machine for SGM China is delivered
- **2012:** Robotics business begins with first projects including FAB Grinding for Bharat Forge
- **2012:** Technical collaboration for dynamic balancing with Balance Engineering
- **2012:** Expanded Grind Master with a new factory for building microfinishing machines
- **2013:** Rebranding exercise undertaken with new logo and identity
- **2014:** Grind Master's China office opened in Beijing – a representative office later converted into a trading company
- **2014:** Technical collaboration for gear chamfering with Samputensili Italy
- **2014:** Grind Master completes 30 years and wins Emerging India Award
- **2015:** Management team restructured with the goal to move towards professional management. Sameer Kelkar appointed CEO.
- **2016:** Expanded Grind Master with a new factory. Unit 2 is dedicated to manufacturing parts

INNOVATING FOR THE WORLD

- **2017:** Acquired SPMS France near Paris
- **2019:** Established Grind Master US in Lansing, Michigan
- **2020:** Installed microfinishing machine at Nissan Japan
- **2020:** Covid pandemic hits. The company utilises the time to improve capability and reduce costs
- **2020:** SPMS France closed
- **2020:** Technical collaboration with Roberts Sinto Corporation USA
- **2021:** ROBOFINISH delivers prestigious projects to Nemak Mexico and Forja Mexico
- **2021:** Metalfinish delivers advanced deburring technology to the US
- **2021:** NANOFINISH develops hydraulic piston rod superfinishing technology for SANY China, Carter, and Taylor in the US
- **2022:** NANOFINISH develops ballscrew superfinishing machine for Hiwin with a global patent
- **2022:** ROBOFINISH delivers breakthrough technology to Bradken
- **2023:** Grind Master US closes but continues collaboration with IMPCO USA
- **2024:** A new paradigm unfolds
- **2024:** Rebranding of Grind Master as a global technology leader with the mission to be the world's best in focused businessest

Acknowledgements

The process of writing a book is a solitary one. But I was never alone through the journey. Many people came to help me along the path. Some helped with memories from the company's rich history while some others helped with packaging the ideas into a book with a coherent structure and flow. Every helping hand was welcome, and every help, big or small, contributed significantly to shaping this book.

First and foremost, I would like to thank my parents Milind and Mohini Kelkar. There would be no Grind Master without their courage and conviction. And there would be no book to write if not for their perseverance and spirit of entrepreneurship. I thank my wife Natasha, who has been a constant source of unwavering love and patience as I wrote this book and went through its many iterations. Thank you!

I am deeply grateful to my mentor Mr. Shailesh Sheth, whose insightful feedback profoundly shaped this book. It hurts me deeply that Mr. Sheth passed away before he was able to hold in his hands the book that he conceptualised and so generously contributed to. As a guide, friend and philosopher, Mr. Sheth will be deeply missed. Sir, your ideas will continue to inspire me, as they will an entire generation of entrepreneurs.

I am thankful to the book editor Sumaa Tekur, whose meticulous attention to detail refined the book. Your expertise and patience were invaluable in the telling of this company's story.

I am grateful to the book designer, Binu, for giving of his design essence and for understanding how I wanted the book to look and feel. I also thank the printers Pragati for producing a quality book by converting our ideas into reality.

There are too many people to thank in the journey of Grind Master – those who work here and those who have impacted the company in some way over the years. Many of their names are mentioned in the many stories of the book. I would like to extend a special thanks to all my friends, colleagues and partners for their encouragement, brainstorming, and honest feedback throughout this journey. Your support has meant more to me than you can know.

Finally, thank you to you, dear reader, without whom this book would have no purpose. I hope that you find as much joy and insight in reading this as I did in writing it.

Thank you, all, for being part of this journey.

Sumaa Tekur
Editor

Binu Philip
Designer

Sameer Kelkar

Author

Sameer is the CEO and R&D Head at Grind Master Machines. He has over 15 years of experience in specialized machine building with domain expertise in metalfinishing technologies and Robotics.

A silver medalist from IIT Bombay and post graduate from University of California and Berkeley, Sameer has multiple passions including mountain biking, trail running, hiking. He believes in living life in the moment - "Here and Now" giving 100%.

Sameer lives in Aurangabad (now Sambhaji Nagar) with his family in a forest house.

www.ingramcontent.com/pod-product-compliance
Lightning Source LLC
LaVergne TN
LVHW042345150826
845671LV00001B/23

* 9 7 9 8 8 9 6 7 3 4 2 4 6 *